Total Q

For Susan and Norma

Total Quality Management

Text with cases

John S. Oakland
PhD, CChem, MRSC, FIQA, FSS, MASQC

Exxon Chemical Professor of
Total Quality Management,
European Centre for TQM,
Management Centre, University of Bradford

Case Study co-author

Leslie J. Porter
BSc, MSc, MBA, PhD, CPhys, MIM, FInstD, MIQA, MASQC

Prudential Assurance Lecturer in
Business Improvement, European
Centre for TQM, Management Centre,
University of Bradford

Butterworth-Heinemann Ltd
Linacre House, Jordan Hill, Oxford OX2 8DP

℞ A member of the Reed Elsevier plc group

OXFORD LONDON BOSTON
MUNICH NEW DELHI SINGAPORE SYDNEY
TOKYO TORONTO WELLINGTON

First published 1995

British Library Cataloguing in Publication Data
Oakland, John S.
   Total Quality Management: Text with
   Cases. – Student ed
   I. Title II. Porter, Leslie J.
   658.5

ISBN 0 7506 2124 9

Typeset by Deltatype Ltd, Ellesmere Port, Cheshire
Printed and bound in Great Britain by
Martins The Printers Ltd, Berwick upon Tweed

Contents

Preface

When I wrote the first edition of *Total Quality Management* in 1988, there were very few books on the subject. Since its publication, the interest in TQM and business process improvement has exploded. There are now many many texts on TQM and its various aspects.

So much has been learned during the last four to five years of TQM implementation that it has been necessary to rewrite the book. This student edition is based on the first, but its structure and content have changed substantially to reflect the developments, current understanding, and experience gained of TQM, and illustrative cases have been added.

Continuous cost reduction, productivity and quality improvement have proved essential for organizations to stay in operation. We cannot avoid seeing how quality has developed into the most important competitive weapon, and many organizations have realized that TQM is *the* way of managing for the future. TQM is far wider in its application than assuring product or service quality – it is a way of managing business processes to ensure complete 'customer' satisfaction at every stage, internally and externally.

This book is about how to manage in a total quality way. It is structured around five parts of a model for TQM. The core of the model is the *customer–supplier* interfaces, both externally and internally, and the fact that at each interface there lies a number of *processes*. This sensitive core must be surrounded by *commitment* to quality, meeting the customer requirements, *communication* of the quality message, and recognition of the need to change the *culture* of most organizations to create total quality. These are the soft FOUNDATIONS, to which must be added the SYSTEMS, the TOOLS, and the TEAMS – the hard management necessities.

Under these headings the essential steps for the successful IMPLEMENTATION of TQM are set out in what I hope is a meaningful and practical way. The book should guide the reader through the language of TQM and sets down a clear way to proceed for organizations.

Many of the 'gurus' appear to present different theories of quality management. In reality they are talking the same 'language' but they use different dialects; the basic principles of defining quality and taking it into account throughout all the activities of the 'business' are common. Quality has to be managed – it does not just happen. Understanding and commitment by senior management, effective leadership and teamwork are fundamental parts of the recipe for success. I have tried to use my extensive research and consultancy experience to take what is to many a jigsaw puzzle and assemble a comprehensive, practical, working model for total quality – the rewards of which are greater efficiencies, lower costs, improved reputation and greater market share.

The book should meet the requirements of the increasing number of students who need to understand the part TQM may play in their courses on science, engineering, or management. I hope that those engaged in the pursuit of professional qualifications in the management of quality assurance, such as membership of the Institute of Quality

Assurance, the American Society of Quality Control, or the Australian Organization for Quality, will make this book an essential part of their library. With its companion book, *Statistical Process Control* (now in its second edition), *Total Quality Management* documents a comprehensive approach, one that has been used successfully in many organizations throughout the world.

I would like to thank my colleagues at the European Centre for TQM, Bradford, and in O&F Quality Management Consultants Ltd for the sharing of ideas and help in their development. The book is the result of many years of collaboration in assisting organizations to introduce good methods of management and embrace the concepts of total quality. I am most grateful to Barbara Ward who converted a patchwork quilt of scribble and typescript into error-free electronic form.

John Oakland

Reading, using, analysing the cases

The cases in this book provide a description of what occurred in nine different organizations, regarding various aspects of their quality improvement efforts. They may each be used as a learning vehicle as well as providing information and description which demonstrate the application of the concepts and techniques of TQM.

The objective of writing the cases has been to offer a resource through which the student of TQM (including many practising managers) understands how TQM companies operate. We hope that the cases will provide a useful and distinct contribution to TQM education and training.

The case material is suitable for practising managers, students on undergraduate and postgraduate courses, and all teachers of the various aspects of business management and TQM. No real prior knowledge is assumed, but the selected highlights from John Oakland's book *Total Quality Management 2* have been drawn together in the five parts of this book to provide a good platform from which to read the cases. Further study of that full text is recommended for those engaged in serious study of TQM or its implementation.

The cases have been written so that they may be used in three ways:

1 As orthodox cases for student preparation and discussion.
2 As illustrations, which teachers may also use as support for their other methods of training and education.
3 As supporting/background reading on TQM.

If used in the orthodox way, it is recommended that firstly the case is read to gain an understanding of the issues and to raise questions which may lead to a collective and more complete understanding of the company, TQM and the issues in the particular case. Secondly, case discussion or presentations in groups will give practice in putting forward thoughts and ideas persuasively.

The greater the effort put into case study, preparation, analysis and discussion in groups, the greater will be the individual benefit. There are, of course, no correct and tidy cases in any subject area. What the directors and managers of an organization actually did is not necessarily the best way forward. One object of the cases is to make the reader think about the situation, the problems and the progress made, and what improvements or developments are possible.

The writing of each case emphasizes particular problems or issues which were apparent for the organization. This may have obscured other more important ones. The diagnostic skill of the student will allow the symptoms to be separated from the disease. Imagination, innovation and intuition should be as much a part of the study of a case as observation and analysis of the facts and any data available.

TQM cases, by their nature, will be very complicated and, to render the cases in this book useful for study, some of the complexity has been omitted. This simplification is accompanied by the danger of making the implementation seem clear-cut and obvious. Believe us, that is never the case with TQM!

TQM case analysis

The main objective of each description is to enable the reader to understand the situation and its implications, and to learn from the particular experiences. The cases are not, in the main, offering specific problems to be solved. In using the cases, the reader/student should try to:

- *Recognize or imagine* the situation in the organization.
- *Understand* the context and objectives of the process(es) described.
- *Analyse* the different parts of the case (including any data) and their interrelationships.
- *Determine* the overall structure of the situation/problem(s)/case.
- *Consider* the different options facing the organization.
- *Evaluate* the options and the course of action chosen, using any results stated.
- *Consider any recommendations* which should be made to the organization for further work, action, or implementation.

The set of cases has been chosen to provide a good coverage across different types of industry and organization, including those in the service, manufacturing and public sectors. The cases have been arranged in a sequence which follows the various parts of the Oakland Model of TQM:

- The foundations.
- The role of the quality systems.
- The role of tools, techniques and measurement.
- The organization, communication and teamwork aspects.
- The implementation and integration into strategy.

The value of illustrative cases in an area such as TQM is that they inject reality into the conceptual frameworks developed by authors in the subject. The cases are all based on real situations and are designed to illustrate certain aspects of managing change in organizations, rather than to reflect good or poor management practice. The cases may be used for analysis, discussion, evaluation, and even decision-making within groups without risk to the individuals, groups, or organization(s) involved. In this way students of TQM may become 'involved' in many different organizations and their approaches to TQM implementation, over a short period and in an efficient and effective way.

The organizations described here have faced translating TQM theory into practice, and the description of their experiences should provide an opportunity for the reader of TQM literature to test his/her preconceptions and understanding of this topic. All the cases describe real TQM processes in real organizations and we are grateful to the people involved for their contribution to this book.

John S. Oakland
Les Porter

Further reading

Easton, G., *Learning from Case Studies* (2nd edn), Prentice-Hall, UK, 1992.

Part One

The Foundations – A Model for TQM

Good order is the foundation of all good things.

Edmund Burke, 1791

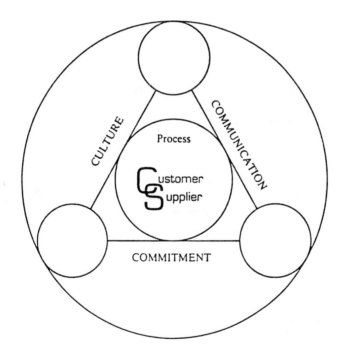

1

Understanding quality

1.1 Quality and competitiveness

There was a company outside Japan that tried to manufacture motor cars. Its name does not matter – it has changed its name now anyway – let's call it B. Motors. The company did a deal with a Japanese car manufacturer that allowed the Japanese-named cars, let's call them HO, to be manufactured by B. Motors. What happened in the boardroom of HO motor cars when that deal was announced can only be described as mass hara-kiri. Clearly, rather a lot of depression had settled over those particular Japanese gentlemen. Why should they behave in this way? What was the difference between the two companies? In a word, image or reputation. Reputation for what? Reputation for quality, reliability, price, and delivery – all the things we *compete* on.

Whatever type of organization you work in – a hospital, a university, a bank, an insurance company, local government, an airline, a factory – competition is rife: competition for customers, for students, for patients, for resources, for funds. There are very few people around in most types of organization who remain to be convinced that quality is the most important of the competitive weapons. If you doubt that, just look at the way some organizations, even whole industries in certain countries, have used quality to take the heads off their competitors. And they are not only Japanese companies. British, American, French, German, Italian, Spanish, Swiss, Swedish organizations, and organizations from other countries, have used quality strategically to win customers, steal business resources or funding, and be competitive. Moreover, attention to quality improves performance in reliability, delivery, and price.

The reputation of Japanese companies once was anything but good. Not too long ago they were most famous for 'cheap oriental trash'. They have clearly *learned* something. This has not as much to do with differences in national cultures as many people think it has. The Japanese culture, which is much older than most western cultures has not changed significantly in 40–50 years.

One of the lessons many Japanese companies learned after the Second World War was to manage quality, and the other things on which we compete. They learned it from a handful of Americans – people like Joseph M. Juran and W. Edwards Deming, who have since reached fame as 'gurus' of quality management.

The company we called B. Motors also learned a thing or two about quality and competition. It lost market share, but started to put things right by a better understanding of quality management and the needs of its customers. Unfortunately its previous reputation was so bad that it is taking it many years to change people's view. It may never do so. Moreover, the country in which it operates gained a poor reputation for shoddy goods and services, in contrast to the 'Japanese', who seem to take so many industries by storm. Even the trains run on time there!

For any organization, there are several lessons to be learned about reputation from this story:

1   It is built upon the competitive elements of quality, reliability, delivery, and price, of which quality has become strategically the most important.
2   Once an organization acquires a poor reputation for quality, it takes a very long time to change it.
3   Reputations, good or bad, can quickly become national reputations.
4   The management of the competitive weapons, such as quality, can be learned like any other skill, and used to turn round a poor reputation, in time.

Before anyone will buy the idea that quality is an important consideration, they would have to know what was meant by it.

What is quality?

'Is this a quality watch?' Pointing to my wrist, I ask this question of a class of students – undergraduates, postgraduates, experienced managers – it matters not who. The answers vary:

*   'No, it's made in Japan.'
*   'No, it's cheap.'
*   'No, the face is scratched.'
*   'How reliable is it?'
*   'I wouldn't wear it.'

My watch has been insulted all over the world – London, New York, Paris, Sydney, Brussels, Amsterdam, Bradford! Very rarely am I told that the quality of the watch depends on what the wearer requires from a watch – perhaps a piece of jewellery to give an impression of wealth; a timepiece that gives the required data, including the date, in digital form; or one with the ability to perform at 50 metres under the sea? Clearly these requirements determine the quality.

Quality is often used to signify 'excellence' of a product or service – people talk about 'Rolls-Royce quality' and 'top quality'. In some engineering companies the word may be used to indicate that a piece of metal conforms to certain physical dimensional characteristics often set down in the form of a particularly 'tight' specification. In a hospital it might be used to indicate some sort of 'professionalism'. If we are to define quality in a way that is useful in its *management*, then we must recognize the need to include in the assessment of quality the true requirements of the 'customer' – the needs and expectations.

Quality then is simply *meeting the customer requirements*, and this has been expressed in many ways by other authors:

*   'Fitness for purpose or use' – Juran.
*   'The totality of features and characteristics of a product or service that bear on its

ability to satisfy stated or implied needs' – BS 4778, 1987 (ISO 8402, 1986) *Quality Vocabulary*: Part 1, *International Terms*.

- 'Quality should be aimed at the needs of the consumer, present and future' – Deming.
- 'The total composite product and service characteristics of marketing, engineering, manufacture and maintenance through which the product and service in use will meet the expectation by the customer' – Feigenbaum.
- 'Conformance to requirements' – Crosby.

Another word that we should define properly is *reliability*. 'Why do you buy a Volkswagen car?' 'Quality and reliability' comes back the answer. The two are used synonymously, often in a totally confused way. Clearly, part of the acceptability of a product or service will depend on its ability to function satisfactorily *over a period of time*, and it is this aspect of performance that is given the name *reliability*. It is the ability of the product or service to *continue* to meet the customer requirements. Reliability ranks with quality in importance, since it is a key factor in many purchasing decisions where alternatives are being considered. Many of the general management issues related to achieving product or service quality are also applicable to reliability.

It is important to realize that the 'meeting the customer requirements' definition of quality is not restrictive to the functional characteristics of products or services. Anyone with children knows that the quality of some of the products they purchase is more associated with *satisfaction in ownership* than some functional property. This is also true of many items, from antiques to certain items of clothing. The requirements for status symbols account for the sale of some executive cars, certain bank accounts and charge cards, and even hospital beds! The requirements are of paramount importance in the assessment of the quality of any product or service.

By *consistently* meeting customer requirements, we can move to a different plane of satisfaction – *delighting the customer*. There is no doubt that many organizations have so well ordered their capability to meet their customers' requirements, time and time again, that this has created a reputation for 'excellence'.

1.2 Understanding and building the quality chains

The ability to meet the customer requirements is vital, not only between two separate organizations, but within the same organization.

When the air hostess pulled back the curtain across the aisle and set off with a trolley full of breakfasts to feed the early morning travellers on the short domestic flight into an international airport, she was not thinking of quality problems. Having stopped at the row of seats marked 1ABC, she passed the first tray onto the lap of the man sitting by the window. By the time the second tray had reached the lady beside him, the first tray was on its way back to the air hostess with a complaint that the bread roll and jam were missing. She calmly replaced it in her trolley and reached for another – which also had no roll and jam.

The calm exterior of the girl began to evaporate as she discovered two more trays without a complete breakfast. Then she found a good one and, thankfully, passed it over. This search for complete breakfast trays continued down the aeroplane, causing inevitable delays, so much so that several passengers did not receive their breakfasts until the plane had begun its descent. At the rear of the plane could be heard the mutterings of discontent. 'Aren't they slow with breakfast this morning?' 'What is she doing with those trays?' 'We will have indigestion by the time we've landed.'

The problem was perceived by many to be one of delivery or service. They could smell food but they weren't getting any of it, and they were getting really wound up! The air hostess, who had suffered the embarrassment of being the purveyor of defective product and service, was quite wound up and flushed herself, as she returned to the curtain and almost ripped it from the hooks in her haste to hide. She was heard to say through clenched teeth, 'What a bloody mess!'

A problem of quality? Yes, of course, requirements not being met, but where? The passengers or customers suffered from it on the aircraft, but down in the bowels of the organization there was a little man whose job it was to assemble the breakfast trays. On this day the system had broken down – perhaps he ran out of bread rolls, perhaps he was called away to refuel the aircraft (it was a small airport!), perhaps he didn't know or understand, perhaps he didn't care.

Three hundred miles away in a chemical factory . . . 'What the hell is Quality Control doing? We've just sent 15,000 litres of lawn weedkiller to CIC and there it is back at our gate – they've returned it as out of spec.' This was followed by an avalanche of verbal abuse, which will not be repeated here, but poured all over the shrinking Quality Control Manager as he backed through his office door, followed by a red faced Technical Director advancing menacingly from behind the bottles of sulphuric acid racked across the adjoining laboratory.

'Yes, what is QC doing?' thought the Production Manager, who was behind a door two offices along the corridor, but could hear the torrent of language now being used to beat the QC man into an admission of guilt. He knew the poor devil couldn't possibly do anything about the rubbish that had been produced except test it, but why should he volunteer for the unpleasant and embarrassing ritual now being experienced by his colleague – for the second time this month. No wonder the QC manager had been studying the middle pages of the *Telegraph* on Thursday – what a job!

Do you recognize these two situations? Do they not happen every day of the week – possibly every minute somewhere in manufacturing or the service industries? Is it any different in banking, insurance, the health service? The inquisition of checkers and testers is the last bastion of desperate systems trying in vain to catch mistakes, stop defectives, hold lousy materials, before they reach the external customer – and woe betide the idiot who lets them pass through!

Two everyday incidents, but why are events like these so common? The answer is the acceptance of one thing – *failure*. Not doing it right the first time at every stage of the process.

Why do we accept failure in the production of artefacts, the provision of a service, or even the transfer of information? In many walks of life we do not accept it. We do not say, 'Well, the nurse is bound to drop the odd baby in a thousand – it's just going to happen'. We do not accept that!

In each department, each office, even each household, there are a series of suppliers and customers. The typist is a supplier to her boss. Is she meeting his requirements?

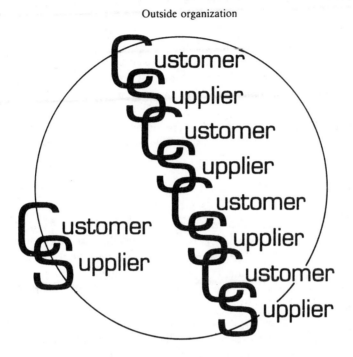

Outside organization

Figure 1.1 *The quality chains*

Does he receive error-free typing set out as he wants it, when he wants it? If so, then we have a quality typing service. Does the air hostess receive from her supplier in the airline the correct food trays in the right quantity?

Throughout and beyond all organizations, whether they be manufacturing concerns, banks, retail stores, universities, hospitals or hotels, there is a series of *quality chains* of customer and suppliers (Figure 1.1) that may be broken at any point by one person or one piece of equipment not meeting the requirements of the customer, internal or external. The interesting point is that this failure usually finds its way to the interface between the organization and its outside customers, and the people who operate at that interface – like the air hostess – usually experience the ramifications. The concept of internal and external customers/suppliers forms the *core* of total quality.

A great deal is written and spoken about employee motivation as a separate issue. In fact the key to motivation *and* quality is for everyone in the organization to have well-defined customers – an extension of the word beyond the outsider that actually purchases or uses the ultimate product or service to anyone to whom an individual gives a part, a service, information – in other words the results of his or her work.

Quality has to be managed – it will not just happen. Clearly it must involve everyone in the process and be applied throughout the organization. Many people in the support functions of organizations never see, experience, or touch the products or services that their organizations buy or provide, but they do handle or produce things like purchase orders or invoices. If every fourth invoice carries at least one error, what image of quality is transmitted!

Failure to meet the requirements in any part of a quality chain has a way of multiplying, and failure in one part of the system creates problems elsewhere, leading to yet more failure, more problems and so on. The price of quality is the continual examination of the requirements and our ability to meet them. This alone will lead to a 'continuing improvement' philosophy. The benefits of making sure the requirements are met at every stage, every time, are truly enormous in terms of increased competitiveness and market share, reduced costs, improved productivity and delivery performance, and the elimination of waste. The Japanese have called this 'company-wide quality improvement' or CWQI.

Meeting the requirements

If quality is meeting the customer requirements, then this has wide implications. The requirements may include availability, delivery, reliability, maintainability and cost-effectiveness, among many other features. The first item on the list of things to do is find out what the requirements are. If we are dealing with a customer/supplier relationship crossing two organizations, then the supplier must establish a 'marketing' activity charged with this task.

The marketers must of course understand not only the needs of the customer but also the ability of their own organization to meet them. If my customer places a requirement on me to run 1,500 metres in 4 minutes, then I know I am unable to meet this demand, unless something is done to improve my running performance. Of course I may never be able to achieve this requirement.

Within organizations, between internal customers and suppliers, the transfer of information regarding requirements is frequently poor to totally absent. How many executives really bother to find out what their customers' – their secretaries' – requirements are? Can their handwriting be read, do they leave clear instructions, do the secretaries always know where the boss is? Equally, do the secretaries establish what their bosses need – error-free typing, clear messages, a tidy office? Internal supplier/customer relationships are often the most difficult to manage in terms of establishing the requirements. To achieve quality throughout an organization, each person in the quality chain must interrogate every interface as follows:

Customers
- Who are my immediate customers?
- What are their true requirements?
- How do or can I find out what the requirements are?
- How can I measure my ability to meet the requirements?
- Do I have the necessary capability to meet the requirements? (If not, then what must change to improve the capability?)
- Do I continually meet the requirements? (If not, then what prevents this from happening, when the capability exists?)
- How do I monitor changes in the requirements?

Suppliers
- Who are my immediate suppliers?
- What are my true requirements?
- How do I communicate my requirements?
- Do my suppliers have the capability to measure and meet the requirements?
- How do I inform them of changes in the requirements?

The measurement of capability is extremely important if the quality chains are to be formed within and without an organization. Each person in the organization must also realize that the supplier's needs and expectations must be respected if the requirements are to be fully satisfied.

To understand how quality may be built into a product or service, at any stage, it is necessary to examine the two distinct, but interrelated aspects of quality:

- Quality of design
- Quality of conformance to design.

Quality of design

We are all familiar with the old story of the tree swing (Figure 1.2), but in how many places in how many organizations is this chain of activities taking place? To discuss the quality of, say, a chair it is necessary to describe its purpose. What it is to be used for? If it is to be used for watching TV for 3 hours at a stretch, then the typical office chair will not meet this requirement. The difference between the quality of the TV chair and the office chair is not a function of how it was manufactured, but its *design*.

Quality of design is a measure of how well the product or service is designed to achieve the agreed requirements. The beautifully presented gourmet meal will not necessarily please the recipient if he or she is travelling on the highway and has stopped for a quick bite to eat. The most important feature of the design, with regard to achieving quality, is the specification. Specifications must also exist at the internal supplier/customer interfaces if one is to pursue company-wide quality. For example, the company lawyer asked to draw up a contract by the sales manager requires a specification as to its content:

1 Is it a sales, processing or consulting type of contract?
2 Who are the contracting parties?
3 In which countries are the parties located?
4 What are the products involved (if any)?
5 What is the volume?
6 What are the financial, e.g. price, escalation, aspects?

The financial controller must issue a specification of the information he or she needs, and when, to ensure that foreign exchange fluctuations do not cripple the company's finances. The business of sitting down and agreeing a specification at every interface will clarify the true requirements and capabilities. It is the vital first stage for a successful total-quality effort.

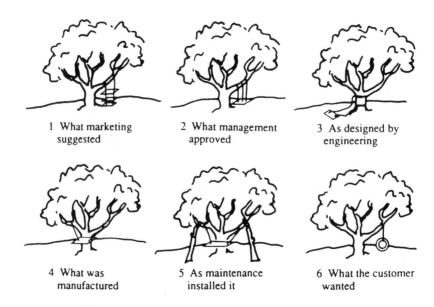

1 What marketing
   suggested

2 What management
   approved

3 As designed by
   engineering

4 What was
   manufactured

5 As maintenance
   installed it

6 What the customer
   wanted

Figure 1.2 *Quality of design*

There must be a corporate understanding of the organization's quality position in the market place. It is not sufficient that marketing specifies the product or service 'because that is what the customer wants'. There must be an agreement that the operating departments can achieve that requirement. Should they be incapable of doing so, then one of two things must happen: either the organization finds a different position in the market place or substantially changes the operational facilities.

Quality of conformance to design

This is the extent to which the product or service achieves the quality of design. What the customer actually receives should conform to the design, and operating costs are tied firmly to the level of conformance achieved. Quality cannot be inspected into products or services; the customer satisfaction must be designed into the whole system. The conformance check then makes sure that things go according to plan.

A high level of inspection or checking at the end is often indicative of attempts to inspect in quality. This may well result in spiralling costs and decreasing viability. The area of conformance to design is concerned largely with the quality performance of the actual operations. It may be salutary for organizations to use the simple matrix of Figure 1.3 to assess how much time they spend doing the right things right. A lot of people, often through no fault of their own, spend a good proportion of the available time doing the right things wrong. There are people (and organizations) who spend time doing the wrong things very well, and even those who occupy themselves doing the wrong things wrong, which can be very confusing!

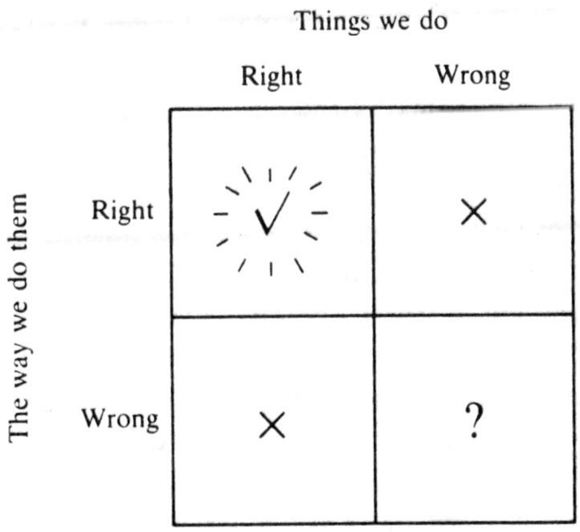

Things we do

Right   Wrong

Figure 1.3 *How much time is spent on doing the right things right?*

1.3 Managing processes

Every day two men who work in a certain factory scrutinize the results of the examination of the previous day's production, and begin the ritual battle over whether the material is suitable for despatch to the customer. One is called the Production Manager, the other the Quality Control Manager. They argue and debate the evidence before them, the rights and wrongs of the specification, and each tries to convince the other of the validity of his argument. Sometimes they nearly start fighting.

This ritual is associated with trying to answer the question, *'Have we done the job correctly?'*, correctly being a flexible word, depending on the interpretation given to the specification on that particular day. This is not quality *control*, it is *detection* – wasteful detection of bad product before it hits the customer. There is still a belief in some quarters that to achieve quality we must check, test, inspect or measure – the ritual pouring on of quality at the end of the process. This is nonsense, but it is frequently practised. In the office one finds staff checking other people's work before it goes out, validating computer input data, checking invoices, typing, etc. There is also quite a lot of looking for things, chasing why things are late, apologising to customers for lateness, and so on. Waste, waste, waste!

To get away from the natural tendency to rush into the detection mode, it is necessary to ask different questions in the first place. We should not ask whether the job has been done correctly, we should ask first *'Are we capable of doing the job correctly?'* This question has wide implications, and this book is devoted largely to the various activities necessary to ensure that the answer is yes. However, we should realize straight away that such an answer will only be obtained by means of satisfactory methods, materials, equipment, skills and instruction, and a satisfactory 'process'.

What is a process?

As we have seen, quality chains can be traced right through the business or service processes used by any organization. A process is the transformation of a set of inputs, which can include actions, methods and operations, into outputs that satisfy customer needs and expectations, in the form of products, information, services or – generally – results. Everything we do is a process, so in each area or function of an organization there will be many processes taking place. For example, a finance department may be engaged in budgeting processes, accounting processes, salary and wage processes, costing processes, etc. Each process in each department or area can be analysed by an examination of the inputs and outputs. This will determine some of the actions necessary to improve quality. There are also functional processes.

The output from a process is that which is transferred to somewhere or to someone – the *customer*. Clearly, to produce an output that meets the requirements of the customer, it is necessary to define, monitor and control the inputs to the process, which in turn may be supplied as output from an earlier process. At every supplier–customer interface then there resides a transformation process (Figure 1.4), and every single task throughout an organization must be viewed as a process in this way.

Once we have established that our process is capable of meeting the requirements, we can address the next question, '*Do we continue to do the job correctly?*', which brings a requirement to monitor the process and the controls on it. If we now re-examine the first question, 'Have we done the job correctly?', we can see that, if we have been able to answer the other two questions with a yes, we *must* have done the job correctly. Any other outcome would be illogical. By asking the questions in the right

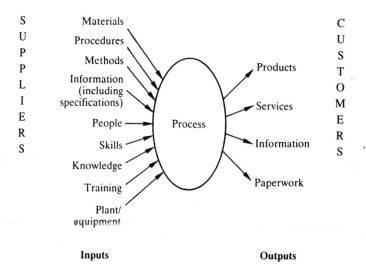

Figure 1.4 *A process*

order, we have moved the need to ask the 'inspection' question and replaced a strategy of *detection* with one of *prevention*. This concentrates all the attention on the front end of any process – the inputs – and changes the emphasis to making sure the inputs are capable of meeting the requirements of the process. This is a managerial responsibility.

These ideas apply to every transformation process; they all must be subject to the same scrutiny of the methods, the people, skills, equipment and so on to make sure they are correct for the job. A person giving a lecture whose overhead projector equipment will not focus correctly, or whose teaching materials are not appropriate, will soon discover how difficult it is to provide a lecture that meets the requirements of the audience.

In every organization there are some very large processes – groups of smaller processes called *key, critical or business processes*. These are activities the organization must carry out especially well if its mission and objectives are to be achieved. The area will be dealt with in some detail in Chapter 13 on the implementation of TQM. It is crucial if the management of quality is to be integrated into the strategy for the organization.

The *control* of quality clearly can only take place at the point of operation or production – where the letter is typed, the sales call made, the patient admitted, or the chemical manufactured. The act of *inspection is not quality control*. When the answer to 'Have we done the job correctly?' is given indirectly by answering the questions of capability and control, then we have *assured* quality, and the activity of checking becomes one of *quality assurance* – making sure that the product or service represents the output from an effective *system* to ensure capability and control. It is frequently found that organizational barriers between departmental empires encouraged the development of testing and checking of services or products in a vacuum, without interaction with other departments.

Quality control then is essentially the activities and techniques employed to achieve and maintain the quality of a product, process, or service. It includes a monitoring activity, but is also concerned with finding and eliminating causes of quality problems so that the requirements of the customer are continually met.

Quality assurance is broadly the prevention of quality problems through planned and systematic activities (including documentation). These will include the establishment of a good quality management system and the assessment of its adequacy, the audit of the operation of the system, and the review of the system itself.

1.4   Quality starts with 'marketing'

The author has been asked on more than one occasion if TQM applies to marketing. The answer to the question is not remarkable – it starts there!

The marketing function of an organization must take the lead in establishing the true requirements for the product or service. Having determined the need, marketing should define the market sector and demand, to determine such product or service features as grade, price, quality, timing, etc. For example, a major hotel chain thinking of opening a new hotel or refurbishing an old one will need to consider its location and accessibility before deciding whether it will be predominantly a budget, first-class, business or family hotel.

Marketing will also need to establish customer requirements by reviewing the market needs, particularly in terms of unclear or unstated expectations or preconceived ideas held by customers. Marketing is responsible for determining the key characteristics that determine the suitability of the product or service in the eyes of the customer. This may of course call for the use of market research techniques, data-gathering, and analysis of customer complaints. If possible, quasi-quantitative methods should be employed, giving proxy variables that can be used to grade the characteristics in importance, and decide in which areas superiority over competitors exists. It is often useful to compare these findings with internal perceptions of quality.

Excellent communication between customers and suppliers is the key to total quality; it will eradicate the 'demanding nuisance/idiot' view of customers, which pervades many organizations. Poor communications often occur in the supply chain between organizations, when neither party realizes how poor they are. Feedback from both customers and suppliers needs to be improved where dissatisfied customers and suppliers do not communicate their problems. In such cases non-conformance of purchased products or services is often due to customers' inability to communicate their requirements clearly. If these ideas are also used within an organization, then the internal supplier/customer interfaces will operate much more smoothly.

All the efforts devoted to finding the nature and timing of the demand will be pointless if marketing fails to communicate the requirements promptly, clearly, and accurately to the remainder of the organization. The marketing function should be capable of supplying the company with a formal statement or outline of the requirements for each product or service. This constitutes a preliminary set of *specifications*, which can be used as the basis for service or product design. The information requirements include:

1   Characteristics of performance and reliability – these must make reference to the conditions of use and any environmental factors that may be important.
2   Aesthetic characteristics, such as style, colour, smell, taste, feel, etc.
3   Any obligatory regulations or standards governing the nature of the product or service.

Marketing must also establish systems for feedback of customer information and reaction, and these systems should be designed on a continuous monitoring basis. Any information pertinent to the product or service should be collected and collated, interpreted, analysed, and communicated, to improve the response to customer experience and expectations. These same principles must also be applied inside the organization if continuous improvement at every transformation process interface is to be achieved. If one department of a company has problems recruiting the correct sort of staff, and personnel has not established mechanisms for gathering, analysing, and responding to information on new employees, then frustration and conflict will replace communication and co-operation.

One aspect of the analysis of market demand that extends back into the organization is the review of market readiness of a new product or service. Items that require some attention include assessment of:

1 The suitability of the distribution and customer-service systems.
2 Training of personnel in the 'field'.
3 Availability of spare parts or support staff.
4 Evidence that the organization is capable of meeting customer requirements.

All organizations receive a wide range of information from customers through invoices, payments, requests for information, letters of complaint, responses to advertisements and promotion, etc. An essential component of a system for the analysis of market demand is that this data is channelled quickly into the appropriate areas for action and, if necessary, response.

There are various techniques of market research, but they will not be described in detail in this book, for they are well documented elsewhere. Nevertheless it is worth listing some of the most common and useful general methods that should be considered for use, both externally and internally:

- Customer surveys.
- Quality panel or focus group techniques.
- In-depth interviews.
- Brainstorming and discussions.
- Role rehearsal and reversal.
- Interrogation of trade associations.

The number of methods and techniques for researching market demand is limited only by imagination and funds. The important point to stress is that the supplier, whether the internal individual or the external organization, keeps very close to the customer. Market research, coupled with analysis of complaints data, is an essential part of finding out what the requirements are, and breaking out from the obsession with inward scrutiny that bedevils quality.

1.5 Quality in all functions

For an organization to be truly effective, each part of it must work properly together. Each part, each activity, each person in the organization affects and is in turn affected by others. Errors have a way of multiplying, and failure to meet the requirements in one part or area creates problems elsewhere, leading to yet more errors, yet more problems, and so on. The benefits of getting it right first time everywhere are enormous.

Everyone experiences – almost accepts – problems in working life. This causes people to spend a large part of their time on useless activities – correcting errors, looking for things, finding out why things are late, checking suspect information, rectifying and reworking, apologizing to customers for mistakes, poor quality and lateness. The list is endless, and it is estimated that about one-third of our efforts are wasted in this way. In the service sector it can be much higher.

Quality, the way we have defined it as meeting the customer requirements, gives people in different functions of an organization a common language for improvement. It enables all the people, with different abilities and priorities, to communicate readily with one another, in pursuit of a common goal. When business and industry were local, the craftsman could manage more or less on his own. Business is now so complex and employs so many different specialist skills that everyone has to rely on the activities of others in doing their jobs.

Some of the most exciting applications of TQM have materialized from departments that could see little relevance when first introduced to its concepts. Following training, many different departments of organizations can show the use of the techniques. Sales staff can monitor and increase successful sales calls, office staff have used TQM methods to prevent errors in word-processing and improve inputting to computers, customer-service people have monitored and reduced complaints, the distribution department has controlled lateness and disruption in deliveries.

It is worthy of mention that the first points of contact for some outside customers are the telephone operator, the security people at the gate, or the person in reception. Equally the paperwork and support services associated with the product, such as invoices and sales literature and their handlers, must match the needs of the customer. Clearly TQM cannot be restricted to the production or operational areas without losing great opportunities to gain maximum benefit.

Managements that rely heavily on exhortation of the workforce to 'do the right job right the first time', or 'accept that quality is your responsibility', will not only fail to achieve quality but will create division and conflict. These calls for improvement infer that faults are caused only by the workforce and that problems are departmental when, in fact, the opposite is true – most problems are inter-departmental. The commitment of all members of an organization is a requirement of 'company-wide quality improvement'. Everyone must work together at every interface to achieve perfection. And that can only happen if the top management is really committed to quality improvement.

Chapter highlights

Quality and competitiveness

- The reputation enjoyed by an organization is built by quality, reliability, delivery and price. Quality is the most important of these competitive weapons.
- Reputations for poor quality last for a long time, and good or bad reputations can become national. The management of quality can be learned and used to improve reputation.
- Quality is meeting the customer requirements, and this is not restricted to the functional characteristics of the product or service.
- Reliability is the ability of the product or service to continue to meet the customer requirements over time.
- Organizations 'delight' the customer by consistently meeting customer requirements, and then achieve a reputation of 'excellence'.

Understanding and building the quality chains

- Throughout all organizations there are a series of internal suppliers and customers. These form the so-called 'quality chains', the core of the company-wide quality improvement (CWQI).
- The internal customer/supplier relationships must be managed by interrogation, i.e. using a set of questions at every interface. Measurement of capability is vital.
- There are two distinct but interrelated aspects of quality, design and conformance to design. *Quality of design* is a measure of how well the product or service is designed to achieve the agreed requirements. *Quality of conformance to design* is the extent to which the product or service achieves the design. Organizations should assess how much time they spend doing the right things right.

Managing processes

- Asking the question 'Have we done the job correctly?' should be replaced by asking 'Are we capable of doing the job correctly?' and 'Do we continue to do the job correctly?'
- Asking the questions in the right order replaces a strategy of *detection* with one of *prevention*.
- Everything we do is a process, which is the transformation of a set of inputs into the desired outputs.
- In every organization there are some key, critical or business processes that must be performed especially well if the mission and objectives are to be achieved.
- Inspection is not *quality control*. The latter is the employment of activities and techniques to achieve and maintain the quality of a product, process or service.
- *Quality assurance* is the prevention of quality problems through planned and systematic activities.

Quality starts with 'marketing'

- Marketing establishes the true requirements for the product or service. These must be communicated properly throughout the organization in the form of specifications.

Quality in all functions

- All members of an organization need to work together on 'company-wide quality improvement'. The co-operation of everyone at every interface is required to achieve perfection.

2

Commitment and leadership

2.1 The total quality management approach

'What is quality management?' Something that is best left to the experts is often the answer to this question. But this is avoiding the issue, because it allows executives and managers to opt out. Quality is too important to leave to the so called 'quality professionals'; it cannot be achieved on a company-wide basis if it is left to the experts. Equally dangerous, however, are the uninformed who try to follow their natural instincts because they 'know what quality is when they see it'. This type of intuitive approach will lead to serious attitude problems, which do no more than reflect the understanding and knowledge of quality that are present in an organization.

The organization which believes that the traditional quality control techniques, and the way they have always been used, will resolve their quality problems is wrong. Employing more inspectors, tightening up standards, developing correction, repair and rework teams do not promote quality. Traditionally, quality has been regarded as the responsibility of the QC department, and still it has not yet been recognized in some organizations that many quality problems originate in the service or administrative areas.

Total Quality Management is far more than shifting the responsibility of *detection* of problems from the customer to the producer. It requires a comprehensive approach that must first be recognized and then implemented if the rewards are to be realized. Today's business environment is such that managers must plan strategically to maintain a hold on market share, let alone increase it. We have known for years that consumers place a higher value on quality than on loyalty to home-based producers, and price is no longer the major determining factor in consumer choice. Price has been replaced by quality, and this is true in industrial, service, hospitality, and many other markets.

TQM is an approach to improving the competitiveness, effectiveness and flexibility of a whole organization. It is essentially a way of planning, organizing and understanding each activity, and depends on each individual at each level. For an organization to be truly effective, each part of it must work properly together towards the same goals, recognizing that each person and each activity affects and in turn is affected by others. TQM is also a way of ridding people's lives of wasted effort by bringing everyone into the processes of improvement, so that results are achieved in less time. The methods and techniques used in TQM can be applied throughout any organization. They are equally useful in the manufacturing, public service, health care, education and hospitality industries. TQM needs to gain ground rapidly and become a way of life in many organizations.

The impact of TQM on an organization is, firstly, to ensure that the management adopts a strategic overview of quality. The approach must focus on developing a *problem-prevention* mentality; but it is easy to underestimate the effort that is required to change attitudes and approaches. Many people will need to undergo a complete change of 'mindset' to unscramble their intuition, which rushes into the detection/inspection mode to solve quality problems – 'We have a quality problem, we had better check every letter – take two samples out of each sack – check every widget twice', etc.

The correct mindset may be achieved by looking at the sort of barriers that exist in key areas. Staff will need to be trained and shown how to reallocate their time and energy to studying their processes in teams, searching for causes of problems, and correcting the causes, not the symptoms, once and for all. This will require of management a positive, thrusting initiative to promote the right-first-time approach to work situations. Through *quality improvement teams*, which will need to be set up, these actions will reduce the inspection-rejection syndrome in due course. If things are done correctly first time round, the usual problems that create the need for inspection for failure will disappear.

The managements of many firms may think that their scale of operation is not sufficiently large, that their resources are too slim, or that the need for action is not important enough to justify implementing TQM. Before arriving at such a conclusion, however, they should examine the existing quality performance by asking the following questions:

1 Is any attempt made to assess the costs arising from errors, defects, waste, customer complaints, lost sales, etc.? If so, are these costs minimal or insignificant?
2 Is the standard of quality managment adequate and are attempts being made to ensure that quality is given proper consideration at the design stage?
3 Are the organization's quality systems – documentation, procedures, operations etc. – in good order?
4 Have personnel been trained in how to prevent errors and quality problems? Do they anticipate and correct potential causes of problems, or do they find and reject?
5 Do job instructions contain the necessary quality elements, are they kept up-to-date, and are employers doing their work in accordance with them?
6 What is being done to motivate and train employees to do work right first time?
7 How many errors and efects, and how much wastage occurred last year? Is this more or less than the previous year?

If satisfactory answers can be given to most of these questions, an organization can be reassured that it is already well on the way to using adequate quality procedures and management. Even so, it may find that the introduction of TQM causes it to reappraise quality activities throughout. If answers to the above questions indicate problem areas, it will be beneficial to review the top management's attitude to quality. Time and money spent on quality-related activities are *not* limitations of profitability; they make significant contributions towards greater efficiency and enhanced profits.

2.2 Commitment and policy

To be successful in promoting business efficiency and effectiveness, TQM must be truly organization-wide, and it must start at the top with the Chief Executive or equivalent. The most senior directors and management must all demonstrate that they are serious about quality. The middle management have a particularly important role to play, since they must not only grasp the principles of TQM, they must go on to explain them to the people for whom they are responsible, and ensure that their own commitment is communicated. Only then will TQM spread effectively throughout the organization. This level of management must also ensure that the efforts and achievements of their subordinates obtain the recognition, attention and reward that they deserve.

The Chief Executive of an organization must accept the responsibility for and commitment to a quality policy in which he/she must really believe. This commitment is part of a broad approach extending well beyond the accepted formalities of the quality assurance function. It creates responsibilities for a chain of quality interactions between the marketing, design, production/operations, purchasing, distribution and service functions. Within each and every department of the organization at all levels, starting at the top, basic changes of attitude will be required to operate TQM. If the owners or directors of the organization do not recognize and accept their responsibilities for the initiation and operation of TQM, then these changes will not happen. Controls, systems and techniques are very important in TQM, but they are not the primary requirement. It is more an attitude of mind, based on pride in the job and teamwork, and it requires from the management total commitment, which must then be extended to all employees at all levels and in all departments.

Senior management commitment must be obsessional, not lip service. It is possible to detect real commitment; it shows on the shop floor, in the offices, in the hospital ward – at the point of operation. Going into organizations sporting poster-campaigning for quality instead of belief, one is quickly able to detect the falseness. The people are told not to worry if quality problems arise, 'just do the best you can', 'the customer will never notice'. The opposite is an organization where total quality means something, can be seen, heard, felt. Things happen at this operating interface as a result of *real* commitment. Material problems are corrected with suppliers, equipment difficulties are put right by improved maintenance programmes or replacement, people are trained, change takes place, partnerships are built, continuous improvement is achieved.

The quality policy

A sound quality policy, together with the organization and facilities to put it into effect, is a fundamental requirement, if a company is to begin to implement TQM. Every organization should develop and state its policy on quality, together with arrangements for its implementation. The contents of the policy shold be made known to all employees. The preparation and implementation of a properly thought out quality policy, together with continuous monitoring, make for smoother production or service operation, minimize errors and reduce waste.

Management must be dedicated to the regular improvement of quality, not simply a one-step improvement to an acceptable plateau. These ideas must be set out in a *quality policy* that requires top management to:

1   Establish an 'organization' for quality.
2   Identify the customer's needs and perception of needs.
3   Assess the ability of the organization to meet these needs economically.
4   Ensure that bought-in materials and services reliably meet the required standards of performance and efficiency.
5   Concentrate on the prevention rather than detection philosophy.
6   Educate and train for quality improvement.
7   Review the quality management systems to maintain progress.

The quality policy must be publicized and understood at all levels of the organization.

An example of a good company quality policy is given below:

- Quality improvement is primarily the responsibility of management.
- In order to involve everyone in the organization in quality improvement, management will enable all employees to participate in the preparation, implementation and evaluation of improvement activities.
- Quality improvement will be tackled and followed up in a systematic and planned manner. This applies to every part of our organization.
- Quality improvement will be a continuous process.
- The organization will concentrate on its customers and suppliers, both external and internal.
- The performance of our competitors will be shown to all relevant units.
- Important suppliers will be closely involved in our quality policy. This relates to both external and internal suppliers of goods, resources, and services.
- Widespread attention will be given to education and training activities, which will be assessed with regard to their contribution to the quality policy.
- Publicity will be given to the quality policy in every part of the organization so that everyone may understand it. All available methods and media will be used for its internal and external promotion and communication.
- Reporting on the progress of the implementation of the policy will be a permanent agenda item in management meetings.

The quality policy must be the concern of all employees, and the principles and objectives communicated as widely as possible. Practical assistance and training should be given, where necessary, to ensure the relevant knowledge and experience are acquired for successful implementation of the policy.

2.3   Creating or changing the culture

The culture within an organization is formed by a number of components:
1   Behaviours based on people interactions.
2   Norms resulting from working groups.
3   Dominant values adopted by the organization.
4   Rules of the game for getting on.
5   The climate.

Culture in any 'business' may be defined then as the beliefs that pervade the organization about how business should be conducted, and how employees should behave and should be treated. Any organization needs a vision framework that includes its *guiding philosophy, core values and beliefs* and a *purpose*. These should be combined into a *mission*, which provides a vivid description of what things will be like when it has been achieved.

The *guiding philosophy* drives the organization and is shaped by the leaders through their thoughts and actions. It should reflect the vision of an organization rather than the vision of a single leader, and should evolve with time, although organizations must hold on to the *core* elements.

The *core values and beliefs* represent the organization's basic principles about what is important in business, its conduct, its social responsibility and its response to changes in the environment. They should act as a guiding force, with clear and authentic values, which are focused on employees, suppliers, customers, society at large, safety, shareholders, and generally stakeholders.

The *purpose* of the organization should be a development from the core values and beliefs and should quickly and clearly convey how the organization is to fulfil its role.

The *mission* will translate the abstractness of philosophy into tangible goals that will move the organization forward and make it perform to its optimum. It should not be limited by the constraints of strategic analysis, and should be proactive not reactive. Strategy is subservient to mission, the strategic analysis being done after, not during, the mission setting process.

Control

The effectiveness of an organization and its people depends on the extent to which each person and department perform their role and move towards the common goals and objectives. Control is the process by which information or feedback is provided so as to keep all functions on track. It is the sum total of the activities that increase the probability of the planned results being achieved. Control mechanisms fall into three categories, depending upon their position in the managerial process:

Before the fact	*Operational*	*After the fact*
Strategic plan	Observation	Annual reports
Action plans	Inspection and correction	Variance reports
Budgets	Progess review	Audits
Job descriptions	Staff meetings	Surveys

| Individual performance objectives | Internal Information and data systems | Performance Review |
| Training and development plans | Training programmes | Evaluation of training |

Many organizations use after-the-fact controls, causing managers to take a reactive rather than a proactive position. Such 'crisis-orientation' needs to be replaced by a more anticipative one in which the focus is on preventive or before-the-fact controls.

Attempting to control performance through systems, procedures, or techniques *external* to the individual is not an effective approach, since it relies on 'controlling' others; individuals should be responsible for their own actions. An externally based control system can result in a high degree of concentrated effort in a specific area if the system is overly structured, but it can also cause negative consequences to surface:

1   Since all rewards are based on external measures, which are imposed, the 'team members' often focus all their efforts on the measure itself, e.g. to have it set lower (or higher) than possible, to manipulate the information which serves to monitor it, or to dismiss it as someone else's goal not theirs. In the budgeting process, for example, distorted figures are often submitted by those who have learned that their 'honest projections' will be automatically altered anyway.
2   When the rewards are dependent on only one or two limited targets, all efforts are directed at those, even at the expense of others. If short-term profitability is the sole criterion for bonus distribution or promotion, it is likely that investment for longer-term growth areas will be substantially reduced. Similarly, strong emphasis and reward for output or production may result in lowered quality.
3   The fear of not being rewarded, or even being criticized, for performance that is less than desirable may cause some to withhold information that is unfavourable but nevertheless should be flowing into the system.
4   When reward and punishment are used to motivate performance, the degree of risk-taking may lessen and be replaced by a more cautious and conservative approach. In essence, the fear of failure replaces the desire to achieve.

The following problem situations have been observed by the author and his colleagues within companies that have taken part in research and consultancy on quality management:

• The goals imposed are seen or known to be unrealistic. If the goals perceived by the subordinate are in fact accomplished, then the subordinate has proved himself wrong. This clearly has a negative effect on the effort expended, since few people are motivated to prove themselves wrong!
• Where individuals are stimulated to commit themselves to a goal, and where their personal pride and self-esteem are at stake, then the level of motivation is at a peak. For most people the toughest critic and the hardest taskmaster they confront is not their immediate boss but themselves.
• Directors and managers are often afraid of allowing subordinates to set the goals for fear of them being set too low, or loss of control over subordinate behaviour. It is

also true that many do not wish to set their own targets, but prefer to be told what is to be accomplished.

TQM is concerned with moving the focus of control from outside the individual to within, the objective being to make everyone accountable for their own performance, and to get them committed to attaining quality in a highly motivated fashion. The assumptions a director or manager must make in order to move in this direction are simply that people do not need to be coerced to perform well, and that people want to achieve, accomplish, influence activity, and challenge their abilities. If there is belief in this, then only the techniques remain to be discussed.

Total Quality Management is user-driven – it cannot be imposed from outside the organization, as perhaps can a quality standard or statistical process control. This means that the ideas for improvement must come from those with knowledge and experience of the processes, activities and tasks; this has massive implications for training and follow-up. TQM is not a cost-cutting or productivity improvement device in the traditional sense, and it must not be used as such. Although the effects of a successful programme will certainly reduce costs and improve productivity, TQM is concerned chiefly with changing attitudes and skills so that the culture of the organization becomes one of preventing failure – doing the right things, right first time, every time.

2.4   Effective leadership

Some management teams have broken away from the traditional style of management; they have made a 'managerial breakthrough'. Their new approach puts their organizations head and shoulders above competitors in the fight for sales, profits, resources, funding and jobs. Many service organizations are beginning to move in the same way, and the successful quality-based strategy they are adopting depends very much on effective leadership.

Effective leadership starts with the Chief Executive's vision, capitalizing on market or service opportunities, continues through a strategy that will give the organization competitive advantage, and leads to business or service success. It goes on to embrace all the beliefs and values held, the decisions taken and the plans made by anyone anywhere in the organization, and the focusing of them into effective, value-adding action.

Together, effective leadership and total quality management result in the company or organization doing the right things, right first time.

The five requirements for effective leadership are the following.

1   Developing and publishing clear documented corporate beliefs and objectives – a mission statement

Executives must express values and beliefs through a clear vision of what they want their company or organization to be, and through objectives – what they specifically want to achieve in line with the basic beliefs. Together, they define what the company or organization is all about. The senior management team will need to spend some time away from the 'coal face' to do this and develop their programme for implementation.

Clearly defined and properly communicated beliefs and objectives, which can be summarized in the form of a mission statement, are essential if the directors, managers and other employees are to work together as a winning team. The beliefs and objectives should address:

- The definition of the business, e.g. the needs that are satisfied or the benefits provided.
- A commitment to effective leadership and quality.
- Target sectors and relationships with customers, and market or service position.
- The role or contribution of the company, organization, or unit, e.g. example, profit-generator, service department, opportunity-seeker.
- The distinctive competence – a brief statement which applies only to that organization, company or unit.
- Indications for future direction – a brief statement of the principal plans which would be considered.
- Commitment to monitoring performance against customers' needs and expectations, and continuous improvement.

The mission statement and the broad beliefs and objectives may then be used to communicate an inspiring vision of the organization's future. The top management must then show *TOTAL COMMITMENT* to it.

2 Developing clear and effective strategies and supporting plans for achieving the mission and objectives

The achievement of the company or service objectives requires the development of business or service strategies, including the strategic positioning in the 'market place'. Plans for implementing the strategies can then be developed. Strategies and plans can be developed by senior managers alone, but there is likely to be more commitment to them if employee participation in their development and implementation is encouraged.

3 Identifying the critical success factors and critical processes

The next step is the identification of the *critical success factors* (CSFs), a term used to mean the most important subgoals of a business or organization. CSFs are what must be accomplished for the mission to be achieved. The CSFs are followed by the key, critical or business processors for the organization – the activities that must be done particularly well for the CSFs to be achieved. This process is described in some detail in Chapter 13 on implementation.

4 Reviewing the management structure

Defining the corporate objectives and strategies, CSFs and critical processes might make it necessary to review the organizational structure. Directors, managers and other employees can be fully effective only if an effective structure based on process management exists. This includes both the definition of responsibilities for the organization's management and the operational procedures they will use. These must be the agreed best ways of carrying out the critical processes.

The review of the management structure should include the establishment of a process quality improvement team structure throughout the organization.

5   *Empowerment – encouraging effective employee participation*

For effective leadership it is necessary for management to get very close to the employees. They must develop effective communications – up, down and across the organization – and take action on what is communicated; and they must encourage good communications between all suppliers and customers.

Particular attention must be paid to the following.

Attitudes

The key attitude for managing any winning company or organization may be expressed as follows: 'I will personally understand who my customers are and what are their needs and expectations of me; I will measure how well I am satisfying their needs and expectations and I will take whatever action is necessary to satisfy them fully. I will also understand and communicate my requirements to my suppliers, inform them of changes and provide feedback on their performance'. This attitude must start at the top – with the Chairman or Chief Executive. It must then percolate down, to be adopted by each and every employee. That will happen only if managers lead by example. Words are cheap and will be meaningless if employees see from managers' actions that they do not actually believe or intend what they say.

Abilities

Every employee must be able to do what is needed and expected of him or her, but it is first necessary to decide what is really needed and expected. If it is not clear what the employees are required to do and what standards of performance are expected, how can managers expect them to do it?

Train, train, train and train again. Training is very important, but it can be expensive if the money is not spent wisely. The training must be related to needs, expectations, and process improvement. It must be planned and *always* its effectiveness must be reviewed.

Participation

If all employees are to participate in making the company or organization successful (directors and managers included), then they must also be trained in the basics of disciplined management.

They must be trained to:

E Evaluate – the situation and define their objectives.
P Plan – to achieve those objectives fully.
D Do, i.e. implement the plans.
C Check – that the objectives are being achieved.
A Amend, i.e. take corrective action if they are not.

The word 'disciplined' applied to people at all levels means that they will do what they say they will do. It also means that in whatever they do they will go through the full process of Evaluate, Plan, Do, Check and Amend, rather than the more traditional and easier option of starting by doing rather than evaluating. This will lead to a never-ending improvement helix (Figure 2.1)

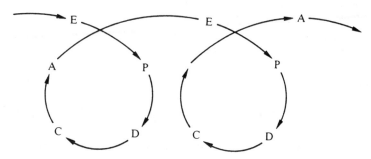

Figure 2.1 *The helix of never-ending improvement*

This basic approach needs to be backed up with good project management, planning techniques and problem-solving methods, which can be taught to anyone in a relatively short period of time. The project management enables changes to be made successfully and the problem-solving helps people to remove the obstacles in their way. Directors and managers need this training as much as other employees.

2.5 Ten points for senior management – the foundations of the TQM model

The vehicle for achieving effective leadership is Total Quality Management. We have seen that it covers the entire organization, all the people and all the functions, including external organizations and suppliers. In the first two chapters, several facets of TQM have been reviewed, including:

- Recognizing customers and discovering their needs.
- Setting standards that are consistent with customer requirements.
- Controlling processes, including systems, and improving their capability.
- Management's responsibility for setting the guiding philosophy, quality policy, etc., and providing motivation through leadership and equipping people to achieve quality.
- Empowerment of people at all levels in the organization to act for quality improvement.

The task of implementing TQM can be daunting, and the Chief Executive and directors faced with it may become confused and irritated by the proliferation of theories and packages. A simplification is required. The *core* of TQM must be the customer–supplier interfaces, both internally and externally, and the fact that at each interface there are processes to convert inputs to outputs. Clearly, there must be commitment to building-in quality through management of the inputs and processes.

How can senior managers and directors be helped in their understanding of what needs to be done to become committed to quality and implement the vision? Some American and Japanese quality 'gurus' have each set down a number of points or absolutes – words of wisdom in management and leadership – and many organizations are using these to establish a policy based on quality. These have been distilled down and modified here to ten points for senior management to adopt.

1   The organization needs long term COMMITMENT to constant improvement

There must be a constancy of purpose, and commitment to it must start from the top. The quality improvement process must be planned on a truly organization-wide basis, i.e. it must embrace all locations and departments and must include customers, suppliers, and subcontractors. It cannot start in 'one department' in the hope that the programme will spread from there.

The place to start the quality process is in the boardroom – leadership must be by example. Then the process must *progressive* expand to embrace all parts of the organization. It is wise to avoid the 'blitz' approach to TQM implementation, for it can lead to a lot of hype but no real changes in behaviour.

2   Adopt the philosophy of zero errors/defects to change the CULTURE to right first time.

This must be based on a thorough understanding of the customer's needs and expectations, and on teamwork, developed through employee participation and rigorous application of the EPDCA helix.

3   Train the people to understand the CUSTOMER–SUPPLIER relationships

Again the commitment to customer needs must start from the top, from the Chairman or Chief Executive. Without that, time and effort will be wasted. Customer orientation must then be achieved for each and every employee, directors and managers. The concept of internal customers and suppliers must be thoroughly understood and used.

4   Do not buy products or services on price alone – look at the TOTAL COST

Demand continuous improvement in everything, including suppliers. This will bring about improvements in product, service and failure rates. Continually improve the product or the service provided externally, so that the total costs of doing business are reduced.

5   Recognize that improvement of the SYSTEMS needs to be managed

Defining the performance standards expected and the systems to achieve them is a managerial responsibility. The rule has to be that the systems will be in line with the shared needs and expectations and will be part of the continuous improvement process.

6   Adopt modern methods of SUPERVISION and TRAINING – eliminate fear

It is all too easy to criticize mistakes, but it often seems difficult to praise efforts and achievements. Recognize and publicize efforts and achievements and provide the right sort of training, facilitation and supervision.

7   Eliminate barriers between departments by managing the PROCESS – improve COMMUNICATIONS and TEAMWORK

Barriers are often created by 'silo management', in which departments are treated like containers that are separate from one another. The customers are not interested in departments; they stand outside the organization and see slices through it – the *processes*. It is necessary to build teams and improve communications around the processes.

8   Eliminate the following:

- Arbitrary goals without methods.
- All standards based only on numbers.
- Barriers to pride of workmanship.
- Fiction. Get *FACTS* by using the correct *TOOLS*.

At all times it is essential to know how well you are doing in terms of satisfying the customers' needs and expectations. Help all employees to know *how* they will achieve their goals and how well they are doing.

Traditional piecework will not survive in a TQM environment, or *vice-versa*, because it creates barriers and conflict. People should be proud of what they do and not be encouraged to behave like monkeys being thrown peanuts.

Train people to measure and report performance in language that the people doing the job can understand. Encourage each employee to measure his/her own performance. Do not stop with measuring performance in the organization – find out how well other organizations (competitive or otherwise) are performing against similar needs and expectations (*benchmark* against best practice).

The costs of quality mismanagement and the level of firefighting are excellent factual indicators of the internal health of an organization. They are relatively easily measured and simple for most people to understand.

9   Constantly educate and retrain – develop the 'EXPERTS' in the business

The experts in any business are the people who do the job every day of their lives. The 'energy' that lies within them can be released into the organization through education, training, encouragement and the chance to participate.

10   Develop a SYSTEMATIC approach to manage the implementation of TQM

TQM should not be regarded as a woolly-minded approach to running an organization. It requires a carefully planned and fully integrated strategy, derived from the mission. That way it will help any organization to realize its vision.

Summary
- Identify *customer–supplier* relationships.
- Manage *processes*.
- Change the *culture*.
- Improve *communication*.
- Show *commitment*.

The right culture, communication, and commitment form the basis of the first part of a model for TQM – the 'soft' outcomes of TQM (Figure 2.2). The process core must be surrounded, however, by some 'hard' management necessities:

1 Systems (based on a good international standard, see Part 2 of this book).
2 Tools (for analysis, correlations, and predictions for action for continuous improvement to be taken, see Part 3 of this book).
3 Teams (the councils, quality improvement teams, quality circles, corrective action teams, etc., see Part 4 of this book).

The model now provides a multi-dimensional TQM 'vision' against which a particular organization's status can be examined, or against which a particular approach to TQM implementation may be compared and weaknesses highlighted. It is difficult to draw in only two dimensions, but Figure 2.3 is an attempt to represent the major features of the model, the implementation of which is dealt with in Part 5.

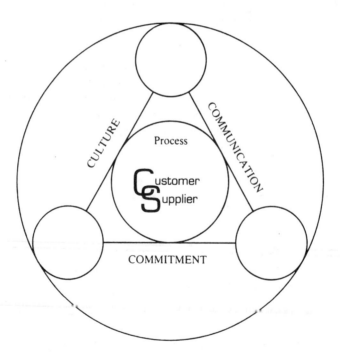

Figure 2.2 *Total quality management model – the 'soft' outcomes*

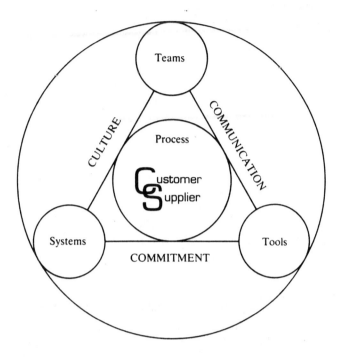

Figure 2.3 *Total quality management model – major features*

One of the greatest tangible benefits of improved quality is the increased market share that results, rather than just the reduction in quality costs. The evidence for this can be seen already in some of the major consumer and industrial markets of the world. Superior quality can also be converted into premium prices. Quality clearly correlates with profit. The less tangible benefit of greater employee participation in quality is equally, if not more, important in the longer term. The pursuit of continual improvement must become a way of life for everyone in an organization if it is to succeed in today's competitive environment.

Chapter highlights

The Total Quality Management approach

- TQM is a comprehensive approach to improving competitiveness, effectiveness and flexibility through planning, organizing and understanding each activity, and involving each individual at each level. It is useful in all types of organization.
- TQM ensures that management adopts a stategic overview of quality and focuses on prevention, not detection, of problems.
- It often requres a mindset change to break down existing barriers. Managements that doubt the applicability of TQM should ask questions about the operation's costs, errors, wastes, standards, systems, training and job instructions.

Commitment and policy

- TQM starts at the top, where serious obsessional commitment to quality must be demonstrated. Middle management also has a key role to play in communicating the message.
- Every Chief Executive must accept the responsibility for commitment to a quality policy that deals with the organization for quality, the customer needs, the ability of the organization, supplied materials and services, education and training, and review of the management systems for never-ending improvement.

Creating or changing the culture

- The culture of an organization is formed by the beliefs, behaviours, norms, dominant values, rules and climate in the organization.
- Any organization needs a vision framework, comprising its guiding philosophy, core values and beliefs, purpose, and mission.
- The effectiveness of an organization depends on the extent to which people perform their roles and move towards the common goals and objectives.
- TQM is concerned with moving the focus of control from the outside to the inside of individuals, so that everyone is accountable for his/her own performance.

Effective leadership

- Effective leadership starts with the Chief Executive's vision and develops into a strategy for implementation.
- Top management must develop the following for effective leadership: clear beliefs and objectives in the form of a mission statement; clear and effective strategies and supporting plans; the critical success factors and critical processes; the appropriate management structure; employee participation through empowerment, and the EPDCA helix.

Ten points for senior management – the foundations

- Total quality is the key to effective leadership through commitment to constant improvement, a right first time philosophy, training people to understand customer–supplier relationships, not buying on price alone, managing systems improvement, modern supervision and training, managing processes through teamwork and improved communications, elimination of barriers and fear, constant education and 'expert' development, a systematic approach to TQM implementation.
- The core of TQM is the customer–supplier relationship, where the processes must be managed. The 'soft' outcomes of TQM – the culture, communications, and commitment provide the foundation for the TQM model.
- The process core must be surrounded by the 'hard' management necessities of systems, tools and teams. The model provides a framework against which an organization's progress towards TQM can be examined.

3

Design for quality

3.1 Innovation, design and improvement

All businesses competing on the basis of quality need to update their products, processes and services periodically. In markets such as electronics, audio and visual goods, and office automation, new variants of products are offered frequently – almost like fashion goods. While in other markets the pace of innovation may not be as fast and furious, there is no doubt that the rate of change for product, service and process design has acclerated on a broad front.

Innovation entails both the invention and design of radically new products and services, embodying novel ideas, discoveries and advanced technologies, *and* the continuous development and improvement of existing products, services, and processes to enhance their performance and quality. It may also be directed at reducing costs of production or operations throughout the life cycle of the product or service system.

In many organizations innovation is predominantly either technology-led, e.g. in some chemical and engineering industries, or marketing-led, e.g. in some food companies. What is always striking about leading product or service innovators is that their developments are market-led, which is different from marketing-led. The latter means that the marketing function takes the lead in product and service developments. But most leading innovators identify and set out to meet the existing and potential demands profitably, and therefore are market-led, constantly striving to meet the requirements even more effectively through appropriate experimentation.

Commitment to quality in the most senior management helps to build quality throughout the design process and to ensure good relationships and communication between various groups and functional areas. Designing customer satisfaction into products and services contributes greatly to competitive success. Clearly, it does not guarantee it, because the conformance aspect of quality must be present and the operational processes must be capable of producing to the design. As in the marketing/operations interfaces, it is never acceptable to design a product, service, system or process that the customer wants but the organization is incapable of achieving.

The design process, then, often concerns technological innovation in response to, or in anticipation of, changing market requirements and trends in technology. Those companies with impressive records of product- or service-led growth have demonstrated a state-of-the-art approach to innovation based on three principles:

- *Strategic balance* to ensure that both old and new product service developments are important. Updating old products, services and processes, ensures continuing cash generation from which completely new products may be funded.
- *Top management approach* to design to set the tone and ensure that commitment is the common objective by visibly supporting the design effort. Direct control should be concentrated on critical decision points, since over-meddling by very senior people in day-to-day project management can delay and demotivate staff.
- *Teamwork*, to ensure that once projects are under way, specialist inputs, e.g. from marketing and technical experts, are fused and problems are tackled simultaneously. The teamwork should be urgent yet informal, for too much formality will stifle initiative, flair and fun of design.

The extent of the design activity should not be underestimated, but it often is. Many people associate design with *styling* of products, and this is certainly an important aspect. But for certain products and many service operations the *secondary design* considerations are vital. Anyone who has bought an 'assemble-it-yourself' kitchen unit will know the importance of the design of the assembly instructions, for example. Aspects of design that affect quality in this way are packaging, customer-service arrangements, maintenance routines, warranty details and their fulfilment, spare-part availability, etc.

An industry that has learned much about the secondary design features of its products is personal computers. Many of the problems of customer dissatisfaction experienced in this market have not been product design features but problems with user manuals, availability and loading of software, and applications. For technically complex products or service systems, the design and marketing of after-sales arrangements are an essential component of the design activity. The design of production equipment and its layout to allow ease of access for repair and essential maintenance, or simple use as intended, widens the management of design quality into suppliers and contractors and requires their total commitment.

Proper design of plant and equipment plays a major role in the elimination of errors, defectives, and waste. Correct initial design also obviates the need for costly and wasteful modifications to be carried out after the plant or equipment has been constructed. It is at the plant design stage that such important matters as variability, reproducibility, ease of use in operation, maintainability, etc. should receive detailed consideration.

Designing

If quality design is taking care of all aspects of the customer's requirements, including cost, production, safe and easy use, and maintainability of products and services, then *designing* must take place in all aspects of:

- Identifying the need (including need for change).
- Developing that which satisfies the need.
- Checking the conformance to the need.
- Ensuring that the need is satisfied.

Designing covers every aspect, from the identification of a problem to be solved, usually a market need, through the development of design concepts and prototypes to the generation of detailed specifications or instructions required to produce the artefact or provide the service. It is the process of presenting needs in some physical form, initially as a solution, and then as a specific configuration or arrangement of materials, resources, equipment, and people.

3.2   Quality function deployment (QFD) – the house of quality

The 'house of quality' is the framework of the approach to design management known as quality function deployment (QFD). It originated in Japan in 1972 at Mitsubishi's Kobe shipyard, but it has been developed in numerous ways by Toyota and its suppliers, and many other organizations. The house of quality (HOQ) concept, initially referred to as quality tables, has been used successfully by manufacturers of integrated circuits, synthetic rubber, construction equipment, engines, home appliances, clothing, and electronics, mostly Japanese. Ford and General Motors use it, and other organizations, including AT&T, Bell Laboratories, Digital Equipment, Hewlett-Packard, Procter & Gamble, ITT, Rank Xerox, Jaguar, and Mercury have applications. In Japan its design applications include public services, retail outlets, and apartment layout.

Quality function deployment (QFD) is a 'system' for designing a product or service, based on customer demands, with the participation of members of all functions of the supplier organization. It translates the customer's requirements into the appropriate technical requirements for each stage. The activities included in QFD are:

1   Market research.
2   Basic research.
3   Invention.
4   Concept design.
5   Prototype testing.
6   Final-product or service testing.
7   After-sales service and trouble-shooting.

These are performed by peoples with different skills in a team whose composition depends on many factors, including the products or services being developed and the size of the operation. In many customer industries, such as cars, video equipment, electronics, and computers, 'engineering' designers are seen to be heavily into designing. But in other industries and service operations designing is carried out by people who do not carry the word 'designer' in their job title. The failure to recognize the design inputs they make, and to provide appropriate training and support, will limit the success of the design activities and result in some offering that does not satisfy the customer. This is particularly true of internal customers.

The QFD team in operation

The first step of a QFD exercise is to form a cross-functional QFD team. Its purpose is to take the needs of the market and translate them into such a form that they can be satisfied within the operating unit and delivered to the customers.

As with all organizational problems, the structure of the QFD Team must be decided on the basis of the detailed requirements of each organization. One thing, however, is clear – close liaison must be maintained at all times between the design, marketing and operational functions represented in the team.

The QFD team must answer three questions – WHO, WHAT and HOW, i.e.

WHO are the customers?
WHAT does the customer need?
HOW will the needs be satisfied?

WHO may be decided by asking 'Who will benefit from the successful introduction of this product, service, or process?' Once the customers have been identified, WHAT can be ascertained through an interview/ questionnaire process, or from the knowledge and judgement of the QFD team members. HOW is more difficult to determine, and will consist of the attributes of the product, service, or process under development. This will constitute many of the action steps in a 'QFD strategic plan'.

WHO, WHAT, and HOW are entered into the QFD matrix or grid of 'house of quality', which is a simple 'quality table'. The *WHAT*s are recorded in rows and the *HOW*s are placed in the columns.

The house of quality provides structure to the design and development cycle, often likened to the construction of a house, because of the shape of matrices when they are fitted together. The key to building the house is the focus on the customer requirements, so that the design and development processes are driven more by what the customer needs than by innovations in technology. This ensures that more effort is used to obtain the vital customer information. It may increase the initial planning time in a particular development project, but the time, including design and redesign, taken to bringing a product of service to the market will be reduced.

This requires that marketing people, design staff (including engineers), and production/operations personnel work closely together from the time the new service, process, or product is conceived. It will need to replace in many organizations the 'throwing it over the wall' approach, where a solid wall exists between each pair of functions (Figure 3.1).

The HOQ provides an organization with the means for inter-departmental or inter-functional planning and communications, starting with the so-called customer attributes (CAs). These are phrases customers use to describe product, process, and service characteristics.

A complete QFD project will lead to the construction of a sequence of house of quality diagrams, which translate the customer requirements into specific operational process steps. For example, the 'feel' that customers like on the steering wheel of a motor car may translate into a specification for 45 standard degrees of synthetic polymer hardness, which in turn translates into specific manufacturing process steps,

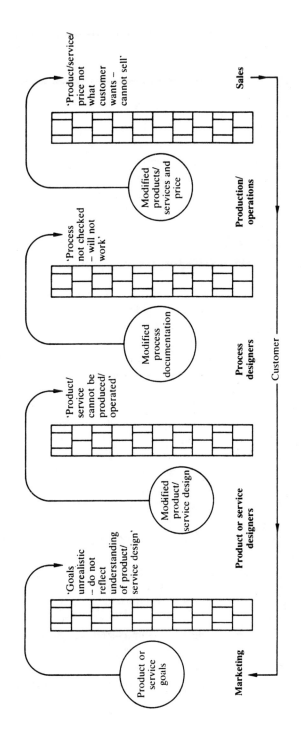

Figure 3.1 'Throw it over the wall.' The design and development process is sequential and walled into separate functions

including the use of certain catalysts, temperatures, processes, and additives.

The first steps in QFD lead to a consideration of the product as a whole, and subsequent steps to consideration of the individual components. For example, a complete hotel service would be considered at the first level, but subsequent QFD exercises would tackle the restaurant, bedrooms and reception. Each of the sub-services would have customer requirements, but they all would need to be compatible with the general service concept.

The QFD or house of quality tables

Figure 3.2 shows the essential components of the quality table or HOQ diagram. The construction begins with the *customer requirements*, which are determined through the 'voice of the customer' – the marketing and market research activities. These are entered into the blocks to the left of the central relationship matrix. Understanding and prioritizing the customer requirements by the QFD team may require the use of competitive and compliant analysis, focus groups, and the analysis of market potential. The prime or broad requirements should lead to the detailed WHATs.

Once the customer requirements have been determined and entered into the table, the *importance* of each is rated and rankings are added. The use of the 'emphasis technique' or paired comparison may be helpful here (see Chapter 8).

Each customer requirement should then be examined in terms of customer rating; a group of customers may be asked how they perceive the performance of the organization's product or service versus those of competitors'. These results are placed to the right of the central matrix. Hence the customer requirements' importance rankings and competition ratings appear from left to right across the house.

The WHATs must now be converted into the HOWs. These are called the *technical design requirements* and appear on the diagram from top to bottom in terms of requirements, rankings (or costs) and ratings against competition (technical benchmarking, see Chapter 7). These will provide the 'voice of the process'.

The technical requirements themselves are placed immediately above the central matrix and may also be given a hierarchy of prime and detailed requirements. Immediately below the central relationship matrix appear the rankings of technical difficulty, development time, or costs. These will enable the QFD team to discuss the efficiency of the various technical solutions. Below the technical rankings on the diagram comes the benchmark data, which compares the technical processes of the organization against its competitors'.

The *central relationship matrix* is the working core of the house of quality diagram. Here the WHATs are matched with the HOWs, and each customer requirement is systematically assessed against each technical design requirement. The nature of any relationship – strong positive, positive, neutral, negative, strong negative – is shown by symbols in the matrix. The QFD team carries out the relationship estimation, using experience and judgement, the aim being to identify HOW the WHATs may be achieved. All the HOWs listed must be necessary and together sufficient to achieve the WHATs. Blank rows (customer requirement not met) and columns (redundant technical characteristics) should not exist.

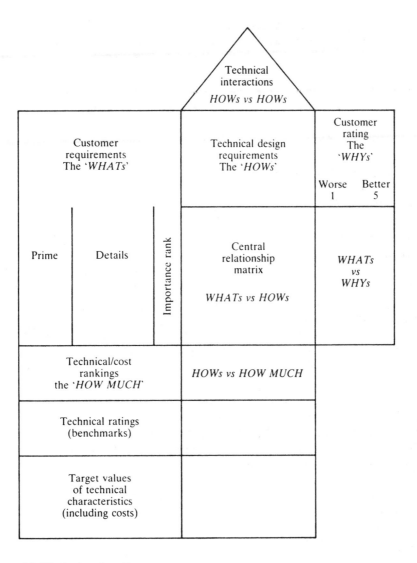

Figure 3.2 *The house of quality*

The roof of the house shows the interactions between the technical design requirements. Each characteristic is matched against the others, and the diagonal format allows
the nature of relationships to be displayed. The symbols used are the same as those in
the central matrix.

The complete QFD process is time-consuming, because each cell in the central and
roof matrices must be examined by the whole team. The team must examine the matrix
to determine which technical requirement will need design attention, and the costs of
that attention will be given in the bottom row. If certain technical costs become a major
issue, the priorities may then be changed. It will be clear from the central matrix if there
is more than one way to achieve a particular customer requirement, and the roof matrix

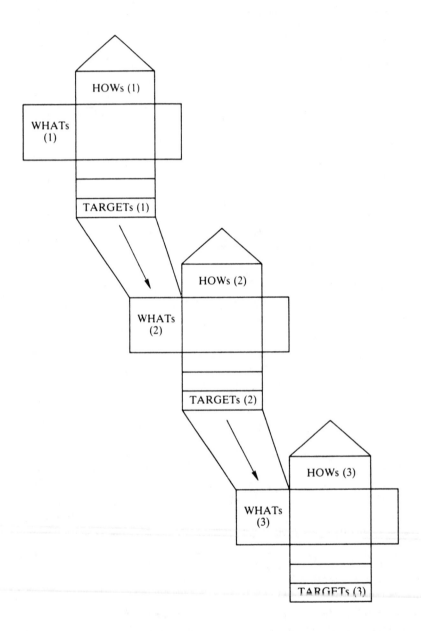

Figure 3.3 *The 'deployment' of the 'voice of the customer' through quality tables*

will show if the technical requirements to achieve one customer requirement will have a negative effect on another technical issue.

The very bottom of the house of quality diagram shows the *target* values of the *technical characteristics*, which are expressed in physical terms. They can only be decided by the team after discussion of the complete house contents. While these targets are the physical output of the QFD exercise, the whole process of information-gathering, structuring, and ranking generates a tremendous improvement in the team's cross-functional understanding of the product/service design delivery system. The target technical characteristics may be used to generate the next level house of quality diagram, where they become the WHATs, and the QFD process determines the further details of HOW they are to be achieved. In this way the process 'deploys' the customer requirements all the way to the final operational stages. Figure 3.3 shows how the target technical characteristics at each level becomes the input to the next level matrix.

QFD progresses now through the use of the 'seven new planning tools'[1] and other standard techniques such as value analysis,[2] experimental design,[3] statistical process control,[4] and so on.

The benefits of QFD

The aim of the HOQ is to co-ordinate the inter-functional activities and skills within an organization. This should lead to products and services designed, produced/operated, and marketed so that customers will want to purchase them and continue doing so.

The use of competitive information in QFD should help to prioritize resources and to structure the existing experience and information. This allows the identification of items that can be acted upon.

There should be reductions in the number of midstream design changes, and these reductions in turn will limit post-introduction problems and reduce implementation time. Because QFD is consensus-based, it promotes teamwork and creates communications at functional interfaces, while also identifying required actions. It should lead to a 'global view' of the development process, from a consideration of all the details.

If QFD is introduced systematically, it should add structure to the information, generate a framework for sensitivity analysis, and provide documentation, which must be 'living' and adaptable to change. In order to understand the full impact of QFD it is necessary to examine the changes that take place in the team and the organization during the design and development process. The main benefit of QFD is of course the increase in customer satisfaction, which may be measured in terms of, for example, reductions in warranty claims.

3.3 Design control

Design, like any other activity, must be carefully managed. A flowchart of the various stages and activities involved in the design and development process appears in Figure 3.4.

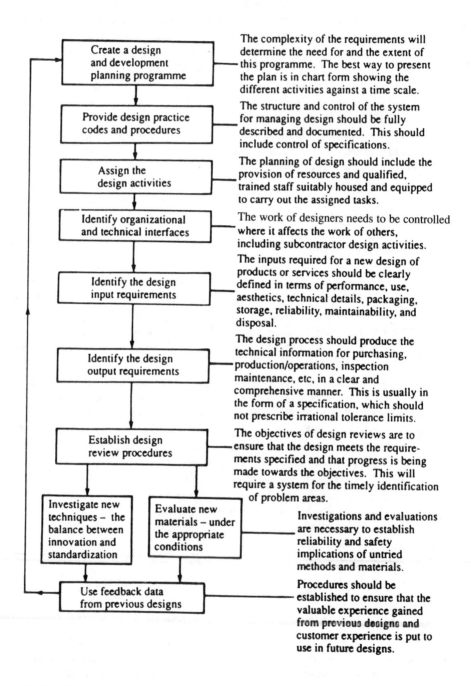

The complexity of the requirements will determine the need for and the extent of this programme. The best way to present the plan is in chart form showing the different activities against a time scale.

The structure and control of the system for managing design should be fully described and documented. This should include control of specifications.

The planning of design should include the provision of resources and qualified, trained staff suitably housed and equipped to carry out the assigned tasks.

The work of designers needs to be controlled where it affects the work of others, including subcontractor design activities.

The inputs required for a new design of products or services should be clearly defined in terms of performance, use, aesthetics, technical details, packaging, storage, reliability, maintainability, and disposal.

The design process should produce the technical information for purchasing, production/operations, inspection maintenance, etc, in a clear and comprehensive manner. This is usually in the form of a specification, which should not prescribe irrational tolerance limits.

The objectives of design reviews are to ensure that the design meets the requirements specified and that progress is being made towards the objectives. This will require a system for the timely identification of problem areas.

Investigations and evaluations are necessary to establish reliability and safety implications of untried methods and materials.

Procedures should be established to ensure that the valuable experience gained from previous designs and customer experience is put to use in future designs.

Figure 3.4 *The design control process*

By structuring the design process in this way, it is possible to:

- Control the various stages.
- Check that they have been completed.
- Decide which management functions need to be brought in and at what stage.
- Estimate the level of resources needed.

The design control must be carefully handled to avoid stifling the creativity of the designer(s), which is crucial in making design solutions a reality.

It is clear that the design process requires a range of specialized skills, and the way in which these skills are managed, the way they interact, and the amount of effort devoted to the different stages of the design and development process is fundamental to the quality, producibility, and price of the service or final product. A QFD team approach to the management of design can play a major role in the success of a project.

It is never possible to exert the same tight control on the design effort as on other operational efforts, yet the cost and the time used are often substantial, and both must appear somewhere within the organization's budget.

Certain features make control of design difficult:

1   No design will ever be 'complete' in the sense that, with effort, some modification or improvement cannot be made.
2   Few designs are entirely novel. An examination of most 'new' products, services or processes will show that they employ existing techniques, components or systems to which have been added a comparatively small novel element.
3   The longer the time spent on a design, the less the increase in the value of the design unless a technological breakthrough is achieved. This diminishing return from the design effort must be carefully managed.
4   External and/or internal customers will impose limitations on design time and cost. It is as difficult to imagine a design project whose completion date is not implicitly fixed, either by a promise to a customer, the opening of a trade show or exhibition, a seasonal 'deadline', a production schedule or, some other constraint, as it is to imagine an organization whose funds are unlimited, or a product whose price has no ceiling.

Total design processes

Quality of design, then, concerns far more than the product or service design and its ability to meet the customer requirements. It is also about the activities of design and development. The appropriateness of the actual *design process* has a profound influence on the quality performance of any organization, and much can be learned by examining successful organizations and how their strategies for research, design, and development are linked to the efforts of marketing and operations. In some quarters this is referred to as 'total design', and the term 'simultaneous engineering' has been used. This is an integrated approach to a new product or service introduction, similar in many ways to QFD in using multifunction teams or task forces to ensure that research, design, development, manufacturing, purchasing, supply, and marketing all work in parallel from concept through to the final launch of the product or service into the market place, including servicing and maintenance.

3.4   Specifications and standards

There is a strong relationship between standardization and specification. To ensure that a product or a service is *standardized* and may be repeated a large number of times in exactly the manner required, *specifications* must be written so that they are open to only one interpretation. The requirements, and therefore the quality, must be built into the design specification. There are national and international standards which, if used, help to ensure that specifications will meet certain accepted criteria of technical or managerial performance, safety, etc.

Standardization does not guarantee that the best design or specification is selected. It may be argued that the whole process of standardization slows down the rate and direction of technological development, and affects what is produced. If standards are used correctly, however, the process of drawing up specifications should provide opportunities to learn more about particular innovations and to change the standards accordingly.

It is possible to strike a balance between innovation and standardization. Clearly, it is desirable for designers to adhere where possible to past-proven materials and methods, in the interests of reliability, maintainability and variety control. Hindering designers from using recently developed materials, components, or techniques, however, can cause the design process to stagnate technologically. A balance must be achieved by analysis of materials, products and processes proposed in the design, against the background of their known reproducibility and reliability. If breakthrough innovations are proposed, then analysis or testing should be indicated objectively, justifying their adoption in preference to the established alternatives.

It is useful to define a specification. The International Standards Organization (ISO) defines it in ISO 8402 (1986) as 'The document that prescribes the requirements with which the product or service has to conform'. A document not giving a detailed statement or description of the requirements to which the product, service or process must comply cannot be regarded as a specification, and this is true of much sales literature.

The specification conveys the customer requirements to the supplier to allow the product or service to be designed, engineered, produced, or operated by means of conventional or stipulated equipment, techniques, and technology. The basic requirements of a specification are that it gives the:

- Performance requirements of the product or service.
- Parameters – such as dimensions, concentration, turn-round time which describe the product or service adequately (these should be quantified and include the units of measurement).
- Materials to be used by stipulating properties or referring to other specifications.
- Method of production or operations.

- Inspection/testing/checking requirements.
- References to other applicable specifications or documents.

To fulfil its purpose the specifications must be written in terminology that is readily understood, and in a manner that is unambiguous and so cannot be subject to differing interpretation. This is not an easy task, and one which requires all the expertise and knowledge available. Good specifications are usually the product of much discussion, deliberation and sifting of information and data, and represent tangible output from a QFD team.

3.5 Quality design in the service sector

The emergence of the services sector has been suggested by economists to be part of the natural progression in which economic dominance changes first from agriculture to manufacturing and then to services. It is argued that if income elasticity of demand is higher for services than it is for goods, then as incomes rise, resources will shift toward services. The continuing growth of services verifies this, and is further explained by changes in culture, fitness, safety, demography and life styles.

In considering the design of services it is important to consider the differences between goods and services. Some authors argue that the marketing and design of goods and services should conform to the same fundamental rules, whereas others claim that there is a need for a different approach to services because of the recognizable differences between the goods and services themselves.

In terms of design, it is possible to recognize three distinct elements in the service package – the physical elements or facilitating goods, the explicit service or sensual benefits, and implicit service or psychological benefits. In addition, the particular characteristics of service delivery systems may be itemized:

- Intangibility.
- Perishability.
- Simultaneity.
- Heterogeneity.

It is difficult, if not impossible, to design the intangible aspects of a service, since consumers often must use experience or the reputation of a service organization and its representatives to judge quality.

Perishability is often an important issue in services, since it is often impossible or undesirable to hold stocks of the explicit service element of the service package. This aspect often requires that service operation and service delivery must exist simultaneously.

Simultaneity occurs because the consumer must be present before many services can take place. Hence, services are often formed in small and dispersed units, and it is difficult to take advantage of economies of scale. There is evidence that the emergence of computer and communications technologies is changing this in sectors such as banking, but contact continues to be necessary for the majority. Design considerations here include the environment and the systems used. Service facilities, procedures, and systems should be designed with the customer in mind, as well as the 'product' and the human resources. Managers need a picture of the total span of the operation, so that factors which are crucial to success are not neglected. This clearly means that the functions of marketing, design, and operations cannot be separated in services, and this must be taken into account in the design of the operational controls, such as the diagnosing of individual customer expectations. A QFD approach here is most appropriate.

Heterogeneity of services occurs in consequence of explicit and implicit service elements relying on individual preferences and perceptions. Differences exist in the outputs of organizations generating the same service, within the same organization, and even the same employee on different occasions. Clearly, unnecessary variation needs to be controlled, but the variation attributed to estimating, and then matching, the consumers' requirements is essential to customer satisfaction and must be designed into the systems. This inherent variability does, however, make it difficult to set precise quantifiable standards for all the elements of the service.

In the design of services it is useful to classify them in some way. Several sources from the literature on the subject help us to place services in one of five categories:

- Service factory.
- Service shop.
- Mass service.
- Professional service.
- Personal services.

Several service attributes have particular significance for the design of service operations:

1 *Labour intensity* – the ratio of labour costs incurred to the value of plant and equipment used (people versus equipment-based services).
2 *Contact* – the proportion of the total time required to provide the service for which the consumer is present in the system.
3 *Interaction* – the extent to which the consumer actively intervenes in the service process to change the content of the service; this includes customer participation to provide information from which needs can be assessed, and customer feedback from which satisfaction levels can be inferred.
4 *Customization* – which includes *choice* (providing one or more selections from a range of options, which can be single or fixed) and *adaptation* (the interaction process in which the requirement is decided, designed and delivered to match the need).
5 *Nature of service act* – either tangible, i.e. perceptible to touch and can be owned, or intangible, i.e. insubstantial.
6 *Recipient of service* – either people or things.

Table 3.1 gives a list of some services with their assigned attribute types and Table 3.2 shows how these may be used to group the services under the various classifications.

Table 3.1 *A classification of selected services*

Service	Labour intensity	Contact	Inter-action	Custom-ization	Nature of act	Recipient of service
Accountant	High	Low	High	Adapt	Intangible	Things
Architect	High	Low	High	Adapt	Intangible	Things
Bank	Low	Low	Low	Fixed	Intangible	Things
Beautician	High	High	High	Adapt	Tangible	People
Bus service	Low	High	Low	Choice	Tangible	People
Cafeteria	Low	High	High	Choice	Tangible	People
Cleaning firm	High	Low	Low	Fixed	Tangible	Things
Clinic	Low	High	High	Adapt	Tangible	People
Coach service	Low	High	Low	Choice	Tangible	People
Sports coaching	High	High	High	Adapt	Intangible	People
College	High	High	Low	Fixed	Intangible	People
Courier firm	High	Low	Low	Adapt	Tangible	Things
Dental practice	High	High	High	Adapt	Tangible	People
Driving school	High	High	High	Adapt	Intangible	People
Equip. hire	Low	Low	Low	Choice	Tangible	Things
Finance consult.	High	Low	High	Adapt	Intangible	Things
Hairdresser	High	High	High	Adapt	Tangible	People
Hotel	High	High	Low	Choice	Tangible	People
Leisure centre	Low	High	High	Choice	Tangible	People
Maintenance	Low	Low	Low	Choice	Tangible	Things
Nursery	High	Low	Low	Fixed	Tangible	People
Optician	High	High	High	Adapt	Tangible	People
Postal service	Low	Low	Low	Adapt	Tangible	Things
Rail service	Low	High	Low	Choice	Tangible	People
Repair firm	Low	Low	Low	Adapt	Tangible	Things
Restaurant	High	High	Low	Choice	Tangible	People
Service station	Low	High	High	Choice	Tangible	People
Solicitors	High	Low	High	Adapt	Intangible	Things
Take away	High	Low	Low	Choice	Tangible	People
Veterinary	High	Low	High	Adapt	Tangible	Things

It is apparent that services are part of almost all organizations and not confined to the service sector. What is clear is that the service classifications and different attributes must be considered in any service design process.

(The author is grateful to the contribution made by John Dotchin to this section of Chapter 3.)

Table 3.2 *Grouping of similar services*

PERSONAL SERVICES	
Driving school	Sports coaching
Beautician	Dental practice
Hairdresser	Optician

SERVICE SHOP	
Clinic	Cafeteria
Leisure centre	Service station

PROFESSIONAL SERVICES	
Accountant	Architect
Finance consultant	Solicitors
Veterinary	

MASS SERVICES	
Hotel	Restaurant
College	Bus service
Coach service	Rail service
Take away	Nursery
Courier firm	

SERVICE FACTORY	
Cleaning firm	Postal service
Repair firm	Equipment hire
Maintenance	Bank

Chapter highlights

Innovation, design and improvement

- All businesses need to update their products, processes and services.
- Innovation entails both invention and design, *and* continuous improvement of existing products, services, and processes.
- Leading product/service innovations are market-led. This requires a commitment at the top to building in quality throughout the design process. Moreover, the operational processes must be capable of achieving the design.
- State-of-the-art approach to innovation is based on a strategic balance of old and new, top management approach to design, and teamwork. The 'styling' of products must also be matched by secondary design considerations, such as operating instructions and software support.

Quality function deployment (QFD) – the house of quality

- The 'house of quality' is the framework of the approach to design management known as quality function deployment (QFD). It provides structure to the design and development cycle, which is driven by customer needs rather than innovation in technology.

- QFD is a system for designing a product or service, based on customer demands, and bringing in all members of the supplier organization.
- A QFD team's purpose is to take the needs of the market and translate them into such a form that they can be satisfied within the operating unit.
- The QFD team answers the following question, WHO are the customers? WHAT do the customers need? HOW will the needs be satisfied?
- The answers to the WHO, WHAT and HOW questions are entered into the QFD matrix or quality table, one of the seven new tools of planning and design.
- The foundations of the house of quality are the customer requirements; the framework is the central planning matrix, which matches the 'voice of the customer' with the 'voice of the processes' (the technical descriptions and capabilities); and the roof is the interrelationships matrix between the technical design requirements.
- The benefits of QFD include customer-driven design, prioritizing of resources, reductions in design changes and implementation time, and improvements in teamwork, communications, functional interfaces, and customer satisfaction.

Design control

- Design must be managed and controlled through planning, practice codes, procedures, activities assignments, identification of organizational and technical interfaces and design input requirements, review investigation and evaluation of new techniques and materials, and use of feedback data from previous designs.
- Total design or 'simultaneous engineering' is similar to QFD and uses multifunction teams to provide an integrated approach to product or service introduction.

Specifications and standards

- There is a strong relation between standardization and specifications. If standards are used correctly, the process of drawing up specifications should provide opportunities to learn more about innovations and change standards accordingly.
- The aim of specifications should be to reflect the true requirements of the product/service that are capable of being achieved.

Quality design in the service sector

- In the design of services three distinct elements may be recognized in the service package: physical (facilitating goods), explicit service (sensual benefits), and implicit service (psychological benefits). Moreover, the characteristics of service delivery may be itemized as intangibility, perishability, simultaneity, and heterogeneity.
- Services may be classified generally as service factory, service shop, mass service, professional service, and personal service. The service attributes that are important in designing services include labour intensity, contact interaction, customerization, nature of service act, and the direct recipient of the act.
- Use of this framework allows services to be grouped under the five classifications.

References

1   See J S Oakland, *Total Quality Management*, 2nd edition, Butterworth-Heinemann, 1993.
2   See K G Lockyer, A P Muhlemann and J S Oakland, *Production and Operations Management*, 6th edition, Pitman, 1992
3   See R Caulcutt, *Statistics in Research and Development*, 2nd edition, Chapman and Hall, 1991.
4   See J S Oakland and R F Followell, *Statistical Process Control*, 2nd edition, Butterworth-Heinemann, 1990.

Case studies

C1

TQM in the research and development environment – a balanced approach between 'hard' and 'soft' quality: Esso Research Centre

Background

The Esso Research Centre is part of Exxon Corporation, the worldwide multinational petrochemical company; the two largest Exxon businesses are petroleum and chemicals, both of which are represented at the Esso Research Centre. The worldwide petroleum business involves the discovery, production, transportation and marketing of petroleum products. The chemicals business manufactures, distributes and markets chemical products ranging from commodities such as ethylene to specialty chemicals used in a wide variety of applications. Research in Exxon is carried out in a number of laboratories specializing in different business aspects, ranging from crude oil production to the quality of the finished petroleum and chemicals used by consumers. The Research Centre, just south of Oxford, UK, has two separate functions, the Petroleum Product Quality Research and Development (R&D) activity, and the Performance Chemicals Technology activity.

The Petroleum R&D is aimed at development of petroleum fuels and lubricant products principally for European use, although some products are developed for worldwide application. The Performance Chemicals Technology Centre focuses on the development of specialty chemicals manufactured worldwide for inclusion in finished fuels and lubricants. In addition to new product development, both organizations provide technical services to assist product manufacture and marketing. A third function of the site is to provide service facilities and resources which support both of the petroleum and chemicals research groups. These range from a common restaurant to the evaluation of the performance of fuels and lubricants, physical and chemical techniques for analysis of products produced, and other operational functions which both groups need in order to operate.

The TQM beginnings

The petroleum research function's history in the total quality process goes back to the mid 1980s, when a mixture of external and internal factors began to affect the site. Externally, the business importance of being certified to the BS5750 (ISO9000) and Ford Q101 standards was increasing in the UK, and needed to be reflected in the technical service role. The chemicals businesses were also beginning to recognize the value of TQM in their operations, and were interested in encouraging the use of quality concepts by their suppliers within the Research Centre. Also at the time, a decision was taken by the Analytical Section to apply for certification to the National Measurement Accreditation Service (NAMAS), in response to some of their customers' interests and an internally driven process called Changing Gear, aimed at increasing employee motivation and self-esteem. Probably the most influential factor at this stage, however, was the appointment of a management team, which was convinced of the need to develop and encourage the people on the site to be more responsive, effective and efficient, in the eyes of the Exxon business groups which fund the petroleum research function. The team believed that the application of some form of TQM was the correct approach to the achievement of this end, so the issue was not whether to, but how to, apply the TQM philosophies.

In the exploratory phase of the site's experience in TQM, virtually no published methodology was available for a research organization to select the right approach. Indeed, some of the language used by some of the quality 'gurus', e.g. 'get it right first time' and 'zero defects', was definitely offputting to people involved in research. In the latter case, the end-result is not always as predictable as in a manufacturing operation, where much of the available TQM experience had been gained.

Searching for some relevant expertise, the management group selected a management consultant, who introduced a model of quality (Figure C1.1), which consisted of two dimensions: the operational and expressive dimensions of quality, both of which must be at a high level for total customer satisfaction to be generated. It

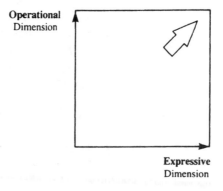

- Need to be good on operational, *and* good on expressive

Figure C1.1 *Two-dimensional model*

emphasized an important feature which needed to be recognized in a research function, that *cooperative relationships* between individuals and teams of people (e.g. R&D, and business groups) are as important as the actual research carried out by R&D groups.

The model was introduced to the whole petroleum site management group, which was then encouraged to develop it. This resulted in several new initiatives with on- and off-site groups, including attempts to measure customer satisfaction in both the operational and expressive dimensions. This model had a significant influence on the future development of the site's quality process, because it emphasized the importance of the 'people' dimension of quality. However, it lacked an important feature, the 'how to' dimension which is needed to achieve good operational and expressive results.

As this exploratory phase progressed, further external developments were occurring. The use of the ISO9002 standard was spreading throughout Europe, including Exxon's lubricant plants and business lines, and the concepts of TQM were becoming more widespread in application in Exxon, particularly in the chemical and petroleum business lines serving the automotive industries.

Consolidating and managing the process

At this stage, the site management group decided to consolidate the site's quality process and appointed a full-time quality manager. Further examination of approaches offered by consultants were made, and one was selected. Although the approach adopted was originally developed by a manufacturing industry leader in quality (Rank Xerox), it was felt to be adaptable to the research process. There were several elements in the appproach, including the 'process' dimension – the 'how to' which was lacking in the earlier experimental phase. The two-dimensional model (Figure C1.1) was, therefore, modified to the three-dimensional model shown in Figure C1.2, the three dimensions being product or service (equivalent to the operational dimension in the earlier mode), people (equivalent to the expressive dimension) and process (how the product and relationships were produced). The training also included a nine-step quality delivery process which covered work group missions, outputs, customers and processors, and a six-step problem-solving process. Tools such as flow-charting, fishbone diagrams, team work and brainstorming were also included.

This training package was given to the whole site over a period of about 12 months and resulted in many quality improvement projects, encompassing how new products were developed, new facilities were installed and scheduled, hazardous waste disposed of, contractor support planned, suppliers paid, and so on.

Although it was also recommended that the site adopt a formal cost of quality measurement system, this recommendation was not adopted. It was felt that it would be difficult to apply the concepts in detail to an R&D operation, where 'failure' can be turned into an important learning point, or where the 'lost opportunities' of a project not taken up at the time of its completion may turn into a positive benefit in later years, when the results and information used in the project may be used in further research work. The principle of a prevention-based approach to maximize research effectiveness was adopted, however.

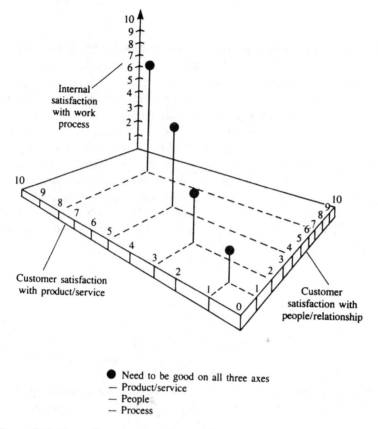

Figure C1.2 *Three-dimensional quality model*

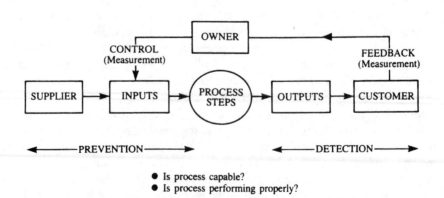

Figure C1.3 *Process management control*

Benefits derived – so soon?

This phase of the development of the Research Centre quality process resulted in many benefits:

- Many of the improvement projects were aimed at site problems which had hindered site effectiveness.
- The importance of the internal customer and quality chain concepts were recognized.
- The process management model (Figure C1.3) was shown to be useful in identifying the process flow, and measurement opportunities.
- An improved image with business groups resulted, which later was seen as vital in obtaining their agreement to future development of the site role.
- The value was demonstrated of the flow-charting and brainstorming quality tools to aid process definition and problem-solving.

Integrating TQM into the strategy

The next development in the process stemmed from a desire to improve the connection between business priorities and some of the improvements generated by staff. In some parts of the site, quality was seen as a separate activity to the normal job, quality behaviour being exhibited during quality improvements projects, which were not translated into equivalent behaviour on the normal, day-to-day job. The measurement of process effectiveness and efficiency also needed building. It was felt that the quality process development so far had been focused on 'the here-and-now', rather than on 'the

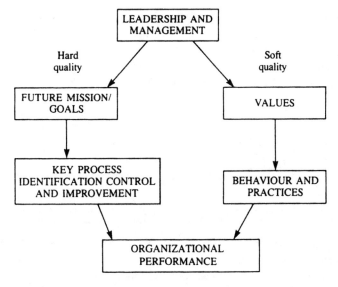

Figure C1.4 *'Hard' and 'soft' quality aspects of the framework*

future'. Fortunately, through contacts that the management group developed with other Exxon groups, and expertise available through the Exxon Chemical chair in TQM at Bradford, an extension to the approach was developed based on an IBM methodology which focused more on the future direction of the site, and led to prioritization of the improvement effort through definition of longer-term goals, critical success factors and key processes. This methodology was supplemented by two other tools, one a method for development of strategic goals, and the other a model of organizational effectiveness which couples work objectives/tasks with values and behaviours. A summary of the final model the site now uses as a framework is show in Figure C1.4.

The site now discusses its quality process as a mixture of 'hard' quality – business goals, driving process control and improvement – and 'soft' quality – values, driving people's behaviour. Both 'hard' and 'soft' quality have to be addressed in a balanced approach. The 'hard' quality track relates to the original operational dimension, the 'soft' quality track to the expressive dimension, in the original two-dimensional model of quality introduced in the early phase. Management workshops have been held on leadership and management style, and values and preferred behaviours defined. Having emphasized that both 'hard' and 'soft' quality tracks need working, it has to be said that the site feels more comfortable dealing with 'hard' quality issues than 'soft' quality issues, as one might expect in the scientific and engineering culture of a research organization.

Further extension of the use of the ISO9000 standards has been made on the site, to support the increased use of this standard by the Exxon business group's customers. This use of quality assurance standards is also seen as a method of providing control for processes such as product development, where control through the conventional use of data and statistical process control (SPC) techniques is slow or inapplicable. Effectively, 80% of the site activity is now included in some form of external quality assurance. This produces the following benefits:

- improved clarity of roles and responsibilities;
- definition of best practices, and written procedures to follow, built on these practices;
- improved communications with business colleagues;
- better documentation of research processes.

The key learning points

So what are the learning points from this experience? The site believes:

- The quality process can be applied to an R&D environment, and can produce useful benefits.
- The concept of the internal customer and the customer–supplier chain has now become well-ingrained in the site culture, with all of the resulting benefits.
- The ISO9000 and NAMAS standards, applied carefully in a 'minimum bureaucracy' style, has added value to key processes, such as product development.

- The process takes much longer than expected to become embedded in the culture of the organization – patience is needed.
- Constancy of purpose is needed to maintain momentum; it is sometimes difficult to concentrate on quality principles when there are pressing and changing business priorities.
- Measurement of the value of the quality process in a research environment is a continuing challenge.
- Achieving the right balance between process discipline, and creativity, which was a concern with adoption of the ISO standards, has not materialized to any great extent; perhaps this is due to the predominance of development versus pure scientific research at the Research Centre and the 'minimize bureaucracy' approach used in writing the quality system.
- There is no 'off-the-shelf' methodology which immediately can be applied to the R&D environment, and one had to be developed in-house. Although this *may* have slowed the process, it is believed that a home-grown methodology is more likely to gain ownership and be sustainable at the Esso Research Centre. This is an important conclusion, judging from other experiences with TQM, in which 'package' approaches have been shown to fail in a research environment.
- The integration of new management group members with different backgrounds has increased in difficulty as quality has increasingly been integrated into the Research Centre culture, rather than being seen as a separate entity.

In the future, the site anticipate continued application of the balanced 'hard' and 'soft' quality approaches using the framework described in Figure C1.4. Continued attention will be given to the collection of data, and use of standards such as the ISO9000 and NAMAS series to support process control and improvement, and the development of cooperative partnerships between the on-site divisions and external business groups.

Acknowledgement

This is from a case study by Dr Roger C. Price, Quality Manager at Esso Research Centre, Abingdon, UK.

C2

Goal deployment in Exxon Chemical

Goal deployment – what is it?

Definitions

Goal: point where race ends; object of effort; destination.
Deployment: taking up positions; fanning out; spread; cascade.

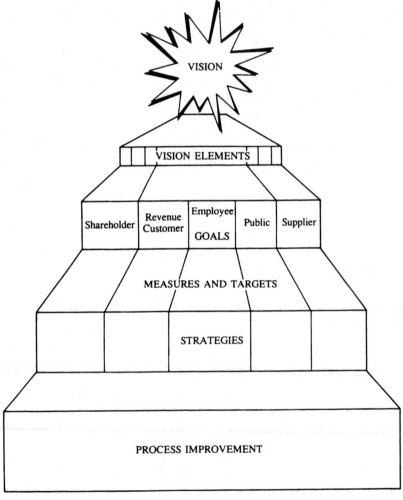

Figure C2.1 *Goal deployment at Exxon Chemical*

These words represent a more meaningful translation of the term policy deployment or policy management, which itself is an American translation of the Japanese phrase *Hoshin Kanri*. *Hoshin Kanri*, translated literally, means 'direction needle management, administration or deployment'. For their purposes, Exxon Chemical take the words 'goal deployment' to refer to the process by which strategic business plans are developed, cascaded and implemented throughout the organization (Figure C2.1)

So – what's new?

For many people, first impressions of goal deployment are that it is not new and that 'we have been here before'. Organizations have always had business plans, quality plans, objectives and improvement targets. Very often, though, these have been only partially successful because they were imposed top-down, were divisive, contradicting or naive, were short-term, were focused on who and what, got lost as another flavour of the month, were just plain unachievable, or were never effectively communicated.

By contrast, the attributes of effective goal deployment are linked to the principles of TQM in that they depend, for example, on two-way communication, on data and information, on the 'how' rather than the 'what', and on effective teamwork.

There are three key attributes of the 'new' goal deployment process in Exxon Chemical. Firstly, it drives towards the organization's mission/vision of the future. Secondly, the goals are made both challenging and achievable by two-way communication and dialogue. Finally, the goals are measurable and measurement is used to prioritize improvement effort and communicate progress.

Why do it?

It is part of TQM

Exxon Chemical believe that one of their critical aims is to progress towards a TQM system, and that having a process by which business strategy is deployed throughout the organization is a vital need. As a framework for TQM, the Malcolm Baldrige Award Criteria (1993) (see Chapter 5) state under Category 3.0 – Strategic Quality Planning:

> examine the company's planning process and how all key quality requirements are integrated into overall business planning. Also examine the company's short and longer term plans and how quality and operational performance requirements are deployed to all work units.

The European Foundation for Quality Management Model for Self-Appraisal (Chapter 5) contains under 2.0 – Policy and Strategy:

> How policy and strategy are based on the concept of TQ.
> How policy and strategy are the basis of business plans.
> How policy and strategy are regularly reviewed and improved.

These requirements can be covered by an effective goal deployment process.

It can be motivational

Goal deployment has provided a focus for Exxon Chemical. It has disciplined management to think out the strategic direction clearly and to translate it into language that the rest of the organization can understand. It has also provided a means for the organization to align and prioritize their activities. In studying job characteristics for motivation at work, Hackman and Oldham (1975) identified three critical psychological states. For people to be motivated they need to experience the feeling that:

- their work is meaningful;
- they are responsible for the outcome of their work;
- they have knowledge of the actual results of their work.

The goal deployment process has helped to support these feelings in Exxon Chemical. Goal deployment indicates to people how they fit into the scheme of things and how their efforts align with and impact on the company's strategic goals, thus making their work more meaningful. The measurement and communication of progress inherent in policy deployment give them both ownership for their efforts and knowledge of results. Overall, goal deployment provides criteria for evaluating work and for rewarding and recognizing achievement.

Why did Exxon Chemical get into it?

There were two influences involved in launching a goal deployment process within Exxon Chemical: one from general thinking about TQM and the other coming more specifically from use of the Baldrige framework.

In general terms, the company came to the view that Total Quality could be seen as three interlocking circles (Figure C2.2). One circle is about teams, people and culture; the second is about work, processes and systems; and the third is about vision, direction and measurement. Since 1986, the company had been putting most effort and attention

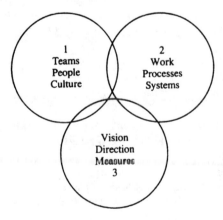

Figure C2.2 *The three interlocking circles of total quality at Exxon Chemical.*

into circles 1 and 2. It was becoming clear that they needed to put more effort into circle 3. This management view was supported by conclusions drawn from worldwide employee surveys.

More specifically, the worldwide and regional business management teams completed a gap analysis against the Baldrige TQM framework. This highlighted that the organization assembled large amounts of data, a lot of which it did not use, and that the company had a vision but no effective trendline measures of progress towards it. A combination of these views and conclusions signalled the need for a coherent set of goals and strategies which would provide organizational direction and a framework to which people could align.

How to do it

Definitions and criteria

There are a number of different terminologies used by different organizations around goal deployment. For the purposes of this case study, the following terms have been adopted by Exxon Chemical:

Vision

A vivid picture of an ambitious, desirable and future state. Its purpose is to inspire the act as a guide for decision-making and planning. It should be:

- memorable;
- involving;
- aligned with company values;
- linked to customer needs;
- a stretch, but not impossible;
- short, clear and communicable;
- within a 5-year horizon.

Goal

A result, milestone or checkpoint in the future which will indicate significant progress towards the vision. Achieving a collection of four to six goals would realize the vision. A goal should be:

- measurable;
- critical for success;
- aggressive, benchmarked targets;
- specific.

Strategy

A specific, medium or long-term plan for making progress towards a goal. A strategy should have the same attributes as a goal but should be more specific and action-oriented. Together a set of strategies, if successfully pursued, will impact the goal measure and eventually achieve the goal.

Creating a vision of the future

In Exxon Chemical the goal deployment process started at the top, where the senior management team created a vision for their organization. They took into account the external environment, the capability of the organization and the desired state versus the competition. The vision was checked against the criteria stated above.

Creating a vision for the organization which is clear and inspiring for people is not easy. However, compared with implementing the changes necessary to achieve it, the Exxon Chemical team felt that it was the simplest step of all!

A technique used by the company to help create the vision (Tichy and Devanna, 1986) was for some senior people to write an article about the company to appear in their favourite business journal 5 years from now. Another version of the same technique was to describe a video documentary made in the future about the successes of the organization. This type of technique was powerful in freeing people from stylized business format and encouraged them to think in creative, journalistic terms about their vision of the future. The composers of the vision were few in number. It is difficult to create a vision by committee. The more people that are involved, the longer and less clear the vision. Faced with a vision which is too long, it becomes necessary to break it down into themes. In Exxon Chemical it was important to identify:

- Organizational themes.
- Individual themes.
- Business themes.

The vision needed to impact on the organization and it needed to wake people up! Without awareness of the need for change, the organization would not have changed: no awareness + no pain + no opportunities = no change.

Setting high-level goals

The top management in Exxon Chemical set a number of goals which, when achieved, would realize the vision. It was helpful to consider the stakeholders in the organization (for example, revenue customers, employees, general public, suppliers, shareholders, etc.) when focusing on the goals. Each goal had a measure. Eventually each measure had a target. These targets were challenging, yet achievable. The organization aspired to be world-class and the targets needed to be benchmarked against world leaders.

The goals themselves became a concise statement which caught people's attention and started the process of communication. This concise statement was backed up with clarifying descriptions, measurements, responsibilities and targets. Measurement was the real key. People in the organization reacted well to understanding what was important enough to be measured by the top management:

- 'What gets measured gets managed'
- 'He who is measured, manages'.

The high-level goals were regarded as a set, together with all their key measures, and checked against the vision and the values of the organization. The following checklist of question were used:

- If we achieve the targets/measures, will we have realized the vision?
- Do the goals/measures cover areas not stated in the vision?
- Is the voice of the customer apparent?
- Are the future needs of the other stakeholders in the organization reflected?
- Is it all compatible with the core values of the organization?

The top management team now needed to gain buy-in and involvement from the organization, starting with the next level down. This started a process called 'catch-ball', a two-way iterative process which ensured the cascade or deployment into the organization. The next-level-down management group took the goals and measures developed by the top team and developed a set of strategies to achieve the goals. If they were unable to get strategies to impact the measures given, then this was a point for feedback. In turn, for each of their key strategies, which should collectively achieve the goals and the vision, the management set measures and targets (Figure C2.3).

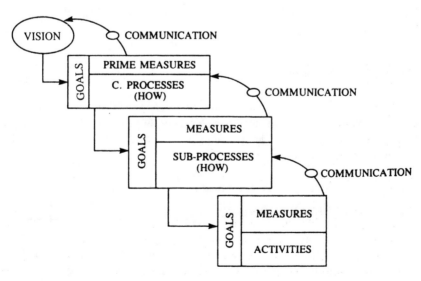

Figure C2.3 *Goal translation process.*

The 'catch-ball' process was the reality check. It required two-way communication and developed a dialogue throughout the organization about the goals, measures and strategies. The strategies of one layer of management became the goals of the next level down. The next level down undertook the goals from above and decided if and how they could achieve them. This was an iterative and often frustratingly long process requiring good communication, dialogue and the ability to be flexible. Managers were prepared to change their goal or measure or target, since they had asked for feedback on them.

Getting buy-in

Management took the responsibility to communicate the goals. When setting the goals and measures they often found it useful to identify a single 'goal-owner' for each goal. In this role a person owned the goal for the management team and coordinated the initial development and review. In communicating the goals further down into the organization, however, it became more important that the whole management team owned all the goals.

The cascade process eventually reached the 'sharp-end' level where real products or services for outside customers were produced. At this point, ownership and responsibility for the business processes which deliver the organization's goods or services were taken. Here it was important to recognize ongoing business process needs and existing improvement efforts. This was done by developing a matrix (similar to the Quality Function Deployment technique) to align existing activities/processes and improvement programmes with the goals (Figure C2.4). This helped to identify:

- which were the activities/work processes critical to attaining the goals;
- which of the existing improvement activities were already aligned with the goals;
- which goals were not going to be achieved without realigning effort;
- how to prioritize the improvement effort.

Communicating progress

The central thrust of effective goal deployment in Exxon Chemical was to enhance the quality of the information available to enable the right people to make the right business decisions, at the right time. The measures generated at each level in the organization were designed to be useful to them and necessary for them to prioritize their efforts and improvement plans.

The measures were also used to communicate progress. This was done in several ways, for example, reports, newsletters and stewardship meetings. Additionally, they used what they called interactive quality stations. A quality station in Exxon Chemical is a place to display goals and strategies, measure progress and communicate about the ongoing improvement effort. The stations also helped to recognize people for their achievement and encouraged improvement ideas. Generally, a quality station was located at some central meeting place frequented by the group. The goals were

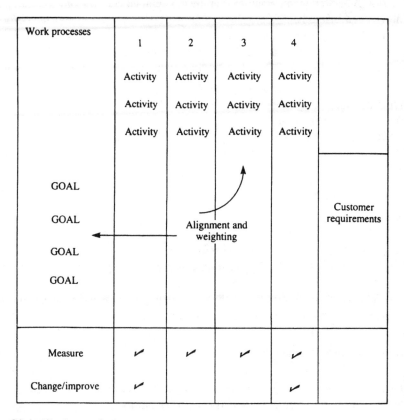

Figure C2.4 *Aligning work processes.*

displayed together with the updated measures and improvement plans. Extensive use was made of pictures, charts and graphs and plenty of room was provided for suggestions and ideas. A quality station is a good tool but it needs the necessary ongoing maintenance: 'Don't create your quality station and then ignore it!'

Some pitfalls

The following lessons have been learned by Exxon Chemical in their goal deployment process.

A powerless vision

A vision or mission can be worthless. It adds no value if it is overambitious and seen to be impossible to achieve by the people. Similarly, it adds no value if it is uninspiring and offers no challenge at all.

A vision generated by a committee can be too detailed and too long.

The vision needs to be tested. It is necessary to get feedback on a vision before it is set in stone by the senior management team. Focus groups, using people from a wide cross-section of the organization, were a good method of getting feedback in Exxon Chemical. The feedback was structured with questions such as:

- What do I like/dislike about it?
- What does it mean to me?
- What themes or aspects are missing?
- How would it be improved?

Overambition

The goals must be deployed with a sense of urgency but also with regard to resources and to the pace at which the organization can accept change. Some prioritization of goals and strategies will be necessary.

A useful concept incorporated into the prioritization process in Exxon Chemical was the universal application of measurement. So, for example:

Priority 1 = measure and improve.

These were areas of strategy that were the key to business needs, where early success was critical. They were selected for early attention and focus.

Priority 0 = measure and maintain.

These were areas of strategy that were the key to success but early improvement was not so critical. However, it was important that the existing standard of achievement was maintained. The vital activity here then was to measure performance and maintain it.

This universal application of performance measurement, independent from priority, made a real difference in how the deployment process was perceived and in its practical implementation. It was recognized that the company did not require a plate-spinning exercise, where some plates are kept spinning whilst others crash to the ground. What was needed was all plates to be kept spinning, but some much faster than others!

Top-down

It is important to recognize the difference between traditional top-down management by objectives and goal deployment. Goal deployment also starts top-down but relies on a cascade of bottom-up feedback processes to achieve alignment throughout the organization.

Management by objectives	*Goal deployment*
Focus on results	Focus on results through improving the process
Top-down	Top-down and bottom-up alignment
Focus on who	Focus on how
Individual responsibility	Group/team responsibility
Work harder	Work smarter
Targets/incentives	Realistic measures
Who failed?	How can we improve?
Manage by dilemma	Prioritize effectively

Bolt-on

Goal deployment should not be perceived as a bolt-on appendage to other company planning systems, for example, strategic quality planning.

In Exxon Chemical, goal deployment encompassed the central and single planning system of the business. This implied two important requirements:

1 The deployed goals, measures and strategies needed to be carefully thought through and of high quality, which took time and management effort.
2 If the alignment process worked, then people would use the goals to prioritize their work. To avoid the negative impact on motivation of realigning people, the goals needed to be long-term and sustainable.

Not invented here

One of the symptoms of empowerment, freedom and diversity, within the goal deployment process, is the strong desire of management and leaders to have their own version of the goals. This sometimes led to a pedantic demand for unnecessary changes to the wording of a goal just to reflect ownership. An example was:

Company level: Be the preferred supplier.
Regional level: Be the supplier of choice.

Generally, this limited differentiation was not helpful. It tended to reduce credibility and led to people wasting effort in trying to analyse what the differences actually meant. Usually it meant that the regional manager simply wanted to be different. Often there was no added value in changing the goal or the measures or strategies from one level to the next. Sometimes people asked what added value a management level was providing!

In translating higher-level goals, especially at senior/middle management levels, it was useful to ask the following sorts of questions:

- Do we agree with the higher-level goals, measures and strategies or not? Are they practical, challenging, viable, etc.? If not, then feedback up recommended changes (catch-ball).
- Do we need, as a management group, to translate these goals? If not, then let us adopt them as they are.
- What value do we add? How is our business/culture different and how should we change the 'what' into 'how'? How can we add value by changing the higher-level goals into our own-level version?
- Have we checked, with the next level down, their views and comments?

Change management

Effectively deploying a set of challenging goals and aligning and motivating people to improve and prioritize their process of work imply change. To succeed, it was important to recognize which elements of change management and awareness of the process of change and transition would be important.

Some fundamental elements of the process of change in Exxon Chemical were:

- The need for change most often comes from outside the organization.
- No need, no pain, no awareness produces no change.
- People do not universally resist change; however, lack of involvement, freedom and choice generates resistance.
- Visioning is easy, implementing is tough.
- Goals and strategy must come first; changes in structure, system and cultural norms come next.
- Complaints during transition are good and a sign of progress.
- Recognize, grieve for and celebrate what was good.
- Three more keys to organizational change:
    communication,
    communication,
    communication.

Benefits and results

The effort required to deploy goals effectively throughout the Exxon Chemical company has been large. The results, however, are multifaceted and substantial and there has been a significant bottom-line payoff.

Benefits for the organization

Goal deployment has disciplined the organization to focus on the long term and identify its key challenges. It has facilitated two-way communication throughout the organization, and provided a framework for decision-making and prioritizing work. It has brought the vision into reality and shown clearly a pathway or staircase for the organization to tread, which will take it towards its vision.

For the management of the organization it has provided a way of educating the workforce about the business and about what is important for the future. It has provided the boundaries and signposts to the pathway forward.

In recent years, a lot of debate has occurred within Exxon Chemical on the subject of empowerment of the workforce. Management have been more or less comfortable with the prospect of unleashing the creativity and resourcefulness of their people, dependent on the culture of their particular part of the organization and the stage or extent of their change process. In the early stages of TQM, for instance, it was important for people to grapple with their work processes, align with their customers and achieve early improvement success. At this stage it was fairly low-risk to empower the workforce to get on with it. There was so much improvement to make in the high-impact, easy-to-do category that almost wherever they focused their attention it added value. In the subsequent stages of TQM, however, improvements became more significant. The potential improvements were larger, having critical impact on the business but needing significant resources to accomplish. In these conditions it was still important to empower the people and seek their creative innovation, but it became more important to provide a focus, a priority and a direction for these more significant improvement efforts. Goal deployment has provided this aligning framework in Exxon Chemical.

Benefits for the people

Goal deployment has indicated to people the role they play and how their efforts are reflected in the achievement of the vision. It has allowed them to context, prioritize their work, and has provided a basis for recognition. It has also provided opportunity for them to contribute and become involved.

Goals, once deployed, have made life generally simpler at Exxon Chemical, and certainly made reporting simpler. Goal deployment has also simplified meetings and reviews by providing a recognized agenda and common language. It has also made leadership more obvious and facilitated followership. This is the concept of upward empowerment. For any worker, if his/her boss has made it crystal-clear, through a goal deployment process, what the measures of success are, the worker can think about how he/she can facilitate success for the boss, how he/she can empower the boss.

Goal deployment in Exxon Chemical

The most senior management group within Exxon Chemical, the Executive Committee, developed a set of goals and measures for the four stakeholders in the chemical company:

1   the shareholder
2   the public
3   the employees
4   the revenue customer

These were consistent with Exxon's vision to be the best (petro) chemical company.

Each of the company's business groups and functions took these goals and measures and, through the interative catch-ball process, developed their own compatible business visions and goals.

The Basic Chemicals business group worldwide management team, for example, developed their own vision 'BC 2000', linked to the company core values. Basic Chemicals Americas and Europe took this vision, and the Exxon Chemical Company goals, and developed a set of aligned regional goals, measures and strategies. Each manufacturing site took the regional strategies and developed their own site goals, measures and strategies. Finally, each working group took the site strategies and developed their own improvement plans. An example of a specific goal deployment was:

Exxon Chemical Company/ Basic Chemicals	Be the preferred supplier.
Basic Chemicals Europe	By having high-quality partnerships with all internal and external customers, always meet or exceed agreed requirements.
Marketing operations	Review Basic Chemicals Europe performance yearly with all customers. Track performance versus agreed requirements. Ensure multilevel contact to maintain the continuity and breadth of our customer relationship. Measure customer satisfaction index.
Manufacturing plant	Measures: product quality capability shipping reliability customer service satisfaction

Specific examples of results

The big impacts of a goal deployment process on a worldwide basis take time to come to fruition. The very nature of the process is long-term. The Exxon Chemical company had always been data-driven, but the deployment process took, on average, about a year to effectively reach the sharp-end or 'shop floor'. The full impact of the process has yet to be fully measured, but it is possible to detect and measure significant improvements at the lower levels in the organization, as people's energy is focused on the goals:

Example 1 – Manufacturing

Company goal	Create the highest shareholder value in our industry.
Business group	Be a major source of earnings growth, maintain a competitive return and be a model of operating integrity.
Regional group	Be the lowest-cost supplier and a leader in the use of feed stocks, hardware and technology and drive quality to the bottom line.
Site group	Reduce fixed and allocated costs versus total erected cost (TEC – project cost) from 25 to 20% in 1 year.

By focusing on the process of how engineering was actually carried out, the organizational structure, and the distribution of costs, the project group was able to reduce engineering costs, on average, to 16% of TEC during the following year. Their ultimate target is 8%, derived from an internal and external benchmarking study.

The group manager stated in his annual report:

It was our second year of systematic performance measurements in all our areas of responsibility. The focus on a small number of key improvement items resulted in major progress in these areas.

Example 2 – Marketing and Sales

Regional group	Improve speed of response to customer.
Area group	Focus on improving our customer complaints management process.

The area sales group completed a goal translation process. They did this by building an alignment matrix of their regional goals against their major work processes. This identified that their complaints management process was critical to several of the goal strategies and measures developed at a regional level. They started to measure complaints overdue, analysed by sales area. This was plotted at a quality station in their group meeting room. Complaints overdue dropped from an average of 25 per month over 3 months to less than 5 over 2 months.

The same group also identified receivables as a critical area. They developed a measure of total cash overdue on a monthly basis and plotted this. Focus in this area reduced overdues by at least $0.5m for the group as a whole.

Example 3 – Manufacturing

Company	Be our customers' preferred supplier.
Regional	Track our performance against agreed requirements and systematically eliminate non-conformances.
Plant	Improve customer satisfaction.

As part of their goal translation effort, the plant group identified several key areas and developed statistical measures which included:

- product quality capability index;
- planned production deviation;
- shipping reliability index.

These are 'traditional' quality assurance measures. In addition, they identified some other customers. These were people and groups in their regional headquarters and venture partners headquarters who had specific requirements for information. They identified the necessary attributes, timing and format for this information. This covered a wide range of daily to monthly performance and planning statistics and information transmitted via a number of different media. They created a charter which defined the specific requirements of this information system as seen through the eyes of their customers. They developed a measurable index of performance against this charter.

Performance increased from 40 to 98% compliance throughout the year. Since this almost met their target of 100%, one of their actions for the following year was to talk to this set of customers about more stretching targets for the future.

Goal deployment outlook

Within Exxon Chemical the goal deployment process has set challenging goals, measures and targets. The deployment has helped to identify key processes, especially those processes which run through all business groups and/or across business groups and functions which are in need of change. Goal deployment has set the criteria for picking out these key processes. With these identified and, through use of tools like benchmarking, work process restructuring and redesign, it has been possible to progress with major improvement and change projects, which have company-, regional- or business-group-wide implications. Several of these major change projects have been identified and are in progress. This wider application represents the combination of TQM, goal deployment and business process re-engineering (Figure C2.5).

Acknowledgement

This is from a case study by Alan Randall, Exxon Chemical.

Bibliography

Baldrige, M., *National Quality Award Criteria*, The American Society for Quality Control, Milwaukee, WI, 1993.

Burke, and Spencer, *Interpretation and Industry Comparisons*, Warner Burke, Pelham, NY, 1990.

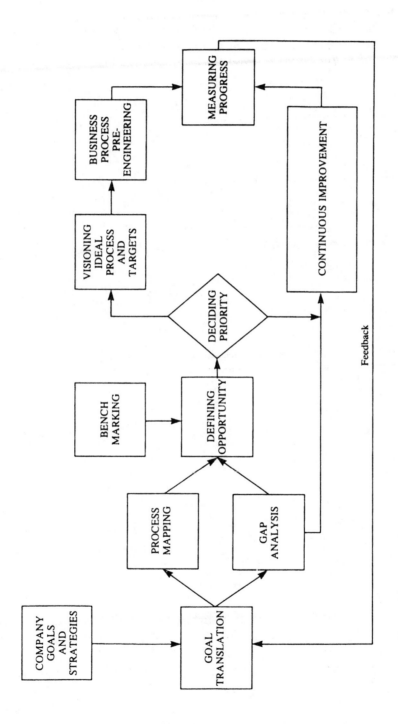

Figure C2.5 *TQM implementation framework*

Hackman, and Oldham, *Development of the job diagnostic survey. Journal of Applied Psychology,* **60**, 1975.

Savage, P. *Who Cares Wins*, Mercury Books, London, 1987.

Tichy, N. M. and Devanna M. A. *The Tranformational Leader,* John Wiley, New York, 1986.

Total Quality Management: The European Model for Self-Appraisal, European Foundation for Quality Management, Brussels, 1994.

Whitely, R. C. *The Customer Driven Company*, Business Books, London, 1991.

Discussion questions

1 You are planning to open a wine bar, and have secured the necessary capital. Your aim is to attract both regular customers and passing trade. Discuss the key implications of this for the management of the business.

2 Discuss the following:
(a) the difference between quality and reliability;
(b) total quality related costs (Part 3);
(c) 100% inspection.

3 Discuss the various facets of the quality control function, paying particular attention to its interfaces with the other functional areas within the organization.

4 Explain what you understand by the term 'Total Quality Management', paying particular attention to the following terms: quality, supplier/customer interfaces, process.

5 Present a 'model' for total quality management, describing briefly the various elements of the model.

6 You are an operations management consultant with particular expertise in the area of product design and development. You are at present working on projects for four firms:
(a) a chain of hotels;
(b) a mail order goods firm;
(c) a furniture manufacture;
(d) a road construction contractor.
What factors do you consider are important generally in your area of specialization? Compare and contrast how these factors apply to your four current projects.

7 Select one of the so-called 'Gurus' of Quality Management, such as Juran, Deming, Crosby, Ishikawa, and explain his approach, with respect to the 'Oakland Model' of TQM. Discuss the strengths and weaknesses of the approach using this framework.

8 Discuss the application of the TQM concept in the service sector, paying particular attention to the nature of services and the customer-supplier interfaces.

9 In your new role as quality manager of the high-tech unit of a large national company, you identify a problem which is typified by the two internal memos shown below. Discuss in some detail the problems illustrated by this conflict, explaining how you would set about trying to make improvements:

From: Marketing Director
To: Managing Director
c.c.
Production Director
Works Manager
Date: 4th August

We have recently carried out a customer survey to examine how well we are doing in the market. With regard to our product range, the reactions were generally good, but the 24 byte microwinkle thrystor is a problem. Without exception everyone we interviewed said that its quality is not good enough. Although it is not yet apparent, we will inevitably lose our market share.
As a matter of urgency, therefore, will you please authorize a complete redesign of this product?

From: Works Manager
To: Production Director
Date: 6th August

This really is ridiculous!
I have all the QC records for the past ten years on this product. How can there be anything seriously wrong with the quality when we only get 0.1% rejects at final inspection and less than 0.01% returns from customers?

10 Discuss the application of quality function deployment (QFD) and the 'house of quality' in:
   (a) a fast moving consumer goods (fmcg) company, such as one which designs, produces, and sells/distributes cosmetic products;
   (b) an industrial company, such as one producing plastic material;
   (c) a commercial service organization such as a bank or insurance company.

Case study assignments

C1 *Esso Research Centre*

What are the particular features of implementing TQM in a research and development environment?

Evaluate the case, as described, in terms of leadership, commitment and policy issues.

What role could quality function deployment (QFD) play in the Research Centre?

C2 *Exxon Chemical*

Discuss the TQM implementation framework developed in this case and its applicability generally to other organizations, including those in the service sector.

How does the 'goal translation' approach relate to TQM, what are the linking factors?

Show how the approach used by Exxon Chemical could be applied to any change management problem

Part Two

TQM – The Role of the Quality System

I must create a System or be enslaved by another man's.
William Blake, 1757–1827, from 'Jerusalem'

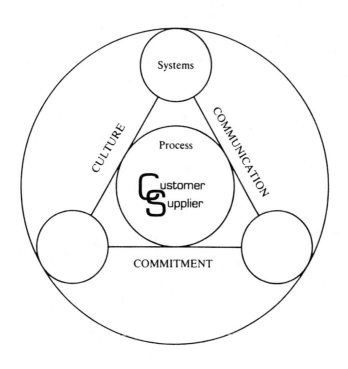

4

Planning for quality

4.1 Quality planning

Systematic planning is a basic requirement for effective quality management in all organizations. For quality planning to be useful, however, it must be part of a continuous review process that has as its objective zero errors or defectives, through a strategy of never ending improvement. Before an appropriate total quality management system can be developed, it is necessary to carry out a preliminary analysis to ensure that a quality organization structure exists, that the resources required will be made available, and that the various assignments will be carried out. This analysis has been outlined in the flowchart of Figure 4.1. The answers to the questions will generate the appropriate action plans.

In quality planning it is always necessary to review existing programmes within the organization's functional areas, and these may be compared with the results of the preliminary analysis to appraise the strengths and weaknesses in quality throughout the business or operation. When this has been done, the required systems and programmes may be defined in terms of detailed operating plans, procedures and techniques. This may proceed through the flowchart of Figure 4.2, which provides a logical approach to developing a multifunctional total quality management system.

A quality plan

A quality plan is a document which is specific to each product, activity or service (or group) that sets out the necessary quality-related activities. The plan should include references to any:

- Purchased material or service specifications.
- Quality system procedures.
- Product formulation or service type.
- Process control.
- Sampling and inspection procedures.
- Packaging or distribution specifications.
- Miscellaneous, relevant procedures.

Such a quality plan might form part of a detailed operating procedure.

For projects relating to new products or services, or to new processes, written quality plans should be prepared to define:

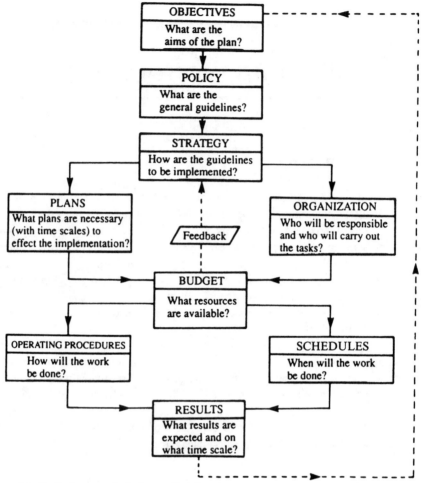

Figure 4.1 *Preliminary analysis for quality planning*

1   Specific allocation of responsibility and authority during the different stages of the project.
2   Specific procedures, methods and instructions to be applied throughout the project.
3   Appropriate inspection, testing, checking, or audit programmes required at various defined stages.
4   Methods of changes or modifications in the plan as the project proceeds.

Some of the main points in the planning of quality relate very much to the *inputs* of processes:

Plant/equipment – the design, layout, and inspection of plant and equipment, including heating, lighting, storage, disposal of waste, etc.

Processes – the design and monitoring of processes to reduce to a minimum the possibility of malfunction and/or failure.

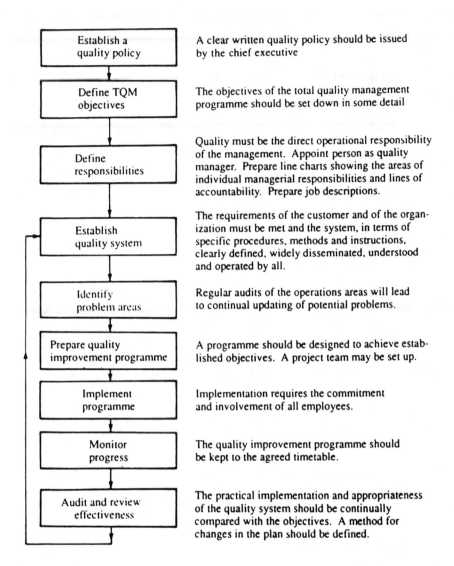

Figure 4.2 *Plan for a quality system*

Workplace – the establishment and maintenance of suitable, clean and orderly places of work.

Facilities – the provision and maintenance of adequate facilities.

Procedures – the preparation of procedures for all operations. These may be in the form of general plans and guides rather than tremendous detail, but they should include specific operational duties and responsibilities.

Training – the provision of effective training in quality, technology, process and plant operation.

Information – the lifeblood of all quality management systems. All processes should be accompanied by good data collection, recording and analysis, followed by appropriate action.

The quality plan should focus on providing action to prevent cash leaking away through waste. If the quality management system does not achieve this, then there is something wrong with the plan and the way it has been set up or operated – not with the principle. The whole approach should be methodical and systematic, and designed to function irrespective of changes in management or personnel.

The principles and practice of setting up a good quality-management system are set out in Chapter 5. The quality system must be planned and developed to take into account all other functions, such as design, development, production or operations, subcontracting, installation, maintenance, and so on. The remainder of this chapter is devoted to certain aspects of the quality-planning process that require specific attention or techniques.

4.2   Flowcharting

In the systematic planning or examination of any process, whether that be a clerical, manufacturing, or managerial activity, it is necessary to record the series of events and activities, stages and decisions in a form that can be easily understood and communicated to all. If improvements are to be made, the facts relating to the existing method must be recorded first. The statements defining the process should lead to its understanding and will provide the basis of any critical examination necessary for the development of improvements. It is essential therefore that the descriptions of processes are accurate, clear and concise.

The usual method of recording facts is to write them down, but this is not suitable for recording the complicated processes that exist in any organization, particularly when an exact record is required of a long process, and its written description would cover several pages requiring careful study to elicit every detail. To overcome this difficulty, certain methods of recording have been developed, and the most powerful of these is flowcharting. This method of describing a process owes much to computer programming, where the technique is used to arrange the sequence of steps required for the operation of the program. It has a much wider application, however, than computing.

Certain standard symbols are used on the chart, and these are shown in Figure 4.3. The starting point of the process is indicated by a circle. Each processing step, indicated by a rectangle, contains a description of the relevant operation, and where the process ends is indicated by an oval. A point where the process branches because of a decision is shown by a diamond. A parallelogram contains useful information but is not a processing step. The arrowed lines are used to connect symbols and to indicate direction of flow. For a complete description of the process all operation steps (rectangles) and decisions (diamonds) should be connected by pathways to the start circle and end oval. If the flowchart cannot be drawn in this way, the process is not fully understood.

It is a salutary experience for most people to sit down and try to draw the flowchart for a process in which they take part every working day. It is often found that:

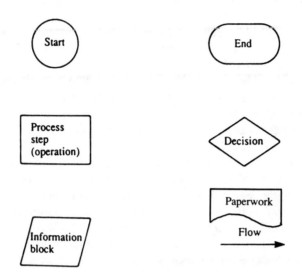

Figure 4.3 *Flowcharting symbols*

- The process flow is not fully understood.
- A single person is unable to complete the flowchart without help from others.

The very act of flowcharting will improve knowledge of the process, and will begin to develop the teamwork necessary to find improvements. In many cases the convoluted flow and octopus-like appearance of the chart will highlight unnecessary movements of people and materials and lead to commonsense suggestions for waste elimination.

Example of flowcharting in use – Improving a travel procedure

We start by describing the original process for a male employee, though clearly it applies equally to females.

The process starts with the employee explaining his travel plans to his secretary. The secretary then calls the travel agent to inquire about the possibilities and gives feedback to the employee. The employee decides if the travel arrangements, e.g. flight numbers and dates, are acceptable and informs his secretary, who calls the agent to make the necessary bookings or examine alternatives. The administrative procedure, which starts as soon as the bookings have been made, is as follows:

1   The employee's secretary prepares the travel request (which is in four parts, A, B, C and D), and gives it to his secretary. The request is then sent to the employee's manager, who approves it. The manager's secretary sends it back to the employee's secretary.

2   The employee's secretary sends copies A, B and C to the agent and gives copy D to the employee. The travel agent delivers the ticket to the employee's secretary, together with copy B of the travel request. The secretary endorses copy B for receipt of the ticket, sends it to Accounting, and gives ticket to employee.
3   The travel agent bills the credit-card company, and sends Accounting a pro-forma invoice with copy C of the travel request. Accounting matches copies B and C, and charges the employee's 181 account.
4   Accounting receives the monthly bill from the credit-card company, matches it against the travel request, then books and pays the credit-card company.
5   The employee reports the travel request on his expense statement. Accounting matches and books to balance the employee's 181 account.

The total time taken for the administrative procedure, excluding the correction of errors and the preparation of overview reports, is 23 minutes per travel request.

The flowchart for the process is drawn in Figure 4.4. A quality-improvement team was set up to analyse the process and make recommendations for improvement, using brainstorming and questioning techniques. They made the following proposal to change the procedure. The preparation for the trip remained the same but the administrative steps, following the bookings being made became:

1   The travel agent sends the ticket to the secretary, along with a receipt document, which is returned to the agent with the secretary's signature.
2   The agent sends the receipt to the credit-card company, which bills the company on a monthly basis with a copy of all the receipts. Accounting pays the credit-card company and charges the employee's 181 account.
3   The employee reports the travel on his expense statement, and Accounting books to balance the employee's 181 account.

The flowchart for the improved process is shown in Figure 4.5. The proposal reduced the total administrative effort per travel request (or per travel arrangement, because the travel request was eliminated) from 23 minutes to 5 minutes.

The details that appear on a flowchart for an existing process must be obtained from direct observatioin of the process, not by imagining what is done or what should be done. The latter may be useful, however, in the planning phase, or for outlining the stages in the introduction of a new concept. Such an application is illustrated in Figure 4.6 for the installation of statistical process control charting systems (see Chapter 8). Similar charts may be used in the planning of quality management systems.

It is surprisingly difficult to draw flowcharts for even the simplest processes, particularly managerial ones, and following the first attempt it is useful to ask whether:

● The facts have been correctly recorded.
● Any over-simplifying assumptions have been made.
● All the factors concerning the process have been recorded.

The author has seen too many process flowcharts that are so incomplete as to be grossly inaccurate.

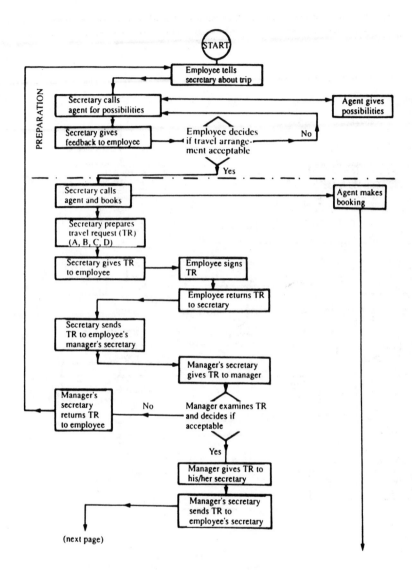

Figure 4.4 *Original process for travel procedure*

Summarizing, then, a flowchart is a picture of the steps used in performing a function. This function can be anything from a process step to accounting procedures, even preparing a meal. Lines connect the steps to show the flow of the various functions. Flowcharts provide excellent documentation and are useful trouble-shooting tools to determine how each step is related to the others. By reviewing the flowchart, it is often possible to discover inconsistencies and determine potential sources of variation and problems. For this reason, flowcharts are very useful in process improvement when examining an existing process to highlight the problem areas. A

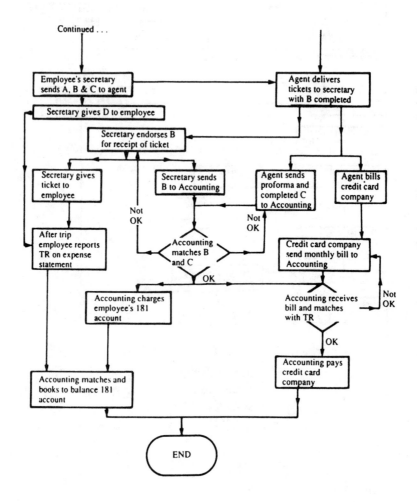

Figure 4.4 *(continued)*

group of people, with the knowledge about the process, should take the following simple steps:

1 Draw a flowchart of existing process.
2 Draw a second chart of the flow the process could or should follow.
3 Compare the two to highlight the changes necessary.

4.3 Planning for purchasing

Very few organizations are self-contained to the extent that their products and services are all generated at one location, from basic materials. Some materials or services are usually purchased from outside organizations, and the primary objective of purchasing is to obtain the correct equipment, materials, and services in the right quantity, of the right quality, from the right origin, at the right time and cost. Purchasing also plays a vital role as the organization's 'window-on-the-world', providing information on any new products, processes, materials and services. It should also advise on probable

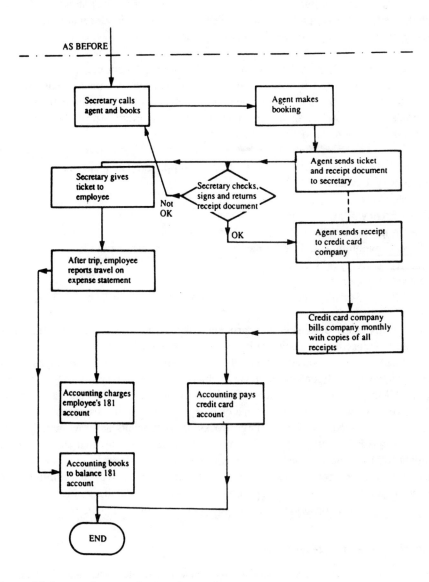

Figure 4.5 *Improved process for travel procedure*

prices, deliveries, and performance of products under consideration by the research, design and development functions.

Although purchasing is clearly an important area of managerial activity, it is often neglected by both manufacturing and service industries. The separation of purchasing from selling has, however, been removed in many large retail organizations, which have recognized that the purchaser must be responsible for the whole 'product line' – its selection, quality, specification, delivery, price, acceptability, and reliability. If any part of this chain is wrong, the purchasing function must resolve the problem. This concept is clearly very appropriate in retailing, where transformation activities on the product itself, between purchase and sale, are small or zero, but it shows the need to include market information in the buying decision processes in all organizations.

The purchasing system should be set out in a written manual which:

1   Assigns responsibilities for and within the purchasing function.
2   Defines the manner in which suppliers are selected, to ensure that they are continually capable of supplying the requirements in terms of material and services.
3   Indicates the purchasing documentation – written orders, specifications, etc. – required in any modern purchasing activity.

So what does an organization require from its suppliers? The goals are easy to state, but less easy to reach:

* Consistency – low variability.
* Centring – on target.
* Process evolution and development to continually reduce variability.
* Correct delivery performance.
* Speed of response.
* A *systematic* quality management approach to achieve the above.

Historically many organizations, particularly in the manufacturing industries, have operated an inspection-oriented quality system for bought-in parts and materials. Such an approach has many disadvantages. It is expensive, imprecise, and impossible to apply evenly across all material and parts, which all lead to variability in the degree of appraisal. Many organizations, such as Ford, have found that survival and future growth in both volume and variety demand that changes be made to this approach.

The prohibitive cost of holding large stocks of components and raw materials also pushed forward the 'just-in-time' (JIT) concept. As this requires that suppliers make frequent, on time, deliveries of small quantities of material, parts, components, etc., often straight to the point of use, in order that stocks can be kept to a minimum, the approach requires an effective supplier network – one producing goods and services that can be trusted to conform to the real requirements with a high degree of confidence.

Commitment and involvement

The process of improving suppliers' performance is complex and clearly relies very heavily on securing real commitment from the senior management of the supplier orga-

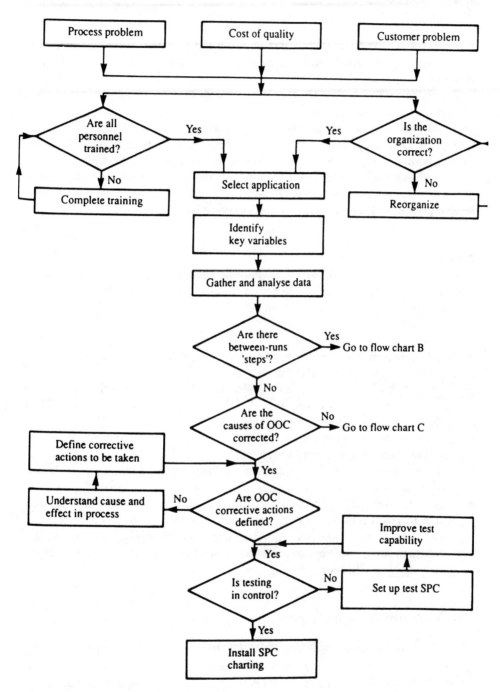

Figure 4.6 *Flowchart (A) for installation of SPC charting systems. (The author is grateful to Exxon Chemical International for permission to use and modify this chart.)*

nizations. This may be aided by presentations made to groups of directors of the suppliers brought together to share the realization of the importance of their organizations' performance in the quality chains. The synergy derived from different suppliers meeting together, being educated, and discussing mutual problems, will be tremendous. If this can be achieved, within the constraints of business and technical confidentiality, it is always a better aproach than separate meetings and presentations on the suppliers' premises.

The author recalls the benefits that accrued from bringing together suppliers of a photocopier, paper, and ring binders to explain to them the way their inputs were used to generate training-course materials and how they in turn were used during the courses themselves. The suppliers were able to understand the business in which their customers were engaged, and play their part in the whole process. A supplier of goods *or* services that has received such attention, education, and training, and understands the role its inputs play, is less likely knowingly to offer nonconforming materials and services, and more likely to alert customers to potential problems.

Policy

One of the first things to communicate to any external supplier is the purchasing organization's policy on quality of incoming goods and services. This can include such statements as:

- It is the policy of this company to ensure that the quality of all purchased materials and services meets its requirements.
- Suppliers who incorporate a quality management system into their operations will be selected. This system should be designed, implemented and operated according to the International Standards Organization (ISO) 9000 series (see Chapter 5).
- Suppliers who incorporate statistical process control (SPC) methods into their operations (see Chapter 8) will be selected.
- Routine inspection, checking, measurement and testing of incoming goods and services will *not* be carried out by this company on receipt.
- Suppliers will be audited and their operating procedures, systems, and SPC methods will be reviewed periodically to ensure a never ending improvement approach.
- It is the policy of this company to pursue uniformity of supply, and to encourage suppliers to strive for continual reduction in variability. (This may well lead to the narrowing of specification ranges.)

Quality system assessment certification

Many customers examine their suppliers' quality management systems themselves, operating a second party assessment scheme (see Chapter 6). Inevitably this leads to high costs and duplication of activity, for both the customer and supplier. If a qualified, independent third party is used instead to carry out the assessment, attention may be focused by the customer on any special needs and in developing closer partnerships with suppliers. Visits and dialogue across the customer–supplier interface are a necessity for the true requirements to be met, and for future growth of the whole business chain. Visits should be concentrated, however, on improving understanding and capability, rather than on close scrutiny of operating procedures, which is best left to experts, including those within the supplier organizations charged with carrying out internal system audits and reviews.

4.4 Planning for just-in-time (JIT) management

There are so many organizations throughout the world that are looking at, introducing, or practising just-in-time (JIT) management principles that the probability of encountering it is very high. JIT, like many modern management concepts, is credited to the Japanese, who developed and began to use it in the late 1950s. It took approximately 20 years for JIT methods to reach Western hardgoods industries and a further 10 years before businesses realized the generality of the concepts.

Basically JIT is a programme directed towards ensuring that the right quantities are purchased or produced at the right time, and that there is no waste. Anyone who perceives it purely as a material-control system, however, is bound to fail with JIT. JIT fits well under the TQM umbrella, for many of the ideas and techniques are very similar and, moreover, JIT will not work without TQM in operation. Writing down a definition of JIT for all types of organization is extremely difficult, because the range of products, services and organization structures leads to different impressions of the nature and scope of JIT. It is essentially:

* A series of operating concepts that allows systematic identification of operational problems.
* A series of technology-based tools for correcting problems following their identification.

The Kanban system

Kanban is a Japanese word meaning visible record, but in the West it is generally taken to mean a card that signals the need to deliver or produce more parts or components. In manufacturing, various types of record cards, e.g. job orders or tickets and route cards, are used for ordering more parts in a *push* type, schedule-based system. In a push system a multi-period master production schedule of future demands is prepared, and a computer explodes this into detailed schedules for producing or purchasing the appropriate parts or materials. The schedules then *push* the production of the parts or components, out and onward. These systems, when computer-based, are usually called Material Requirements Planning (MRP) or the more recent Manufacturing Resource Planning (MRPII).

The main feature of the Kanban system is that it *pulls* parts and components through the production processes when they are needed. Each material, component, or part has its own special container designed to hold a precise, preferably small, quantity. The number of containers for each part is a carefully considered management decision. Only standard containers are used, and they are always filled with the prescribed quantity.

A Kanban system provides parts when they are needed but without guesswork, and therefore without the excess inventory that results from bad guesses. The system will only work well, however, within the context of a JIT system in general, and the reduction of set-up times and lot sizes in particular. A JIT programme can succeed without a Kanban-based operation, but Kanbans will not function effectively independently of JIT.

Just-in-time purchasing

Purchasing is an important feature of JIT. The development of long-term relationships with a few suppliers, rather than short-term ones with many, leads to the concept of *co-producers* in networks of trust providing dependable quality and delivery of goods and services. Each organization in the chain of supply is encouraged to extend JIT methods to its suppliers. The requirements of JIT mean that suppliers are usually located near the purchaser's premises, delivering small quantities, often several times per day, to match the usage rate. Paperwork is kept to a minimum and standard quantities in standard containers are usual. The requirement for suppliers to be located near the buying organization, which places those at some distance at a competitive disadvantage, causes lead times to be shorter and deliveries to be more reliable.

It can be argued that JIT purchasing and delivery are suitable mainly for assembly line operations, and less so for certain process and service industries, but the reduction in the inventory and transport costs that it brings should encourage innovations to lead to its widespread adoption. Those committed to open competition and finding the lowest price will find most difficulty. Nevertheless, there must be a recognition of the need to develop closer relationships and to begin the dialogue – the sharing of information and problems – that leads to the product or service of the right quality, being delivered in the right quantity, at the right time.

Chapter highlights

Quality planning

- Systematic planning is a basic requirement for TQM.
- A quality plan sets out details for systems, procedures, purchased materials or services, products/services, plant/equipment, process control, sampling/ inspection, training, packaging and distribution.

Flowcharting

- Flowcharting is a method of describing a process in pictures, using symbols – rectangles for operation steps, diamonds for decision, parallelograms for information, and circles/ovals for the start/end points. Arrow lines connect the symbols to show the 'flow'.
- Flowcharting improves knowledge of the process and helps to develop the team of people involved.
- Flowcharts document processes and are useful as trouble-shooting tools and in process improvement. An improvement team would flowchart the existing process and the improved or desired process, comparing the two to highlight the changes necessary.

Planning for purchasing

- The prime objective of purchasing is to obtain the correct equipment, materials, and services in the right quantity, of the right quality, from the right origin, at the right time and cost. Purchasing also acts as a 'window-on-the-world'.
- The separation of purchasing from selling has been eliminated in many retail organizations, to give responsibility for a whole 'product line'. Market information must be included in *any* buying decision.
- The purchasing system should be set out in a written manual, which gives responsibilities, the means of selecting suppliers, and the documentation to be used.
- An organization requires from its suppliers consistency, on target, process evolution, good delivery performance, speed of response, and systematic quality management.
- Improving supplier performance requires from the suppliers' senior management commitment, education, a policy, an assessed quality system, and supplier approval.

Planning for just-in-time (JIT) management

- JIT fits well under the TQM umbrella and is essentially a series of operating concepts that allow the systematic identification of problems, *and* tools for correcting them.
- Kanban cards signal the need to deliver or produce more parts or components. The system of Kanbans will work well only in the context of JIT.
- Purchasing is an important feature of JIT. Long-term relationships with a few suppliers, or 'co-producers', are developed in networks of trust to provide quality goods and services.

System design and contents

5.1 Why a documented system?

In earlier chapters we have seen how the keystone of quality management is the concept of customer and supplier working together for their mutual advantage. For any particular organization this becomes 'total' quality management if the supplier/customer interfaces extend beyond the immediate customers, back inside the organization, and beyond the immediate suppliers. In order to achieve this, a company must organize itself in such a way that the human, administrative and technical factors affecting quality will be under control. This leads to the requirement for the development and implementation of a quality system that enables the objectives set out in the quality policy to be accomplished. Clearly, for maximum effectiveness and to meet individual customer requirements, the quality system in use must be appropriate to the type of activity and product or service being offered.

It may be useful to reflect on why such a device is necessary to achieve control of processes. The author remembers being at a table in a restaurant with eight people who all ordered the 'Chef's Special Individual Soufflé'. All eight soufflés arrived together at the table, magnificent in their appearance and consistency, each one exhibiting an almost identical size and shape – a truly remarkable demonstration of culinary skill. How had this been achieved? The chef had *managed* such consistency by making sure that, for each soufflé, he used the same ingredients (materials), the same equipment (plant), the same method (procedure) in exactly the same way every time. The process was under control. This is the aim of a good quality system, to provide the 'operator' of the process with consistency and satisfaction in terms of methods, materials, equipment, etc. (Figure 5.1). Two feedback loops are also required: the 'voice' of the customer (marketing activities) and the 'voice' of the process (measurement activities).

The chef's soufflés were not British Standard, NIST Standard, Australian Standard, or ISO Standard soufflés – they were the chef's special soufflés. It is not conceivable that the chef sat down with a blank piece of paper to invent a soufflé recipe. Why re-invent wheels? He probably used a standard formula and changed it slightly to make it his own. This is exactly the way in which organizations must use the international standards on quality systems that are available. The 'wheel' has been invented but it must be built in a way that meets the specific organizational and product or service requirements. The International Organization for Standardization (ISO) Standard 9000 Series (1994) sets out the methods by which a management system, incorporating all the activities associated with quality, can be implemented in an organization to ensure that all the specified performance requirements and needs of the customer are fully met.

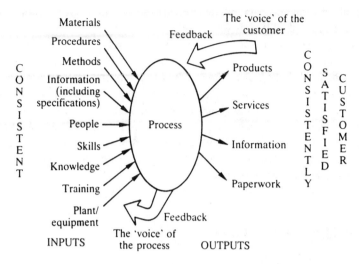

Figure 5.1 *The systematic approach to process management*

Let us return to the chef in the restaurant and propose that his success leads to a desire to open eight restaurants in which are served his special soufflés. Clearly he cannot rush from each one of these establishments to another every evening making soufflés. The only course open to him to ensure consistency of output, in all eight restaurants, is for him to write down in some detail the system he uses, and then make sure that it is used on all sites, every time a soufflé is produced. Moreover, he must periodically visit the different sites to ensure that:

1 The people involved are operating according to the documented system (a system audit).
2 The soufflé system still meets the requirements (a system review).

If in his system audits and reviews he discovers that an even better product or less waste can be achieved by changing the method or one of the materials, then he may wish to effect a change. To maintain consistency, he must ensure that the appropriate changes are made to the documented system, *and* that everyone concerned is issued with the revision and begins to operate accordingly.

A fully documented quality management system will ensure that two important requirements are met:

- *The customer's requirements* – for confidence in the ability of the organization to deliver the desired product or service consistently.
- *The organization's requirements* – both internally and externally, and at an optimum cost, with efficient utilization of the resources available – material, human, technological, and administrative.

These requirements can be truly met only if objective evidence is provided, in the form of information and data, which supports the system activities, from the ultimate supplier through to the ultimate customer.

A *quality system* may be defined, then, as an assembly of components, such as the organizational structure, responsibilities, procedures, processes and resources for implementing total quality management. These components interact and are affected by being in the system, so the isolation and study of each one in detail will not necessarily lead to an understanding of the system as a whole. Often the interactions between the components – such as materials and processes, procedures and responsibilities – are just as important as the components themselves, and problems can arise from these interactions as much as from the components. Clearly, if one of the components is removed from the system, the whole thing will change.

5.2   Quality system design

The quality system should apply to and interact with all activities of the organization. It begins with the identification of the requirements and ends with their satisfaction, at every transaction interface. The activities may be classified in several ways – generally as processing, communicating and controlling, but more usefully and specifically as:

1   Marketing.
2   Market research.
3   Design.
4   Specifying.
5   Development.
6   Procurement.
7   Process planning.
8   Process development and assessment.
9   Process operation and control.
10 Product- or service-testing or checking.
11 Packaging (if required).
12 Storage (if required).
13 Sales.
14 Distribution or installation/operation.
15 Technical service.
16 Maintenance.

These may be regarded as slats on a rotating drum rolling towards a satisfied customer, who becomes 'delighted' by the consistency of the product or service (Figure 5.2). The driving force of the drum is the centralized quality system, and the drum will not operate until the system is in place and working. The first step in getting the drum rolling is to prepare the necessary documentation. This means, in very basic terms, that procedures should be written down, preferably in such a way that the system conforms to one of the national or international standards. This is probably best done in the form of a quality manual.

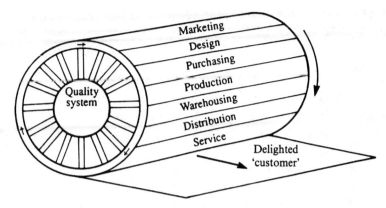

Figure 5.2 *The quality system power unit to the delighted 'customer'*

It is interesting to bring together the concept of Deming's Cycle of continuous improvement – PLAN DO CHECK ACT – and quality systems. A simplification of what a good quality system is trying to do is given in Figure 5.3, which follows the improvement cycle.

In most organizations established methods of working already exist, and all that is required is the writing down of what is currently done. In some instances companies may not have procedures to satisfy the requirements of a good standard, and they may have to begin to devise them. Alternatively, it may be found that two people, supposedly performing the same task, are working in different ways, and there is a need to standardize the procedure. Some organizations use the effective slogan 'If it isn't written down, it doesn't exist'. This can be a useful discipline, provided it doesn't lead to paper bureaucracy.

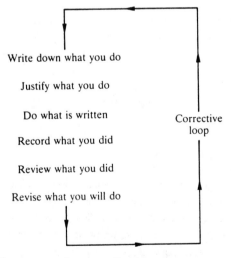

Figure 5.3 *The quality system and never ending improvement*

Justify that the *system* as it is designed *meets the requirements of a good international standard*, such as ISO 9001. There are other excellent standards that are used, and these provide similar checklists of things to consider in the establishment of the quality system.

The system must be a working one with the documents well fingered in use. One person alone cannot document a quality system; the task is the job of all personnel who have responsibility for any part of it. The quality manual must be a *practical working document* – that way it ensures that consistency of operation is maintained and it may be used as a training aid.

In the operation of any process, a useful guide is:

- No process without data collection.
- No data collection without analysis.
- No analysis without decisions.
- No decisions without actions, which can include doing nothing.

This excellent discipline is built into any good quality system, primarily through the audit and review systems. The requirement to *audit or 'check'* that the system is functioning according to plan, and to *review* possible system improvements, utilizing audit results, should ensure that the *improvement* cycle is engaged through the *corrective action* procedures. The overriding requirement is that the systems must reflect the established practices of the organization, improved where necessary to bring them into line with current and future requirements.

5.3   Quality system requirements

The special methods and procedures that need to be documented and implemented will be determined by the nature of the process or processes carried out. Certain fundamental principles are applicable, however, throughout industry, commerce, and the services. These fall into generally well defined categories, as follows.

1   Management responsibility

Quality policy (see Chapter 2)

The organization should define and publish its quality policy, which forms one element of the corporate policy. Full commitment is required from the most senior management to ensure that the policy is communicated, understood, implemented and maintained at all levels in the organization. It should therefore be authorized by top management and signed by the Chief Executive, or equivalent, who must also ensure that it is updated as appropriate to meet organizational changes.

Organization

Organizations should have an organization chart, and define the responsibilities of those shown in the chart, which should include all functions that affect quality. One manager with the necessary authority, resources, support, and ability should be given the responsibility to co-ordinate, implement, and monitor the quality system, resolve any problems and ensure prompt and effective corrective action. This includes responsiblity for ensuring proper handling of the quality system. Those who control sales, service, processing, warehousing, delivery, and reworking of nonconforming product or service must also be identified.

Management review

Management reviews of the system must be carried out, with records to indicate the actions decided upon. The effectiveness of these actions should be considered during subsequent reviews. Reviews typically include data on the internal quality audits, customer complaints, non-conforming materials, the performance of sub-contractors, and the training plan.

Table 5.1 *Quality management and quality assurance standards BS EN ISO 9000 series*

ISO Standard	BS5750 Part	Title
	0	Principal concepts and applications.
9000-1		Guidelines for selection and use.
9000-2		Generic guidelines for application of ISO 9001, 9002, 9003. Quality systems specifications:
9001		for design, development, production, installation and servicing,
9002		for production, installation and servicing
9003		for final inspection and test.
	4	Guide to the use of BS5750: Part 1 'Specification for design/development, production, installation and servicing', Part 2 'Specification for production and installation', Part 3 'Specification for final inspection and test'
9004	0.2	Guide to quality management and quality system elements.
9004-1		Guidelines.
9004-2	8	Guide to quality management and quality system elements for services.
9004-3	9[1]	Guide for processed materials.
9004-4	10[1]	Guide to quality improvement.
9004-5	11[1]	Guide to use of quality plans.
9004-6	12[1]	Guide to configuration management.
9000-3	13	Guide to the application of BS5750: Part 1 to the development, supply, and maintenance of software.
9000-4	14	Guide to dependability programme management.

[1] In preparation at time of printing.

2 *Quality system*

The organization should prepare a quality plan and a quality manual that is appropriate for the 'level' of quality system required.

A *Level 1* system relates to design, production or operation, and installation, and applies when the customer specifies the goods or services in terms of how they are to peform, rather than in established technical terms.

A *Level 2* system is relevant when an organization is producing goods or services to a customer's or a published specification.

A *Level 3* system applies only to final production or service inspection, check, or test procedures.

The reader is referred to the International Standard, ISO 9000 (British Standard BS EN 9000 series) and Table 5.1.

A quality manual should set out the general quality policies, procedures, and practices of the organization. In the quality manual for large organizations it may be convenient to indicate simply the existence and contents of other manuals, those containing the details of procedures and practices in operation in specific areas of the system.

Before an organization can agree to supply to a specification, it must ensure that:

(a) The processes and equipment (including any that are subcontracted) are capable of meeting the requirements.
(b) The operators have the necessary skills and training.
(c) The operating procedures are written down and not simply passed on verbally.
(d) The plant and equipment instrumentation is capable (e.g. measuring the process variables with the appropriate accuracy and precision)
(e) The quality-control procedures and any inspection, check, or test methods available, provide results to the required accuracy and precision, and are documented.
(f) Any subjective phrases in the specification, such as 'finely ground', 'low moisture content', 'in good time', are understood, and procedures to establish the exact customer requirements exist.

3 *Contract review*

It is difficult to over-emphasize the importance of this aspect of the system. Each accepted customer order should be regarded as a contract, and 'order entry procedures' should be developed and documented. These should ensure that:

(a) The customer requirements are absolutely clear and in writing, including the recording of any verbal communication, e.g. telephone instructions or orders.
(b) Differences between the order and any original enquiry and/or quotation are agreed or resolved.
(c) The terms of the order (contract) can be met, including verifying that dates promised to customers on acceptance of the contract can be met.

Clearly, a procedural dialogue should be established between customer and supplier with regard to the specification, interfaces and the communication of changes. The system must ensure that everyone in the organization understands the commitment, skills, and resources required to meet any particular contract, and that these have been scheduled.

4 Design control

Where a Level 1 system is required, there must be procedures that control and verify design of products or services to ensure that the customer requirements will be met. The translation of the information derived from market research into practical designs that are achievable by the operating units should be the core of the documented design-control system. This will include the following activities, which were dealt with in more detail in Chapter 3:

- Planning of research, design and development.
- Assignment of design activities to qualified staff.
- Identification of the organizational and technical interfaces between different groups.
- Preparation of a design brief relating to the requirements of the product or service (inputs).
- Production of clear and comprehensive technical data to enable complete operation of the service or production and delivery of the product, according to the requirements (outputs).
- Verification that the design outputs meet the requirements of the inputs.
- Identification and control of all design changes and modifications and the associated documentation.

Attention, in detail, to the above areas will form the basis of a research, design and development programme. With correct implementation it will maintain a balance between innovation and standardization, which encourages the use of new techniques whilst retaining reliable, proven designs, materials and methods.

5 Document and data control

All documents relating to quality, including the following, should be 'controlled':

(a) Quality manual and supplementary manuals.
(b) Departmental operating manuals.
(c) Written procedures.
(d) Purchasing specifications.
(e) Lists of approved suppliers.
(f) Product, parts, or service formulations.
(g) Intermediate, part, or component formulations and specifications.

(h) Service manuals.
(i) Relevant international and national standards.

'Control' is necessary to ensure that only the most up-to-date issues are used and referred to at the various locations. Clearly this will require records of what documents exist and/or are needed, and of who holds the documents; plus a written procedure for the issue of amendments and revisions, and for re-issues, together with some form of acknowledgement of receipt. Computerized techniques may be very helpful here. If additional copies of 'controlled' documents are produced for temporary purposes, procedures should exist to prevent their misuse. Sales literature is not usually regarded as controlled documentation, unless it forms the basis of a contract. In industries where continuous innovation, redesign and/or improvements are major features, good document change control is vital.

6 Purchasing (see also Chapter 4)

The objective of the purchasing system is very simple – to ensure that purchased products and services conform to the requirements of the organization. The means of achieving this should be concentrated on assessments of the suppliers' own quality systems, rather than by an elaborate scheme of checking, testing and inspection on receipt. The system should essentially consider the 'contract review' from the view of the purchaser.

Suppliers or subcontractors should be selected on the basis of their ability to meet the defined requirements, and objective documentary evidence will be required to show that the supplier:

(a) Has the capability to do so.
(b) Will do so reliably and consistently.

When the extent of *vendor appraisal* necessary has to be decided, the following factors should be taken into consideration:

- Feasibility of appraisal.
- Objective evidence, from records and analysis of acceptable past performance (not 'reputation', which is subjective).
- Any independent third-party quality system assessment, certification, or registration to a recognized standard, e.g. ISO 9000 series.
- Any assessments by means of questionnaires or visits, which should be documented.

Vendor appraisal of any product or service subcontractors is often necessary to ensure that their quality sysem matches the standard of the purchasing organization, and appraisal visits may form part of the corrective action following unsatisfactory performance. The basic requirements of purchasing documents are that they:

(a) Are written.
(b) Include the specification, or reference to it, to describe clearly the product/ service required.
(c) Are made available to the supplier.
(d) Are reviewed and approved by authorized personnel before issue.

Purchases can be made by telephone or computer means, but must refer to the appropriate purchasing documentation. The system should allow customers to impose quality-system requirements on their suppliers' suppliers, and so on, if specified in the contract. This may include independent third-party certification, assessment of products, services or records, or even the use of such specific techniques as statistical process control (SPC). (See Chapter 8.)

Records of acceptable suppliers and subcontractors should be maintained, together with their monitored performance.

7 Customer-supplied product or services

Where a customer supplies material or services on which further transformation work is required, it is necessary to have systems that ensure the material's suitability for use and that enable monitoring and traceability of the material or service through all processes and storage. Any material that is damaged, lost, or not suitable for use should be recorded and reported to the customer. Special considerations may be necessary when the customer supplies material that is to be used in a continuous process with other purchased material. Clearly a supplier cannot be held responsible for the quality of the customer's material handled, but he is responsible for maintaining its condition while it is in his care.

8 Identification and traceability

Identification and traceability from purchased materials to finished products and services are essential if effective methods of process control are to be applied and quality problems are to be related to cause. Materials in process or bulk storage should be identified, if necessary by virtue of their location and time, and the design of procedures and record-keeping should allow for this. Traceability requirements are an optional part of an agreed specification or contract, and may be the subject of special contract conditions. In a garage, for example, a system should be developed to identify any parts removed from vehicles as either for re-use, requiring repair, etc.

9 Process control

To control the operation of any process clearly requires some planning activity, i.e. careful consideration of the inputs to the process so that they become suitable for the purpose. This requirement covers the core of any operation. It may be difficult to imagine, but the author has seen too often the operation of processes about which too little is known in terms of the capability to meet the requirements.

To operate processes under controlled conditions, documented work instructions must be available to staff. These do not need to repeat the basic skills of the operator's profession, but they must contain sufficient detail to enable the process to be carried out under the specified conditions. A fully documented 'process manual' should contain, where appropriate:

(a) A description of the process, with appropriate technological information; this may be in the form of a process flowchart.
(b) A description of the plant or equipment required.
(c) Any special process 'set-up' or 'start-up' procedures.
(d) Reference to any instrumentation, calibration procedures, and measures related to control of the process.
(e) Simplified operator instruction or a summary that includes the quantity of materials required and the order in which the process is to be carried out. This may take the form of service handbooks or bulletins, etc.

For certain special processes, such as welding, plastic moulding, heat treatment, application of protective treatments, vehicle servicing, and cooking, where deficiencies may become apparent only after the product is in use, continuous monitoring of adherence to the documented procedures is the only effective method of process control.

10   Inspection and testing

All need to be either inspected or otherwise verified. The amount of inspection is clearly a function of the situation, and might consist simply of:

- Checking a product label or delivery note against a purchase order.
- Visual examination for damage in transit.
- Checking the evidence from a certificate of conformity or of analysis.

These checks are valid only if an adequate assessment of the supplier's quality system has been carried out.

Whatever the system, it must be operated in accordance with the written procedures. If bought-in materials have to be released into production before adequate verification or checking can take place, the system should ensure that it is possible to identify the material and recall it if problems arise. This may prevent the acceptance of certain bulk materials without the appropriate receiving inspection.

In process monitoring

This answers the 'Are we doing the job OK?' question, which calls for some form of process monitoring and control. Ideally it is the actual process parameters, such as temperature, cutting speed, feed rate, pressure, typing speed, flow rate, which should be monitored to ensure feedforward control of the process. The work instructions should also indicate the frequency of any in-process inspections or checks, and the action to be taken in the event of process parameters being found to be incorrect, or 'out-of-control'.

Checking finished product and/or service

Whatever final checking, inspecting or testing activities have been set out in the quality plan should be documented, including any delaying of despatch, or release of service, until the checks have been carried out. Records must be kept of all the checks, tests, measurements, etc., carried out at inwards goods or services receipt, during operation of the process, or at the final product or service stage, which are required to demonstrate conformance to the requirements or specifications. These may include certificates of conformity or analysis, and evidence on plant records or in a computer that process control parameters were actually monitored. There should also be a statement of what records are kept, for how long, and by whom.

11 Measuring, inspection and test equipment

All measuring and the test equipment relevant to the quality system must be controlled, calibrated and maintained. This includes equipments used for in-process parameter measurements and control, such as temperature and pressure gauges, as well as that used in laboratories or test/measurement areas. Where equipment is used only for observation, safety, or faulty diagnosis reasons, it may be excluded from the fully documented inspection calibration system.

The system for the instrumentation should:

(a) Refer to the measurements to be made, their accuracy and precision, and the equipment to be used to ensure the necessary capability.
(b) Identify the equipment and ensure its calibration against the appropriate standard(s) with suitable procedures, and its correct handling, preservation, storage etc.
(c) Maintain calibration records for all inspection, measuring and test equipment.
(d) Allow, where appropriate, tracking back to national standards.

12 Inspection and test status

There are essentially three statuses for all materials and services – incoming, intermediate or in-process, and finished:

- Awaiting inspection, check or test.
- Passed requirements of inspection, check or test.
- Failed requirements of inspection, check or test.

The test status of material is identified by any suitable means: labels, location, stamps markings, position in the process, records (including computers), etc. These should be used to ensure that only material or services conforming to the requirements are passed on to the next stage, or despatched. The test or check carried out may of course refer to a process-control parameter.

13   Nonconforming products or services

To prevent inadvertent use or delivery of materials or provision of services that do not conform to the specified requirements, there should be a documented system that clearly identifies and, if possible, 'segregates' them. The procedures should also show how the nonconforming output will be reworked, disposed of, accepted with concession, or regraded, and what corrective action will take place.

14   Corrective and preventive action

This is a very important part of the system in any organization, since it provides the means to never ending improvement of process operation. Systematic planning is a basic requirement for effective corrective action programmes. The procedures for major corrective action should be in the form of general guidance and should define the duties of the managers, supervisors and key personnel. The detailed action to be taken will be dependent upon the circumstances prevailing at the time, and it is not therefore appropriate for the written procedures to be too detailed. All employees must be made fully aware of the general corrective action procedures appertaining to their own processes and activities. The written procedures for corrective action should be implemented when there are:

- Failures in *any* part of the quality system.
- Complaints from customers (internal or external).
- Complaints to suppliers (internal or external) and to subcontractors.

The underlying purpose of this part of the system is to eliminate the causes of non-conformance by initiation of investigations, analyses, and preventive actions. Controls must be built in to make sure that the corrective actions are taken, that they are effective, and that any necessary changes in procedures are recorded and implemented. The provision of *corrective action teams*, with regular training and updating, enables people to become used to working together to solve problems.

15   Protection of product or service quality

The sight of a warehouseman, in dirty wellington boots, climbing over clean sacks of finished product to count them, still remains in the author's memory. A great deal of damage can be done to products and service between their 'production' and their transfer to the customer. This highlights the need for the quality system to cover such things as handling, storage, packaging, transport, and delivery of final product or services. The written procedures should be aimed at preventing damage or deterioration. The use of the correct type of packaging and labelling may invoke national or international regulations and/or codes of practice. Where contract hauliers or outside transport are employed, their ability to meet the requirements of cleanliness, schedules, etc., should be established, and appropriate procedures documented.

16   Quality records

The records provide objective evidence that work is being carried out in accordance with the documented procedures. Attention should be paid to identifying which records need to be retained, and to their easy retrieval. One of the author's colleagues was, on one occasion, performing a vertical audit for traceability purposes in a garment manufacturer. He selected some items from stock and, on attempting to trace back to purchased materials, discovered that final inspection records on certain items were missing. It transpired that one of the final inspectors spent 3 months in hospital, and the chief inspector, who insisted that she had stood in and carried out the necessary inspection, was too busy to write down the results. This represents a failure of the system to *demonstrate* compliance with its own requirements, and can be as serious as an ineffective procedure.

Records will have been established if the documented quality system has been set up as described above, but there must be procedures for the collection, indexing, filing or storage, retrieval, and disposition of records. Serious thought should be given to the retention time of records, which should then be stated in the documented system.

The quality records should include training and management audit and review records.

17   Quality system audits and reviews

An internal audit sets out to establish whether the quality system is being operated according to the written procedures. A *review* addresses the much wider issue of whether the quality system actually meets the requirements, and aims to determine the system's effectiveness. Clearly the results of quality audits will be used in the reviews for, if procedures are not being operated according to plan, it may be that improvements in the system are required, rather than enforcing adherence to unsuitable methods. Organizations should plan to self-police the quality system by carrying out both internal audits and reviews, and the person responsible for organizing these is the manager with responsibility for co-ordinating and monitoring the whole quality system. Auditor training is now recognized as a key element in quality system implementation.

18   Training (see Chapter 12)

For *all* staff, written procedures should be established and maintained for:

- Identifying and reviewing individual training needs.
- Carrying out the training.
- Keeping records of training, including qualifications.

On-the-job training may frequently be appropriate in meeting the training requirements. It should be possible to go to the training records and establish from them objectively whether an individual has been instructed to carry out the various tasks associated with his/her job.

Training procedures may also include methods of ensuring the quality policy is understood, implemented and maintained at all levels in the organization, for existing and new employees.

19   Servicing

If servicing is an important part of the customer requirements, e.g. in the provision of a burglar alarm service, procedures should be documented for its operation and to verify that it satisfies the needs. The servicing system may well include some or all of the contents of the quality system: design, documentation control, process control, training, review, etc. In particular it must ensure that:

(a) The servicing procedures are effectively carried out.
(b) Adequate resources are made available, in terms of people, time, equipment, materials, information, etc.
(c) Good interfaces exist for dealing with the customer, in terms of regular service contracts, items returned, customer complaints or call-outs.

20   Statistical techniques (see Chapter 8)

In most organizations it is necessary to measure and establish the so-called 'capability of the process'. In many industries this requires the use of certain procedures, which are grouped under the general heading of *statistical process control* (SPC).

In addition to measuring capability, controlling and improving processes through the use of statistical techniques, it might also be necessary to identify and classify lots of batches of material by their characteristics, select samples, determine any rules for acceptance or rejection of material or for adjusting the severity of inspection, and the segregation and screening of rejected materials. The system should refer to the statistical procedures used, giving the areas from their application, but always remember that statistics is simply the collection and use of data.

In considering the detailed quality system requirements, the system *must* be tailored to the needs of the 'business'. It must be seen to be an integral part of the way the business is run, and the system must be usable by all employees in never ending improvement.

5.4   Environmental management systems

Organizations of all kinds are increasingly concerned to achieve and demonstrate sound environmental performance. Many have undertaken enviromental audits and review to assess this. To be effective, these need to be conducted within a structured management system, which in turn is integrated with the management activities dealing with all aspects of desired environmental performance.

A cell containing a • represents a connection between the relevant sub-clauses of the two standards.

Requirement of BS EN ISO 9001 Subclause	Requirement of BS7750 Subclause										
	4.1	4.2	4.3	4.4	4.5	4.6	4.7	4.8	4.9	4.10	4.11
	Management system	Environmental policy	Organization and personnel	Environmental effects	Objectives and targets	Management programme	Manual and documentation	Operational control	Records	Audits	Reviews
4.1 Management responsibility	•	•	•							•	
4.2 Quality system	•						•				
4.3 Contract review				•	•	•					
4.4 Design control						•	•	•			
4.5 Document control							•				
4.6 Purchasing				•				•			
4.7 Purchaser supplied product				•							
4.8 Product identification									•		
4.9 Process control								•			
4.10 Inspection and testing								•			
4.11 Inspection, measuring and test equipment								•			
4.12 Inspection and test status								•			
4.13 Control of nonconforming product								•			
4.14 Corrective action								•			
4.15 Handling, storage, packaging and delivery				•				•			
4.16 Quality records									•		
4.17 Internal quality audits										•	
4.18 Training			•								
4.19 Servicing				•				•			
4.20 Statistical techniques								•			

Source – BS7750: 1992 (British Standards)

Table 5.2 *The links between BS7750: 1992 and BS EN ISO 9001: 1994*

Such a system should establish procedures for setting environmental policy and objectives, and achieving compliance to them. It should be designed to place emphasis on the prevention of adverse environmental effects rather than on detection after occurrence. It should also identify and assess the environmental effects arising from the organization's existing or proposed activities, products, or services, and from incidents, accidents, and potential emergency situations. The system must identify the relevant regulatory requirements, the priorities, and pertinent environmental objectives and targets. It needs also to facilitate planning, control, monitoring, auditing and review activities to ensure that the policy is complied with, that it remains relevant, and that it is capable of evolution to suit changing circumstances.

In 1992 a British Standard BS7750 was prepared under the direction of the Environment and Pollution Standards Policy Committee in response to the increasing concerns about environmental protection and performance. It contains a specification for environmental management systems for ensuring and demonstrating compliance with stated policies and objectives. The standard is designed to enable any organization to establish an effective management system as a foundation for both sound environmental performance and participation in environmental auditing schemes.

BS7750 shares common management system principles with BS EN ISO 9001, and organizations may elect to use an existing management system, developed in conformity with the BS EN ISO 9001 series, as a basis for environmental management. The new standard defines environmental policy, objectives, targets, effect, management, systems, manuals, evaluation, audits and reviews. It mirrors the ISO 9000 series requirements in many of its own eleven requirements, and it includes a guide to these in the informative Annex A.

The link to BS EN ISO 9001 is spelled out in a table that is reproduced in Table 5.2. The standard has also been developed in such a way as to complement the European Community ECO-Audit Regulations and as a foundation for registration under them.

5.5   The rings of confidence

Quality systems are needed in all areas of activity, whether large or small businesses, manufacturing, service or public sector. The advantages of systems in manufacturing are obvious, but they are just as applicable in areas such as marketing, sales, personnel, finance, research and development, as well as in the service industries and public sectors.

No matter where it is implemented, a good quality system will improve process control, reduce wastage, lower costs, increase market share (or funding), facilitate training, increase staff participation, and raise morale.

The activities to be addressed in the design and implementation of a good quality-management system may be considered to be attached to a 'ring of confidence', which starts and ends with the customer (Figure 5.4). It is possible to group these into two spheres of activities:

• Those directly interacting with the customer.

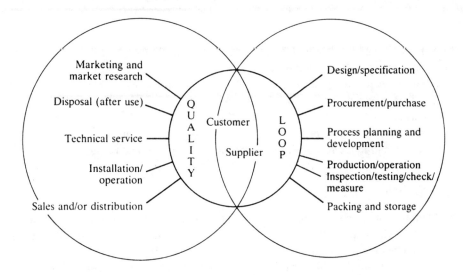

Figure 5.4 *The rings of confidence*

- Those directly interacting with the customer.
- Those concerning primarily the internal activities of the supplier.

The overlap necessary between customer and supplier is clearly illustrated by this model. Equally obvious is that separation will lead to disfunction and disaster.

It cannot be stated too often that the customer–supplier interactions, which generate satisfaction of needs, are just as necessary internally. The principles of quality-system design, documentation and implementation set out in this and the next chapter must apply to every single person, every department, every process transaction, and every type of organization. The vocabulary in the engineering factory system may be different from that used in the hotel, the hospital system will be set out differently to that of the drug manufacturer, but the underlying concepts will be the same.

It is not acceptable for the managers in industries, or parts of organizations, less often associated with standards on quality systems to find 'technological' reasons for avoiding the requirements to manage quality. The author and his colleagues have heard the excuse that 'our industry (or organization) differs from any other industry (or organization)', in almost every industry or organization with which they have come into contact. Clearly there are technological differences between all industries and nearly all organizations, but in terms of managing total quality there are hardly any at all.

Senior managers in every type and size of organization must take the responsibility for the adoption of the appropriate documented quality system. If this requires translation from 'engineering language', so be it – get someone from inside or outside the organization to do it. Do not wait for the message to be translated into different forms – inefficiencies, waste, high costs, crippling competition, loss of market.

Chapter highlights

Why a documented system?

- An appropriate documented quality system will enable the objectives set out in the quality policy to be accomplished.
- The International Organization for Standardization (ISO) 9000 series set out methods by which a system can be implemented to ensure that the specified requirements are met.
- A quality system may be defined as an assembly of components, such as the organizational structure responsibilities, procedures, process, and resources.

Quality system design

- Quality systems should apply to and interact with all activities of the organization. The activities are generally processing, communicating, and controlling. These should be documented in the form of a quality manual.
- The system should follow the PLAN DO CHECK ACT cycle, through documentation, implementation, audit and review.

Quality system requirements

- The general categories of ISO-based standards include management responsibility, quality system, contract review, design control, document and data control, purchasing, customer-supplied products or services, identification and traceability, process control, checking/measuring/inspecting of incoming materials or services, measuring/inspection/test equipment, inspection/test status, nonconforming products or services, corrective action, protection of product or service quality, quality records, quality-system audits and reviews, training, servicing and statistical techniques.

Environmental management systems

- The British Standard BS7750 contains a specification for environmental management systems for ensuring and demonstrating compliance with the stated policies and objectives, and acting as a base for auditing and review schemes. It shares common management-system principles with the ISO 9000 series.

The rings of confidence

- The activities needed in the design and implementation of a good quality system start and end with the customer, in two spheres – a customer sphere and a supplier sphere.
- Senior management in all types of industry must take responsibility for the adoption and documentation of the appropriate quality system in their organization.

Quality system audit/review and self-assessment

6.1 Securing prevention by audit and review of the system

Error or defect prevention is the process of removing or controlling error/defect causes in the system. There are two major elements of this:

- Checking the system.
- Error/defect investigation and follow-up

These have the same objectives – to find, record and report *possible* causes of error, and to recommend future corrective action.

Checking the system

There are six methods in general use:

(a) *Quality audits and reviews*, which subject each area of an organization's activity to a systematic critical examination. Every component of the total system is included, i.e., quality policy, attitudes, training, process, decision features, operating procedures, documentation. Audits and reviews, as in the field of accountancy, aim to disclose the strengths and weaknesses and the main areas of vulnerability or risk.

(b) *Quality survey*, a detailed, in-depth examination of a narrower field of activity, i.e. major key areas revealed by quality audits, individual plants, procedures or specific problems common to an organization as a whole.

(c) *Quality inspection*, which takes the form of a routine scheduled inspection of a unit or department. The inspection should check standards, employee involvement and working practices, and that work is carried out in accordance with the procedures, etc.

(d) *Quality tour*, which is an unscheduled examination of a work area to ensure that, for example, the standards of operation are acceptable, obvious causes of errors are removed, and in general quality standards are maintained.

(e) *Quality sampling*, which measures by random sampling, similar to activity sampling, the error potential. Trained observers perform short tours of specific locations by prescribed routes and record the number of potential errors or defects seen. The results may be used to portray trends in the general quality situation.

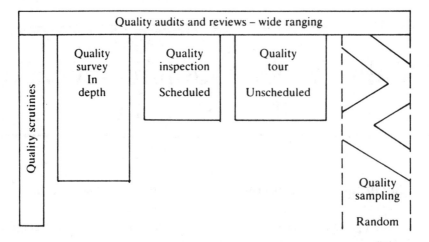

Figure 6.1 *A prevention programme combining various elements of 'checking' the system.*

(f) *Quality scrutinies*, which are the application of a formal, critical examination of the process and technological intentions for new or existing facilities, or to assess the potential for mal-operation or malfunction of equipment and the consequential effects of quality. There are similarities between quality scrutinies and FMECA studies (see Chapter 8).

The design of a prevention programme, combining all these elements, is represented in Figure 6.1.

6.2   Error or defect investigations and follow-up

The investigation of errors and defects can provide valuable error prevention information. The method is based on:

- *Collecting* data and information relating to the error or defect.
- *Checking* the validity of the evidence.
- *Selecting* the evidence without making assumptions or jumping to conclusions.

The results of the analysis are then used to:

- *Decide* the most likely cause(s) of the errors or defects.
- *Notify* immediately the person(s) able to take corrective action.
- *Record* the findings and outcomes.
- *Report* them to everyone concerned, to prevent a recurrence.

The investigation should not become an inquisition to apportion blame, but focus on the positive preventive aspects. The types of follow-up to errors and their effects is shown in Table 6.1.

It is hoped that errors or defects are not normally investigated so frequently that the required skills are developed by experience, nor are these skills easily learned in a classroom. One suggested way to overcome this problem is the development of a programmed sequence of questions to form the skeleton of an error or defect investigation questionnaire. This can be set out with the following structure:

(a) *Plant equipment* – description, condition, controls, maintenance, suitability, etc.
(b) *Environment* – climatic, space, humidity, noise, etc.
(c) *People* – duties, information, supervision, instruction, training, attitudes, etc.
(d) *Systems* – procedures, instructions, monitoring, control methods, etc.

Table 6.1 *Following up errors*

System type	Aim	General effects
Investigation	To prevent a similar error or defect	*Positive:* identification notification correction
Inquisition	To identify responsibility	*Negative:* blame claims defence

6.3   Internal and external quality-system audits and reviews

A good quality system will not function without adequate audits and reviews. The system reviews, which need to be carried out periodically and systematically, are conducted to ensure that the system achieves the required effect, while audits are carried out to make sure that actual methods are adhering to the documented procedures. The reviews should use the findings of the audits, for failure to operate according to the plan often signifies difficulties in doing so. A re-examination of the procedures actually being used may lead to system improvements unobtainable by other means.

A schedule for carrying out the *audits* should be drawn up, different activities perhaps requiring different frequencies. All procedures and systems should be audited at least once during a specified cycle, but not necessarily all at the same audit. For example, every 3 months a selected random sample of work instructions and test methods could be audited, with the selection designed so that each procedure is audited at least once per year. There must be, however, a facility to adjust this on the basis of the audit results.

A quality-system *review* should be instituted, perhaps every 12 months, with the aims of:

- Ensuring that the system is achieving the desired results.
- Revealing defects or irregularities in the system.
- Indicating any necessary improvements and/or corrective actions to eliminate waste or loss.
- Checking on all levels of management.
- Uncovering potential danger areas.
- Verifying that improvements or corrective action procedures are effective.

Clearly, the procedures for carrying out the audits and reviews and the results from them should be documented, and themselves be subject to review.

The assessment of a quality system against a particular standard or set of requirements by internal audit and review is known as a *first-party* assessment or approval scheme. If an *external* customer makes the assessment of a supplier against either its own or a national or international standard, a *second-party* scheme is in operation. The external assessment by an independent organization not connected with any contract between customer and supplier, but acceptable to them both, is known as an *independent third-party* assessment scheme. The latter usually results in some form of certification or registration by the assessment body.

One advantage of the third-party schemes is that they obviate the need for customers to make their own detailed checks, saving both suppliers and customers time and money, and avoiding issues of commercial confidentiality. Just one knowledgeable organization has to be satisfied, rather than a multitude with varying levels of competence. This method often certifies suppliers for quality assurance based contracts without further checking.

Each certification body usually has its own recognized mark, which may be used by registered organizations of assessed capability in their literature, letter headings, and marketing activities. There are also publications containing lists of organizations whose quality systems and/or products and services have been assessed. To be of value, the certification body must itself be recognized and, usually, assessed and registered with a national or international accreditation scheme, such as the National Accreditation Council for Certification Bodies (NACCB) in the UK.

Many organizations have found that the effort of designing and implementing a written quality system good enough to stand up to external independent third-party assessment has been extremely rewarding in:

- Encouraging staff and improving morale.
- Better process control.
- Reduced wastage.
- Reduced customer service costs.

This is also true of those organizations that have obtained third-party registrations and supply companies that still insist on their own second-party assessment. The reason for this is that most of the standards on quality systems, whether national, international, or company-specific, are now very similar indeed. A system that meets the requirements of the ISO 9000 series will meet the requirements of all other standards, with only the slight modifications and small emphases here and there required for specific customers. It is the author's experience, and that of his immediate colleagues, that an assessment carried out by one of the independent certified assessment bodies is at least as rigorous and delving as any carried out by a second-part representative.

Internal system audits and reviews must be positive, and conducted as part of the preventive strategy and not as a matter of expediency resulting from quality problems. They should not be carried out only before external audits, nor should they be left to the external auditor – whether second or third party. An external auditor discovering discrepancies between actual and documented systems will be inclined to ask why the internal review methods did not discover and correct them. As this type of behaviour in financial control and auditing is commonplace, why should things be different in the control of quality?

Managements anxious to display that they are serious about quality must become fully committed to operating an effective quality system for all personnel within the organization, not just the staff in the quality department. They system must be planned to be effective and achieve its objectives in an uncomplicated way. Having established and documented the procedures, an organization must ensure that they are working and that everyone is operating in accordance with them. The system once established is not static; it should be flexible, to enable the constant seeking of improvements or stream-lining.

Quality auditing standard

There is a British and International Standard Guide to quality-systems auditing (BS 7229, ISO 10011: 1991). This points out that audits are required to verify whether the individual elements making up quality systems are effective in achieving the stated objectives. The growing use of standards internationally emphasizes the importance of auditing as a management tool for this purpose. The guidance provided in the standard can be applied equally to any one of the three specific and yet different auditing activities:

(a) *First-party or internal audits*, carried out by an organization on its own systems, either by staff who are independent of the systems being audited, or by an outside agency.
(b) *Second-party audits*, carried out by one organization (a purchaser or its outside agent) on another with which it either has contracts to purchase goods or services or intends to do so.
(c) *Third-party audits*, carried out by independent agencies, to provide assurance to existing and prospective customers for the product or service.

ISO 10011 (BS 7229) overs audit objectives and responsibilities, including the roles of auditors and their independence, and those of the 'client' or auditee. It provides the following detailed guidance on audit:

- *Initiation*, including its scope and frequency.
- *Preparation*, including review of documentation, the programme, and working documents.

- *Execution*, including the opening meeting, examination and evaluation, collecting evidence, observations, and closing the meeting with the auditee.
- *Report*, including its preparation, content and distribution.
- *Completion*, including report submission and retention.

Attention is given at the end of the standard to corrective action and follow-up, where it is stressed that the improvement process should be continued by the auditee after the publication of the audit report. This may include a call by the client for a verification audit of the implementation of any corrective actions specified.

6.4   Towards a TQM standard for self-assessment

'Total quality' is the goal of many organizations, but it is difficult to find a universally accepted definition of what this actually means. For some people TQM means SPC or quality systems, for others teamwork and involvement of the workforce. Clearly there are many different views on what constitutes the 'total quality organization' and, even with an understanding of the framework of TQM, there is the difficulty of calibrating the performance or progress of any organization towards it.

The philosophy of TQM recognizes that customer satisfaction, business objectives, safety, and environment considerations are mutually dependent, and applicable in any organization. Clearly, the application of TQM calls for investment primarily in people and time; time to implement new concepts, time to train, time for people to recognize the benefits and move forward into new or different organizational cultures. But how will organizations know when they are getting close to TQM, or whether they are even on the right road? How will they *measure* their progress?

There have been many recent developments and there will continue to be many more, in the search for a TQM standard or framework against which organizations may be assessed or measure themselves, and carry out the so-called 'gap analysis'. To many companies the ability to judge their TQM progress against an accepted set of criteria would be most valuable and informative.

Quality award criteria

Most TQM approaches strongly emphasize measurement, especially in the quality assurance and control areas. Some insist on the use of cost of quality. The recognition that total quality management is a broad culture change vehicle with internal and external focus embracing behavioural and service issues, as well as quality assurance and process control, prompted the United States to develop a widely used framework for TQM – the Malcolm Baldrige National Quality Award (MBNQA). The award itself, which is composed of two solid crystal forms 14 inches high, is presented annually to recognize companies in the USA that have 'excelled in quality management and quality achievement'. Up to two awards may be given in each of three categories: manufacturing, service, and small businesses. But it is not the award itself, or even the fact that it is presented each year by the President of the USA, which has attracted the attention of most organizations. It is the excellent framework, which is one of the closest things we have to an international standard for TQM.

The value of a structured discipline using a points scoring system has been well established in quality and safety *assurance* systems (for example, ISO 9000/BS 5750, Vendor Auditing). The extension of this approach to a *total* quality-auditing process has been long established in the Japanese-based 'Deming Prize', which is perhaps the most demanding and intrusive auditing process. There are other excellent models and standards used throughout the world: the British Standard BS 7850 Guide to TQM, the Marketing Quality Assurance (MQA) Specification, the UK Quality Award, and the European Quality Award.

In 1987 and MBNQA was introduced for US-based organizations. Many US companies have realized the necessity to assess themselves against the Baldrige criteria, if not to enter for the Baldrige Award then certainly as an excellent basis for self-audit and review, to highlight areas for priority attention and provide internal and external benchmarking.

The MBNQA aims to promote:

- Awareness of quality as an increasingly important element in competitiveness.
- Understanding of the requirements for quality excellence.
- Sharing of information on successful quality strategies and the benefits to be derived from their implementation.

The award criteria are built upon a set of core values and concepts:

1 Customer-driven quality.
2 Leadership.
3 Continuous improvement and learning.
4 Employee participation and development.
5 Fast response.
6 Design quality and prevention.
7 Long-range view of the future.
8 Management by fact.
9 Partnership development.
10 Corporate responsibility and citizenship.
11 Results orientation.

These are embodied in a criteria framework of seven first level categories, which are used to assess organization. These are given in Table 6.2, along with the ten first level categories of the Deming Prize.

Figure 6.2 shows how the framework connects and integrates the categories. This has four basic elements: driver, system, measures of progress, and goal. The driver is the senior executive leadership that creates the values, goals, and systems, and guides the sustained pursuit of quality and performance objectives. The system includes a set of well-defined and designed processes for meeting the organization's quality and performance requirements. Measures of progress provide a results-oriented basis for channelling actions to deliver ever-improving customer values and organizational performance. The goal is the basic aim of the quality process in delivering the above to the customers.

Table 6.2 *The first-level categories of the Baldrige Award and the Deming Prize*

Baldrige	Deming
1 Leadership	1 Policy
2 Information and analysis	2 Organization and management
3 Strategic planning	3 Education and dissemination
4 Human resource development and management	4 Collection, dissemination, and use of information on quality
5 Process management	5 Analysis
6 Business results	6 Standardization
7 Customer focus and satisfaction	7 Control
	8 Quality assurance
	9 Results
	10 Planning for the future

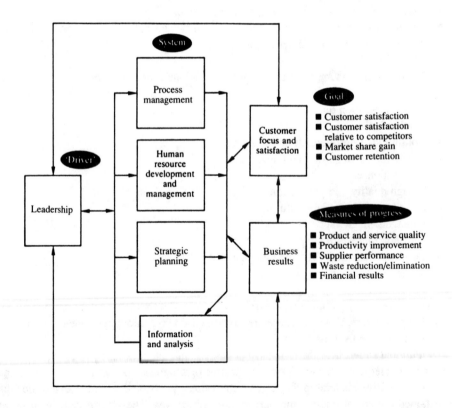

Figure 6.2 *Baldrige Award criteria framework – dynamic relationships. Source: Malcolm Baldrige National Quality Award criteria, US National Institute of Standards and Technology*

Figure 6.2 shows how the framework connects and integrates the categories. This has four basic elements: driver, system, measures of progress, and goal. The driver is the senior executive leadership that creates the values, goals, and systems, and guides the sustained pursuit of quality and performance objectives. The system includes a set of well-defined and designed processes for meeting the organization's quality and performance requirements. Measures of progress provide a results-oriented basis for channelling actions to deliver ever-improving customer values and organizational performance. The goal is the basic aim of the quality process in delivering the above to the customers.

The seven criteria categories are further subdivided into examination items and areas to address. These are described in some detail in the 'Award Criteria', available from the US National Institute of Standards and Technology.

In Europe it has also been recognized that the technique of self-assessment is very useful for any organization wishing to develop and monitor its quality culture. The European Foundation for Quality Management (EFQM) has launched a European Quality Award, which can be used effectively for a systematic review and measurement of operations. The EQA self-assessment model recognizes that *processes* are the means by which a company or organization harnesses and releases the talents of its *people* to produce *results*. Moreover, the processes and the people are the enablers which produce results.

Figure 6.3 displays graphically the principle of the European Quality Award. Essentially this states that customer satisfaction, employee satisfaction, and impact on society are achieved through leadership driving policy and strategy, people management, resources, and process, which lead ultimately to excellence in business results.

Using the European Quality Award's nine categories, it is possible to build a model of criteria and a review framework against which an organization may face and measure itself, to examine any 'gaps'.

Many managers feel the need for a rational basis on which to measure TQM in their organization, especially in those companies 3 or more years 'into TQM' that would like the answer to questions such as 'Where are we now?' 'Where do we need/want to be?' and 'What have we got to do to get there?' These questions need to be answered from internal employees' views, the customers' views, and the views of suppliers. A business excellence review process, which uses the EQA model criteria and lists questions that

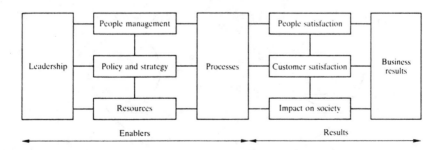

Figure 6.3 *The European Quality Award assessment model. Source: Total Quality Management: The European Model of Self-Appraisal. EFQM*

should be asked under each heading, will help any organization to identify opportunities for improvement.

Clearly, it is necessary for any organization to rationalize all the criteria used by the various awards. There is great overlap between them, and the main components must be the organization's processes, quality management system, human-resource management, results and customer satisfaction.

Self-assessments provide an organization with vital information in monitoring its progress towards its goals and total quality. The external assessments used in the processes of making awards must be based on those self-assessments that are performed as prerequisites for improvement.

The systematic measurement and review of operations are two of the most important management activities of any TQM system. Self-assessment allows an organization clearly to discern its strengths and areas for improvement by focusing on the relationship between the people, processes, and performance. Within any quality-conscious organization it should be a regular activity.

6.5   Adding the systems to the TQM model

In Chapters 1 and 2 the foundations for TQM were set down. The core of total quality was established as the customer/supplier chains that extend through and out from an organization. It was recognized that if the chains are 'cut' anywhere, processes that

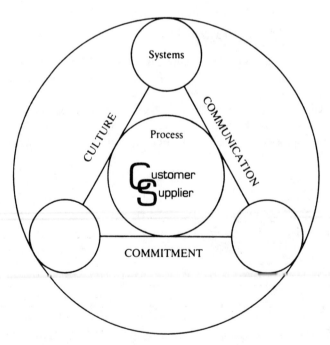

Figure 6.4 *Total quality management model – the quality system*

must be managed will be found. Within the TQM framework were identified the 'soft' outcomes of total quality, namely culture change, communication improvements and commitment.

To this foundation must be added the first hard management necessity – a quality system, based on any good international standard. This is shown in Figure 6.4.

Chapter highlights

Securing prevention by audit and review of the system

- There are two major elements of error or defect prevention: checking the system, and error/defect investigations and follow-up. Six methods of checking quality systems are in general use: audits and reviews, surveys, inspections, tours, sampling and scrutinies.

Error or defect investigations and follow-up

- Investigations proceed by collecting, checking and selecting data, and analysing it by deciding causes, notifying people, recording and reporting findings and outcomes.

Internal and external quality-system audits and reviews

- A good quality system will not function without adequate audits and reviews. Audits make sure the actual methods are adhering to documented procedures. Reviews ensure the system achieves the desired effect.
- System assessment by internal audit and review is known as first-party, by external customer as second-party, and by an independent organization as third-party certification. For the latter to be of real value the certification body must itself be recognized.

Towards a TQM standard for self-assessment

- One of the most widely used frameworks for TQM self-assessment in the USA is the Malcolm Baldrige National Quality Award (MBNQA).
- The MBNQA criteria are built on ten core values and concepts, which are embodied on a framework of seven first level categories: leadership (driver), information and analyses, strategic process planning, human resource development and management, management business (system), business results (measures of progress, and customer focus and satisfaction (goal). These are comparable with the ten categories of the Japanese Deming Prize, and the nine components of the European Quality Award: leadership, people management, policy and strategy, resources, and

processes (ENABLERS), people satisfaction, customer satisfaction, impact on society, and business results (RESULTS).

● The various award criteria provide rational bases against which to measure progress towards TQM in organizations. Self-assessment against, for example, the EQA model should be a regular activity, as it identifies opportunities for improvement in performance through processes and people.

Adding the systems to the TQM model

● To the foundation framework of the customer-supplier chain, processes and the 'soft' outcomes of TQM, must be added the first hard management necessity – a quality system based on a good international standard.

Case studies

C3

Quality systems in CarnaudMetalbox PLC, Foodcan UK, Perry Wood Factory

Introduction

The CarnaudMetalbox Perry Wood Factory in Worcester is part of the Foodcan UK business, a major manufacturer of cans and components in the UK. The Perry Wood factory produces three-piece cans for the food industry. The company's customers cover a wide range of well-known brand names, in both human and pet foods.

Following some very tough problems in the market place, CarnaudMetalbox Foodcan (then Metalbox Food Packaging), decided to look at its business strategy very closely. While it had established itself as a leading manufacturer of packaging (particularly in metals), customers were demanding a more responsive and cost effective service. They started to look at alternative sources of supply and CarnaudMetalbox began to lose market share.

In analysing why this had come about, managers recognized that prices needed to be more competitve and they had to address costs and organizational issues. However, they also knew that their competitive advantage was based on quality and customer service and they needed to strengthen this advantage. The senior management set about examining how they could sharpen that edge whilst at the same time reducing operating costs.

Quality management at Perry Wood

Various senior managers at Perry Wood were aware of the ideas of the quality gurus, but it all seemed rather remote and theoretical to these hard-nosed can makers at the time. However, they became convinced that TQM was the right route for the business to succeed, a practical route forward was required and quality systems such as BS5750/ISO9000 seemed to be an appropriate vehicle.

Some managers were certainly attracted to the idea that you could apply for and get a certificate which implied that your quality was better than those who did not have such a certificate. For most managers this was their first impression of

BS5750/ISO9000. They were later to discover that these initial impressions were ill-founded. Furthermore, they also discovered that the use of a sound quality management system was far more important to them than outside certification. However, these first impressions did help to build up in managers at the time a blind faith in the cause of quality without which they would probably not have achieved their mission in the planned timescale.

Towards the end of that year, the company decided that all Metalbox Food Packaging sites would be registered to BS5750 Part 2/ISO 9002 by the end of the following year.

The senior management team at Perry Wood quickly recognized two things:

1 Pulling together a quality management system would require a full-time input from at least one of the management team if they were to succeed in the timescale (approximately nine months).
2 A quality management system was only a starting point as far as TQM was concerned.

They responded by apppointing a full-time total quality manager, a role that now exists at all Foodcan UK plants.

The initial review

The initial task was first of all to establish what BS5750 required them to do. For this they assembled a multi-disciplined team of people from all levels within the factory – shift managers, supervisors, line engineers, QA inspectors, operators, etc. to review the situation.

Within 6 weeks, the following had been established.

1 They did not have a comprehensive quality management system that would meet the requirements of the standard.
2 What they already had documented was either out of date because of changes that had occurred, or was not complied with for various reasons.
3 They had no formal managed calibration system, something very important to BS5750/ISO9000 certification.
4 Their system for traceability was not good enough to prompt effective corrective action.
5 No-one knew of, or understood, the quality policy.
6 The sixty-year-old factory did not exude a quality image.
7 The system for quarantine of sub-standard product was not consistent.
8 People did not understand all the quality jargon being bandied about.
9 If a quality system was to be successfully created, it would need to be created by the workforce and not for the workforce.

The implementation process

In order to enhance the management involvement and commitment, Perry Wood soon disbanded the original full-time task force and created eight major projects geared to completing the work needed for a successful audit and certification. The objectives of these projects were allocated to departmental managers and they were encouraged to set up teams to include relevant supervisors and shop floor personnel. These were Perry Wood's first embryonic TQM teams. Networking with other plants also contributed to the development of TQM across the company.

Each project team discovered previously unrecognized staff who would later form the foundations upon which they could start to build a TQM culture. An additional asset, built in at this stage, which was also unrecognized as such at the time, was the time-scale for the process. From conception to delivery of a healthy quality system took nine months. According to the total quality manager, this is as near to the experience of pregnancy as any man is likely to get! Such a tight time-scale is generally not to be recommended but many companies fail to achieve the necessary momentum to get their system running because they fail to target a date for audit, or make the date far too remote. In this respect the external audit is a useful spur rather than an end in itself. Nerves before the full audit were quite natural – no-one, however, was prepared to let the workforce down and put off the audit. Despite the doubters, all tasks were completed with enthusiasm and determination and in the target year the Perry Wood site gained registration to BS5750: Part 2.

Elements of their implementation approach fitted well into Perry Wood's evolving TQM Strategy, and they have since built upon these early foundations. The experience showed that a documented quality system that establishes where you are now is not a bad place to start for any company uncertain of where to begin their TQM journey. For Perry Wood, formal review of quality started to change the emphasis for measuring business performance; traceability helped problem identification and problem solving and corrective action laid a foundation for continuous improvement.

Recommendations for successful implementation of a quality system

Looking back on their BS5750 programme, the Perry Wood team have drawn up the following advice for other organizations about to embark on the registration journey.

1 Do it because you believe it can help you improve, not because everyone else is doing it.
2 Find someone in the organization who will passionately believe in it. There will be days when everyone else will want to ditch it.
3 Set up a team of multi-disciplined people to determine what you specifically will need to do. This should consist of staff at all levels. This gives the task a higher profile and also creates some grass roots enthusiasts for later on.
4 Disband the team as soon as they have accomplished the task, otherwise ownership of the system will never develop.

5 Set up teams led by managers to carry out the work needed. Make sure as many people as is practically possible get involved.

6 Keep your workforce informed and interested. Perry Wood gave every employee a three hour quality induction to explain what the audits would entail, what the jargon meant, why they were doing it, etc.

7 Set yourself a challenging time-scale. However, keep your eye on the ball. No customer will thank you for letting them down whilst you put together your system. Key resources need to be dedicated to putting the system together so you need to plan availability as well as maintenance of existing control systems.

8 Believe in your people. The experts for writing your quality procedures are not the QA manager or an outside consultant, but the people actually carrying out the tasks concerned. Ask yourself this question: 'If your employees are not capable of documenting, or telling you what they do, what likelihood is there that they will consistently comply with an imposed procedure, written by someone who, at best, could not perform the task as well or, at worst, could not perform the task at all.'

9 Be prepared for continuous change. Most companies find that the major difference between a successful system and an unsuccessful one is the extent to which it allows for and encourages change. In today's climate a quality management system that you start to put together today will be going out of date by the time it is implemented.

10 Talk to other companies who have been through the process. Much time can be saved avoiding common problems already faced and solved.

Developing the TQM programme

Eighteen months after third part certification of the system, statistical process control (SPC) became a key issue for CarnaudMetalbox and was seen as the next step in the quality journey. Leading experts in the field of SPC made presentations to the company and one of its leading customers. The increasing interest of customers in SPC generated renewed commitment at many of the CarnaudMetalbox factories.

At the Perry Wood Factory there had been an earlier attempt to introduce SPC but this had failed due to an over-emphasis on statistics rather than the practicalities of process control. The project started in a similar way to their ISO9002 project with a review of current practices.

The SPC review

An initial review by the authors working as consultants with staff from the quality department quickly established that:

1 A comprehensive set of log sheets and, in some cases charts, was used to monitor the process.

2 Existing mean charts used internal manufacturing specification limits instead of statistically based action and warning lines (see Chapter 8).

3 There was a general reluctance to take corrective action based on action signals from these charts. Supervisors were responsible for corrective actions, but more accountable for production targets.

4 Line operators generally found the tolerance based charts to be useful, whereas supervisors considered the charts a hindrance to production. Line operators could take corrective actions only when authorized by supervisors.

5 There was a lot of data collection at various stages of the production process, but little use was made of this other than simply to classify it as OK/ not OK.

6 Many processes offered improvement opportunities using SPC techniques.

7 The seven basic tools of TQM (see Chapter 8) could be used in an effective way to identify and solve problems. Many production problems were of a recurring nature.

The SPC programme

The Perry Wood Management Team demonstrated their commitment to SPC by attending a one-day SPC awareness seminar and subsequently sponsoring a series of three-day SPC workshops for middle managers and supervisors. An SPC co-ordinator, reporting to the total quality manager was appointed at an early stage of the programme. In-house SPC training materials were developed by the SPC co-ordinator and during the first year of the programme, the majority of operators received some SPC training.

A series of SPC projects was set up and many teams were involved in the successful solution of critical problems. This project work was complemented by development work in the field of SPC systems and techniques appropriate to Perry Wood's production processes.

Since introducing SPC, Perry Wood has improved the stability and capability of many of its production processes. There has also been a considerable drop in the level of defects and waste. People are also playing an increasingly active role in continuous improvement activities using SPC techniques. The SPC initiative encouraged a wider participation in teamwork and gave the TQM programme a new boost. The earlier ISO9002 programme provided an ideal foundation for the SPC initiative.

The next steps

The quality system at Perry Wood is a framework on which a quality culture has been built. Since establishing the system, Perry Wood has moved on to develop its TQM process further. A clear focus on continuous improvement, closer relationships with customers and suppliers, and the measurement and improvement of proccesses using tools and techniques like SPC, are part of this ongoing process.

Perry Wood has tackled the issue of team organization of work into customer-driven cell manufacturing where the workforce are organized into self-managing groups with clear goals and authority to run their own processes and solve their own problems. Other techniques such as failure mode and effect analysis (FMEA – see Chapter 8) have been used to improve key areas of the process.

Building on information they now have on process capability, CarnaudMetalbox world-wide have embarked upon a major commitment to total productive maintenance which will help improve overall equipment effectiveness and continue to harness the efforts and ideas of all the people in the organization. Already, building on its TQM foundations, Perry Wood is a committed factory to this process.

Perry Wood is a good example of a learning organization that is constantly harnessing the ideas of TQM to improve its business.

C4

Assessing TQM implementation in the Prudential Assurance Co. Ltd, Life Administration Home Service Division

Introduction

Prudential Corporation is one of the world's largest and strongest financial services groups. The Corporation's UK core business is conducted by the Home Service Division of the Prudential Assurance Co. Ltd. Home Service's main business are life assurance, pensions, savings and general insurance. These products are serviced by some 9000 field staff working from nearly 180 branch offices.

The Life Administration group, with its offices in Reading and Belfast, supports this activity by providing essential administrative back-up for new business, servicing, accounts and claims for life and pensions business. An indication of the size and complexity of the operation is given by the following statistics:

Computer systems hold over 15 million contract records:

- 30 million direct debit transactions are processed each month.
- 100 000 proposals for new business are processed each month.
- 400 000 pieces of mail are sent to sales staff per month, as well as 500 000 letters to policy-holders.
- 120 000 telephone calls are received every month.

In the early 1990s the Life Administration business plan defined key business targets and activities to be undertaken over a 3-year time frame. Extensive market research was undertaken as part of the planning process. Two main conclusions were drawn:

- Customers' requirements were defined but performance could be improved.

- Life Administration's productivity had to increase if its policy-holders were to receive first-class returns on their investments. Market trends indicated current staffing levels could not be supported.

The preferred way forward was to implement a TQM programme, which became known as the Way of Life. Targets were set for headcount, cost and productivity. Efficiency – doing things right first time – and effectiveness – doing the right things – became key drivers. A team of managers acted as facilitators to plan and support the quality initiative. These managers developed the Life Administration mission statement which was endorsed by the Life Administration Board. The company's TQM programme is detailed below under the heading of the nine European Quality Award categories.

Leadership

Management involvement

The Life Administration management have a style based on effective leadership and TQM. Management commitment, or rather the lack of it, is often cited as the reason why quality programmes fail. Within Life Administration there is no defined strategy for displaying management commitment, just a blend of management style which works. Some key management attributes which support quality improvement are listed below:

- they are champions of the cause
- they participate
- they listen

The board of directors sponsored the TQM programme and senior experienced middle managers were assigned to the project team to facilitate the programme. The first stage was to develop an education package from which a TQM programme, called the Way of Life, was born.

The Life Administration Board was involved in establishing the mission statement, quality policy, and Principles and Values statements which describe the culture aspired to. They were also the first members of staff to be trained and the first to become involved with quality improvement activity. Such was the commitment from the senior management that the training alone represented an investment of over 4000 workdays across all of the group. This training was conducted by Life Administration line management rather than external consultants.

From the point when the decision was made to implement a TQM programme, the first 9 months were spent planning the first education programme before it was launched. The major milestones are summarized in Table C4.1.

Even though the original Way of Life programme was a major success, management were not complacent and were personally involved in the follow-up Business Awareness and Serving Customers – Our Way of Life programme.

Managers at board level actually taught the half-day business awareness modules

Table C4.1 *Life Administration Home Service Division TQM programme*

Way of Life TQM programme

May 1989	Business plan approved
	Selection of consultants and facilitator team
Oct-Nov 1989	Facilitator education
	Review of current position
Nov 1989-Jan 1990	First phase of education prepared
Feb-July 1990	First phase of education delivered
	Second phase of education prepared
Aug 1990-April 1991	Second phase of education delivered

Business Awareness programme

Sep-Dec 1991	Half-day Business Awareness sessions developed and delivered

Serving Customers – Our Way of Life programme

Sep-Dec 1991	Two-day module Serving Customers – Our Way of Life designed and piloted
Jan-Dec 1992	Serving Customers – Our Way of Life modules delivered to all staff

which were given to all staff. They also always opened the 2-day residential customer-care programme, going back to stay overnight at the hotel used for the training, so that they could discuss quality with the staff in a relaxed atmosphere, and then returned again on the second day to close the session and to accept any actions which were beyond the scope of lower-grade staff. These actions became affectionately known as the 'live withs'. The programme was run over 50 times during one year and the senior management team were represented at every single event.

Senior management supported quality improvement in many other ways. For example, they delivered papers at international conferences on quality within Prudential. They promoted quality within Prudential itself, with Life Administration being viewed as a flagship. They also supported staff attending conferences and meetings on quality so that even junior members of staff had the experience of learning about quality from face-to-face contact with other companies.

Within two years of the programme, the Life Administration was awarded the Northern Ireland Quality Award for service. The award was made after Life Administration submitted a written report on eight separate criteria. Of the eight criteria, they came top out of five and were short-listed alongside two other leading organizations in quality. A site visit followed during which the senior management and staff were quizzed for several hours. They were delighted to receive the award, but the reason why they beat the opposition was more significant. In the words of the judges:

> The Award is granted for making rapid progress and achieving inspirational commitment from all managers and staff, so transforming an office working environment into a challenging and stimulating place to work.

Way of Life review

The measurement of employees' perceptions was seen as an important element of the TQM programme. Consultants reviewed the attitudes and behaviour of Life Administration staff at the start of the quality initiative training. This was repeated a year later by the same consultants. Results are on a 1-10 scale.

	Start of survey	*One-year later*
How serious is management about quality	6	9
How serious do you think your staff are about quality?	5	8
How well do individual managers work together?	6	7
How well do departments work together?	5	8
How does the company rate on employee communication?	5	8
How would your subordinate rate you in taking quality seriously?	6	8

The results show significant improvement in all areas. The consultants concluded: 'The initiative has succeeded in bringing about substantial change in communications, behaviour and attitudes to quality throughout the organization. The process has been received with enthusiasm at all levels and as a result the environment for continuous improvement has been established'. Clearly, the training had established a climate for change and a desire to improve. There are now over 150 supervisor-led improvement teams which meet on a regular basis to work on quality improvement activities, working on over 1000 improvement ideas across Life Administration.

The second review, which was conducted by different independent consultants on a group interview basis, used a brainstorming session to list staff's views on the way the TQM programme could be improved. A total of 199 people took part in the review, which included the Life Administration Board itself. A total of 19 questions were addressed by the teams. The results of the review in ascending order are shown below.

Scores are on a 1 (disagreee) to 5 (agree) scale

1	Everyone in the organization shares the same vision of quality	2.38
2	Systems and procedures are up-to-date and reflect best practice with today's technology	2.50
3	The management culture develops employee trust by personal involvement and viability	2.63
4	There are no barriers between internal departments	2.67
5	People are recognized for their contribution and work well done	2.80
6	We conduct regular surveys to determine customers' product and service expectations	2.86
7	Generally decisions here are made based on sound data with good input from my level	2.87
8	Customer satisfaction measures are set and published regularly	2.93
9	Employees feel confident that management will act upon employee initiatives	3.00

10	Management deal promptly with issues for improvement according to resources available	3.01
11	Management communication to all employees is regular and up-to-date	3.33
12	Teamwork is very good here	3.50
13	Training plans are prepared and implemented which are relevant to employee requirements	3.68
14	Throughout the organization there is a commitment to meet internal and external customer requirements	3.69
15	Target setting with measurement and publication of performance	3.90
16	I know and understand the mission statement and quality policy	4.11
17	Employee participation in problem identification and solving is practised and encouraged	4.16
18	I believe in generating ideas for continuous improvement	4.46
19	I have personally participated in an improvement initiative in the past 12 months	4.70

On the positive side, the review found that:

- Way of Life was highly visible and accepted by staff.
- Most people interviewed had personally taken part in quality improvement activity during the year.
- There was no shortage of ideas.
- Commitment to provide customer satisfaction was high.

On the negative side, though:

- Management involvement needed to be more visible.
- The same vision was not shared.
- Computer systems and work procedures needed to be improved.

Action was quickly taken on the results of the review. For example, the Serving Customers – Our Way of Life Business Awareness programme addressed the concern over the shared vision.

Management quality action

Measurement itself is useless unless it leads to action. The main process for review and action is through the contact process. Each 4-week period, a report is compiled listing all failures. This report includes corrective action plans.

The contact report is discussed at board level. It gives board members the opportunity to discuss issues in their area in an open team environment. This can lead to offers of help from other areas or ideas on the way to tackle specific issues.

The contact process concerns itself not only with performance-related measures, but also covers areas such as customer satisfaction results, employee survey results and customer complaints. To ensure staff are kept informed with both achievements and actions, the results of the contact process are cascaded through the team briefing network.

Management structure

The organizational structure project is an excellent example of management commitment to quality improvement. Previously, departments were structured in a functional manner by product and transaction type. This proved to be a major barrier to customer service, since staff were transaction-focused. Often, several departments needed to contribute to a customer response which became delayed and uncoordinated.

The senior management team commissioned a complete review of the management and operational structure. A layer of management was eliminated, which improved the command and communication chain. Products and transactions are now combined into divisional groups which face a major customer, the field staff, with clear lines of access. Complex technical work is concentrated in specialist areas, which allows the divisional departments to focus on customer service.

Restructuring called for a complete redesign of the management roles and competencies, against which more than 150 staff were measured during a thorough and objective process.

With the new management structure in place, attention was turned to redesigning the clerical roles so that an even closer relationship would exist between multiskilled groups of staff providing a comprehensive service to specific district offices. One of the project objectives was to involve the staff directly in the design process. To support all this, the training and development programmes were completely rewritten.

Throughout restructuring, Life Administration have reviewed all the cultural influences, particularly the reward and recognition processes, to ensure that they fully and consistently support quality activities.

Reward and recognition

As previously mentioned, the quality objectives and business objectives are indivisible, and so the focus on quality improvement is kept at all levels through the review of the operating plan and individual objectives. The results of the annual appraisal, which is based on the achievement of the objectives is a key determinant of an employee's remuneration. Every employee has customer satisfaction set as a key objective. But rewarding through the achievement of individual objectives once per year is thought to be too wide a time frame. To overcome this, there are three additional reward schemes which are designed to reward and recognize achievement.

Way of Life awards

First there is the Way of Life award scheme, which has a three-tiered bronze, silver and gold approach. The level of reward and recognition increases with the level of award.

Bronze awards are considered by peers and are controlled by the area quality management teams. To obtain a higher value award, a presentation has to be given to the senior management team. This body either confirms the bronze, recommends a silver, or refers the achievement to the Life Administration Board. The Board then decides on the level of the award, gold or silver. Senior management's involvement in the award process is another visible sign of their commitment. Getting an award is not easy. To date, although there have been numerous bronze awards, there have only been five silver and two gold awards.

Instant incentives

The Way of Life award process is quite lengthy due to its peer recognition element and is aimed mainly at team effort. Each manager has the authority to recommend an individual for an instant award when (s)he witnesses the individual giving exceptional customer service. The awards take the format of shopping vouchers.

Challenge

As mentioned earlier, one of the management-led strategic projects looked at the structure of Life Administration. Challenge was developed to support the changes.

The scheme is based on team performance, with teams being awarded points for meeting certain criteria. The criteria are not only volume-related but include accuracy and customer satisfaction measures.

Review

Staff opinion was sought on these reward and recognition processes and there was a clear recommendation to combine all the schemes into one scheme which made no distinction between quality and business performance. Total quality had to be the way of doing business. The new integrated scheme retained many of the positive features of the earlier scheme, such as instant recognition and peer group recognition where appropriate, but offered more 'exciting' prizes. A tandem parachute jump with the Red Devils was one prize. This was not the 'failed' TQM facilitator's prize!

Policy and strategy

The management team facilitating the quality initiative developed a mission statement which was endorsed by the board of directors.

The Life Administration mission statement affirms:

> We administer Prudential Assurance life business. Our purpose is to delight our customers by delivering a quality service, in a cost-effective manner, through the contribution of everyone.

Quite often, a company will have a top-level mission statement but nothing to support its implementation. In this case, they developed a set of 'principles and values' which translated the words contained in the mission statement into easy-to-understand bullet points which describe the culture they were trying to grow within Life Administration. These bullet points became known as the Way of Life statements.

Our Way of Life

We are committed to delivering a quality service to our customers:

- The customer is the reason we exist and the key consideration in carrying out our day-to-day business.
- The customer is the person or area to whom we are providing a service.
- Everyone is a vital link in the service chain and the successful partnership between the suppliers of services and their customers is of primary importance.
- As individuals and teams we demonstrate our commitment to our customers by 'getting it right first time'.
- We will continually review, redefine and improve the quality of service we provide to meet the changing expectations of our customers.

We recognize that our purpose can only be achieved through people:

- We recognize that everyone wants to provide a quality service.
- Each individual has the right to know what is expected of him/her and the reasons why.
- We are committed to providing continuous education, training and development opportunities to enable everyone to realize their full potential.
- Each individual in responsible for providing a quality service.
- We encourage people throughout the organization to listen actively to each other and to voice their ideas and opinions.

We are committed to creating a business-like and caring working environment:

- We will communicate in an open manner, which mirrors and supports our Way of Life.
- Teamwork will play a vital part in achieving our purpose.
- Opportunity will be given to individuals and teams to make changes at the level where it is most practical.
- We actively support the local community and the wider environment in which we live and work.

The mission statement was not set in tablets of stone. In the later stages of the TQM programme the company used a copywriter to wordsmith the mission. This was then given to all the improvement teams for their comments. The feedback was invaluable and the whole process generated an improved mission with wider ownership.

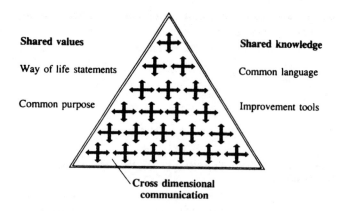

Shared values

Way of life statements

Common purpose

Shared knowledge

Common language

Improvement tools

Cross dimensional
communication

Figure C4.1 *Awareness to action*

The first step to implement the mission statement was to set business measures which focused on the key drivers. These were called the Key Business Indicators (KBIs), and these are related to key words in the mission, as shown below.

Mission	*KBIs*
Quality service	Attitude
	Speed
	Accuracy
Cost-effective	Productivity
Contribution of everyone	Morale

The current KBI targets are contained within the Life Administration business plan, which has Board-level approval. Sitting below the top-level plan are departmental operating plans which reflect the business plan targets on a department-by-department basis. The duration of these plans is 1 year. Although these are prepared by the departmental managers, there is a high level of involvement from the supervisors who contribute to these plans. Alongside the departmental operating plans sit individual objectives and accountabilities which detail the responsibilities of the senior managers, departmental managers and supervisors.

Although the planning process is labelled as a business planning process, Life Administration believe that business goals and quality goals are indivisible. For example, the business plan objectives talk of a 10% year-on-year reduction in the operating budget. This is being achieved through many actions which include ensuring processes are 'right first time' so that inspection can be dispensed with. Other objectives include a maximum 5-day turnaround time with zero non-conformances.

Implementing the TQM programme had two key parts. There were the 'hard' business measures based on the KBIs. But there was also the 'soft' cultural side, which is difficult to measure but easy to experience. Life Administration developed an organization which is best pictured in Figure C4.1. To help them achieve this cultural change, and to achieve their performance target, they developed a four-point quality strategy so that words could be turned into actions. The strategy was based on the following:

Control of processes	Getting processes 'right first time' and having understanding of their interdependence. Service excellence can only be delivered through capable processes.
Customer-focused culture	Listening to customers and reacting quickly to their changing requirements.
Continuous improvement	Adopting continuous improvement as a strategic imperative and striving to exceed customers' expectations.
	Within the continuous improvement segment of the quality strategy they consider six main areas. These are leadership, improvement activity, education, measurement and benchmarking, reward and recognition and continuance.
Communication	Keeping everyone in touch and promoting TQM within both Life Administration and Prudential in general. This involves upward, downward and horizontal communication.

The main activity during the earlier years was that of educating all staff. This education was so successful that it won a UK National Training Award. Following this, the emphasis on effective training continued and Life Administration was awarded another National Training Award for its ISO9000/BS5750 programme.

People management

Prudential had a very traditional culture. Before the TQM programme took hold, there was very little involvement from staff in any form of change. Middle managers spent most of their time protected by office walls, taking decisions in isolation. This was not an environment in which teamwork and employee participation could survive. The only quality improvement vehicle available was strategic projects, where middle managers appointed departmental managers on to project teams. They in turn appointed their first-line managers on to subproject teams, in some cases to do all the work.

Participative teamwork within Life Administration was launched through the Way of Life education programme. The programme made it clear why they had to change, gave the staff the tools so they could change, and empowered the staff to make changes.

There are four types of improvement activity within Life Administration:

1 *Strategic projects:* management-led and sponsored by a Life Administration Board member or other senior manager. These still play a key role.

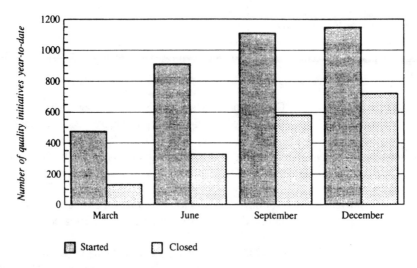

Figure C4.2 *Way of Life workgroup activity during one year*

2 *Cross-department improvement teams:* groups are formed voluntarily when a quality improvement opportunity is identified in one area and action has to be taken in another.
3 *Work groups:* work groups meet regularly to identify and implement quality improvement opportunities within their work area.
4 *Individual action:* individuals are encouraged to take action that will result in an improvement either in their personal performance or to their assigned processes.

The focus on quality improvement is kept by having quality improvement as a key objective written into everyone's objectives and accountabilities. This was necessary as it overcame what was the major obstacle to keeping quality improvement going – the conflict between improvement and work volumes. These problems have been minimized as the business measures are also the quality improvement measures, but it has still been a long education process to get people to understand that the way to achieve the business targets is by quality improvement action and not just by working harder. People had to learn to work smarter, and they did this by eliminating the many problems they faced day in, day out.

Figure C4.2 shows the progress made during one year in terms of the number of quality initiatives started and completed. However, it has not all been plain sailing. One of the drawbacks of the education process is that the training was given to teams by their first-line manager, and the effectiveness of the teams became a function of the competence of the first-line managers in training them. Getting the first-line manager to deliver the training ensured a high degree of line ownership for the quality process, the training was made relevant on an area-by-area basis, and it gave the first-line managers some extra skills as part of the process. To support the first-line managers in their roles there was a support network but into place to control the process and give advice. This network was called the Quality Management Team (QMT) network. Each area has a QMT.

The QMT structure in itself is a good example of teamwork in action. As mentioned

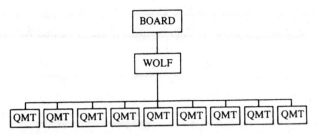

WOLF: Way of life forum
QMT: Quality management team

Figure C4.3 *QMT structure*

above, each area has a QMT, and each QMT has a representative on the Way of Life Forum (WOLF; Figure C4.3). The WOLF had a responsibility to the Life Administration senior management team, and WOLFs are always attended by at least one Life Administration Board member.

When the QMTs were first established, they were chaired by the senior manager in the areas and consisted only of area management. As these groups evolved, a mixture of grades were introduced on to these teams and for the first time they had teams consisting of senior management, management and clerical-grade staff working together in order to achieve common objectives. This illustrates the major shift in culture that has taken place within Life Administration.

It would also be unfair to claim that the major improvements achieved resulted solely from quality training. Many other training initiatives have made a significant contribu-

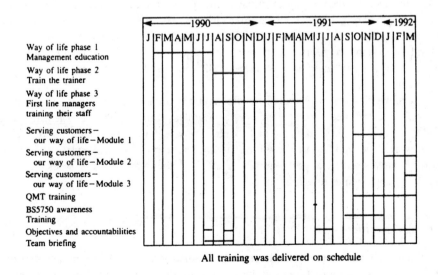

All training was delivered on schedule

Figure C4.4 *TQM training schedule*

tion, good examples being performance management and team briefing. Figure C4.4 shows the training plan for all quality improvement-related training, both planned and delivered. All training was delivered on schedule.

Attendance at conferences or quality events has not been included on the training plan, although these play an important role. This type of training is more on an individual basis, and is monitored like other individual training requirements, through the Life Administration Development Plan process. All the computer-based training packages that are available to staff have also been excluded. A hallmark of the training is that it is all very Life Administrative-specific. It addresses key business needs for Life Administration. The training programmes are designed to be interesting and even fun.

Each of the different training initiatives is discussed briefly below:

Way of Life (TQM) training

The Life Administration TQM programme was launched by educating all staff. This training was so successful it won a National Training Award.

As suitable off-the-shelf training material could not be found, it was written specifically to achieve the stated objectives and was Life Administration branded. All training was conducted by Prudential staff and its effectiveness evaluated by independent consultants.

Training was in three stages. In the first stage, staff from board member to supervisor were trained over a 6-week period. The main objective of this training was to begin to change the culture and gain acceptance, at all levels of management, of the need to improve quality. Whilst this equipped supervisors with knowledge, stage 2 gave training skills, team leadership skills, preparation time and support.

The third stage was a living example of the quality initiative principles in practice, with teams working together to improve quality. The training was delivered to the clerical staff by their own supervisor. This enabled Life Administration to establish natural supervisor-led work groups with the objective of tackling quality improvements. The strategy adopted has successfully delivered a high level of employee involvement.

To achieve the main objective of sustained quality improvement activity, the training material was designed so that there was a 'seamless transition between learning and productive involvement'. It had to be flexible in physical design so that it could be used in the workplace, and had to allow for different learning speeds and styles of delivery. Work groups selected a problem which affected them and took a week-by-week structured approach to its elimination.

Serving Customers – Our Way of Life

Written to the same exacting standards as the original Way of Life programme, Serving Customers – Our Way of Life took the organization a stage further forward. Whereas the focus during Way of Life was on the elimination of workplace problems, the focus

---

Module 1 – Business awareness

Half-day Business Awareness sessions were given to all staff. The first session was presented by the Head of Life Administration, who discussed business results plus the vision for the next year and beyond.

The second session was delivered by an academic from a Business School who gave his own personal view of the outlook for the financial services industry. This session was designed to make staff aware of the business imperative to improve both productivity and service. Finally, a serving Life Administration Board member presented a more local view to the staff in their area. The objective of these sessions was to share the vision for the future and prepare staff for module 2 of the programme.

Module 2 – Barriers to customer service

All staff attended this 2-day module which gave them the opportunity to identify barriers to excellent customer service. The module started by discussing exactly what makes good customer service and what makes bad customer service. Examples were given of 'good companies' and 'bad companies'. Although the programme was given to all staff, the programme given to managers and supervisors had an additional section to enable them to lead customer care. One key learning point consistent with the Way of Life theory was that good customer service can only be delivered with capable processes.

At the end of the programme staff committed themselves to both group and individual improvement actions to remove the barriers to customer service. Barriers which were outside the group's control were accepted by senior management, and there is a process in place to feed back to the groups the management actions which have been taken.

---

of Serving Customers – Our Way of Life was a banner to achieving outstanding customer service. The programme was in two modules.

QMT training

One of the problems with many packaged training programmes is that they are very pre-scriptive. The view within Life Administration was that such prescription destroys innovation and personal ownership. Although this is true, a structured approach can have value in terms of direction. The QMT training package was developed to give QMT some gentle direction. It also provided refresher training in quality improvement tools as one of the prime functions of the QMT is to provide support and consultancy.

Objectives and accountabilities and team briefing

Although these are normally regarded as management processes, they are included here to reinforce the importance given to defining people's responsibilities and communication. Both were taught in a workshop environment.

With their Performance Management System (PMS), staff first draft their accountabilities and objectives themselves, before offering them to their manager for discussion. The objectives reflect the objectives in the area's operating plans. In this way, personal ownership of objectives are ensured.

In order to keep focus on quality, quality objectives and accountabilities are incorporated into the PMS. For example, the actions which staff are committing to at the end of the Serving Customers – Our Way of Life programme are monitored through the PMS.

Life Administration always had a 'cascade' communication process, but a survey revealed that messages were not getting right the way down throughout the organization. A formal team briefing process with a supporting process to allow communication to pass up the chain as well as down it has subsequently been introduced. Weekly, bimonthly and, where appropriate, *ad hoc* newsletters are also used in the communication process.

Team measures

A measurement system supports all improvement activities. The success of the quality improvement action is measured by a subset of the business success measure. A five-point measurement matrix is used:

1 *Customer impact:* evaluation of whether the quality improvement action has a major or minor positive impact on customers.
2 *Time:* Staff in the early stages of the TQM programme did not think that they had time to work on quality improvement activities. Time has therefore been made a measure of success, to reinforce to staff that time spent on quality improvement activity is a profitable investment.
3 *Money*: Direct cost savings in materials are evaluated.
4 *Service:* If a quality improvement has a positive effect on either the accuracy or speed of service, the improvement is classifed in terms of major or minor effect.
5 *Morale:* One of the benefits to staff of quality improvement is that by removing quality problems, it makes their jobs 'hassle-free' and can remove some mundane tasks. Being listened to and having your idea implemented also gives greater job satisfaction.

Each team (or individual) evaluates the effectiveness of their improvement action against the above criteria when they close off their logged quality improvement initiative. The status of all the quality improvement initiatives, and benefits when closed, are recorded by the QMTs.

Each 4 week period the QMTs collate the data from the QMTs from all around their areas, and the total results across all Life Administration are issued back to QMTs in a summary report. The figures also go to senior management for review.

Quality Week

The idea behind Quality Week came about following the attendance of some Life Administration staff at the National Society for Quality through Teamwork Conference. A group of people decided to form a team to try to get more excitement into the quality programme. Several options were considered, but the idea of a Quality Week to celebrate the successes to date was chosen.

The event was also an opportunity to involve everybody in the preparations for the move to new premises. New facilities and a brand new environment were seen to offer a tremendous opportunity. The acronym NBG (new ball game) was adopted for the week and various teamwork events took place throughout the week. The NBG theme manifested itself in teams within 10 leagues competing against each other. The leagues were just convenient groups of Life Administration staff. Will Carling, the England Rugby Team Captain, gave a talk on teamwork. A number of companies and organizations also held workshops and seminars for Life Administration staff. The workshops showed how other organizations were tackling TQM.

A review of the Quality Week found that it had rekindled enthusiasm for quality and proved it could be fun. Many staff benefited from seeing how other companies tackled quality and picked up lots of new ideas. The week certainly stimulated teamwork and the active participation in process improvement.

General comments

The People Management area in Life Administration has seen major changes resulting from the TQM programme. The human resource planning process supports the company's policy and strategy in a dynamic way. Market research is carried out on employees to find out what their true needs are. Every employee has an individual training and development plan and all training is delivered on a project-by-project basis.

A management development section has been set up and this has produced a list of key management competences. In the reorganization accompanying the TQM programme, existing managers had to reapply for management positions to see if they met the new criteria. Those failing to meet the criteria were not appointed to managerial positions in the new structure.

The company runs various counselling processes, including a quarterly review of employee development plans and one-to-one training sessions. A mentoring system also operates. Employees are free to choose a mentor who is then used to the peer group recognition process. Health and Safety issues are managed in a progressive way. For example, the company provides excellent occupational health facilities, with centres staffed by nurses running well-women clinics, heart programmes, etc. A preventive approach is seen as vitally important for the well-being of all employees.

Commitment to people also involved the provision of the previously mentioned new office facilities. The old facilities did not encourage or promote quality. Employees could not be expected to do a good job in inadequate offices. The move to the new offices was also a good demonstration of teamwork in action. The move, involving over

1400 staff, was accomplished over two weekends with no operational disruption. The whole process was managed by a cross-functional team.

Management of resources

The financial management at the Prudential works within the framework laid down by the company's policy and strategy. It is customer-driven and market-based. While the financial and accounting figures are used to track the business performance, the focus is on customer service and the market. Quality objectives are also the company's business objective and all financial decision making supports total quality.

The process of management of cash flow, working capital and costs is well-understood and fully documented. The process is subject to regular review as part of a strategy of never-ending improvement.

A Management Accounting Reporting System (MARS) was introduced, giving ownership of budget down to the department level, whereas before this was controlled at area level. Such ownership has allowed greater participation in the construction of the budget, with acceptance of budget restrictions imposed on Life Administration by the Prudential Board. Within each department, employees are informed about the overall and department budget, and are made aware of their responsibility to meet the targets.

The management of information resources is seen as a key to the success of the TQM programme. Computer systems play a vital role in the Prudential's operations and they are also one of the biggest barriers to quality improvement. Barriers may be the speed at which systems can be realistically changed, or the system designers' failure to meet the true needs of their customers, i.e. the system user within Prudential. A key customer–supplier team has been formed between Life Administration and the computer systems area to break down their barriers. The collaboration has resulted in the formation of a Life User Group, so that Life Administration has an influence on the way in which computer systems projects are resourced. Life Administration has a slice of the overall budget for Home Systems development and has a choice as to how that money is spent. It also reviews the value-for-money aspects, which has provided a key driver for Home Service systems in their own quality programme.

Computer system designers have introduced a process called Home Service Development Life Cycle for the development of new systems. The process, which is a form of phased project management with clearly defined checkpoints, requires a high degree of user involvement as the customer joins a user group to establish true business needs. The process also includes a System Implementation Review where the effectiveness of the development process is reviewed so that improvement action can be taken, if necessary. Three months after system implementation, there is a Post Development Review where the system itself is evaluated against the predefined business requirements. Life Administration takes part in both these reviews in the role of customer.

The involvement of the customer, i.e. Life Administration, will ensure that the systems effort is directed for the best effect. For example, the team has already decided to resource the clearance of the top 100 recorded system 'niggles' before moving on to any major changes. This will have a major impact on staff, who had previously perceived that they had to live with such minor problems. It is demonstrating that management want to 'get it right first time' for them and support their quality improvement activities with good information systems.

Processes

Life Administration's philosophy is one of total continuous improvement. The effectiveness of all activities and processes is regularly reviewed. They learn from this experience and use this information in the planning process.

They have realized that 'doing things right' alone is not enough – they must also 'do the right things'. A tremendous amount of effort is going into reviewing exactly what they, as suppliers of a service, understand by 'the right things'. The way they examine the performance of their processes against targets also plays a key role in improvement activities. This is best summarized in Figure C4.5.

The importance of the ISO9000 Quality Management System was recognized at an early stage of the TQM programme. It was seen as a way of managing processes to deliver consistent outputs. There were no commerical pressures on Prudential to be registered to ISO9000. Registration would have only limited marketing benefit as the majority of the policy-holders would not have heard of ISO9000 unless they had come across it in their own business. However, the Industrial Branch area became the first areas within an insurance company to become a registered firm.

There were many reasons why the decision was taken to register the Industrial

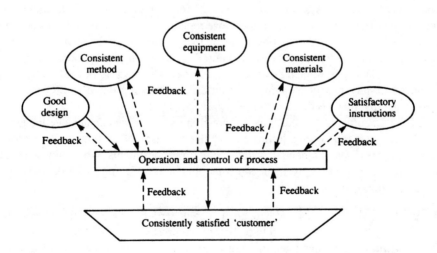

Figure C4.5 *The process approach*

Branch area of Life Administration. The administration of assurance business is by nature highly regulated by legislation. As a consequence, a quality assurance system of sorts had always been in existence. The benefit of extending this system to the ISO9000 standard was that the British Standard, with its focus on process control, contained some additional requirements that were perceived to improve the degree of control. Examples of these requirements are internal quality audits, control of non-conforming material and management review.

A second reason for seeking registration had more to do with the staff than quality assurance. Assurance administration is a complicated business. For some time there had been an interest among staff in reviewing all the existing procedures and documentation which controlled the processes. The ISO9000 registration project provided a necessary focus on procedures so that this desire could be realized. The unannounced surveillance visits would also keep people's attention on ensuring documentation is kept up-to-date, and the procedures are actually operated.

The company recognized the many benefits to ISO9000 registration, including:

- Demonstration of a company commitment to quality
- Improved consistency
- Reduction in waste and increased efficiency
- Management and process control
- A driver for continuous improvement

But the Prudential were looking for some additional benefit. For instance, they saw ISO9000 registration becoming an integral part of their TQM strategy. They believed that it would not be possible to deliver excellent customer service unless they had capable processes. They also saw registration as a useful lever in influencing the quality of service offered by some internal Prudential suppliers.

At the outset staff listed the requirements of the approach they could take. There are many ways of approaching registration. Some companies employ consultants to construct the quality system and others set up an internal project team to do it themselves. The company wanted to achieve registration with 100% staff involvement as it believed this was the only way to ensure total ownership of the quality system and that registration would lead to lasting benefit. Registration had to be more than a badge on the wall. They also wanted ownership of the goal, which was to be the first insurance company to have part of its administration organization registered to ISO9000. This also meant that they needed a fast-track approach.

ISO9000 is often introduced as a top-down initiative which can achieve the goal of registration, but fails to give lasting benefit due to a lack of ownership of procedures and disciplines. The Prudential sought help from consultants to develop a process which generated total involvement and commitment to achieving ISO9000 registration using the following principles:

1 *Humour:* Humour was used to break down barriers and inhibitions, creating a climate where people wanted to be part of the process.
2 *Recognition:* Individual contributions and achievements were rewarded with a variety of recognition awards which served both as a 'thank you' and as evidence that management cared.

3 *Teamwork:* Every employee, including senior management, was a member of a team, which created friendly competition as well as a sense of loyalty and commitment to one's peers.

4 *Deadlines:* By providing a clear timetable for each stage of the process, we ensured that systems, procedures and records were in place in time for assessment.

The awareness process included a wide range of visual materials based around a friendly beaver character by the name of Five-O-Go together with handouts, workbooks, recognition awards and control mechanisms. The principal elements of the process were as follows:

1 *Preparing the manual:* The first step was to write the quality manual, which was submitted to the British Standards Institution for their approval prior to the audit. A project team was given the responsibility of developing the manual, which was subsequently signed off by senior management.

2 *Teaser campaign:* an internal marketing campaign which used surprise, curiosity, humour and competition ensured all employees were aware of the goal – to be the first to achieve ISO9000 certification.

3 *Ready stage:* Commencing with a team briefing, all employees were involved in identifying, reviewing and improving procedures, using the 'beaver brainwave' process. It was important at this stage to identify and draft any missing procedures. All employees completed a checklist which ensured that they understood the process and were committed to the goal of registration.

4 *Steady stage:* Once all procedures had been drafted and agreed, the steady stage provided the opportunity to remove the bugs, establish accurate records and ensure consistency. Each team completed a time for reflection workbook which ensured their understanding of and adherence to the policy statements defined in the quality manual. Once steady stage had been achieved, a spring clean operation was carried out to ensure all out-of-date documentation was either archived or destroyed.

5 *Preassessment audit:* One month prior to assessment, a preassessment audit was carried out by independent auditors. The purpose of this was to expose all employees to the assessment procedures, and identify any major discrepancies. It also helped to eliminate complacency and apathy where necessary.

6 *Go stage:* This stage comprised a countdown to assessment, where employees were briefed on the assessment procedure, and what the auditors would require of them. It also ensured that the auditors received a warm welcome, and that employees responded positively to the assessment process.

7 *Celebration:* Registration was achieved in December 1991. Once registered, there was an oportunity to recognize the involvement and commitment of all employees and celebrate achievement of the goal by holding registration celebration parties.

In addition to gaining total employee commitment to the quaity management system and subsequently gaining registration, the Five-O-Go! process was a major motivational and training success. The approach was perceived as radical but fun, and the staff were proud of their achievement, with significant improvement in morale and self-esteem.

The ISO9000 project was so successful that the company have already started to extend registration to other areas of the business. The benefits are due both to the fact that they achieved registration, plus the way they achieved it with 100% staff involvement. In the words of one of the BSI assessors: 'We have never seen such total enthusiasm and commitment from all staff to achieving the goal of registration'.

They have already begun to feel the benefit of the application of the ISO9000 standard within the Industrial Branch area. Most benefit is coming from the control of management processes, examples being internal audits (which are designed to be constructive and to improve processes), formal local management reviews and purchasing.

ISO9000 has been extended to other areas in a phased programme. Details of all the registrations are listed below.

- Industrial Branch Administration Offices in Belfast and Reading
- Life Administrations Technical Training and Management Training Departments. (At the time, this was only the second company in the UK to achieve registration for its training department.)
- Life Administration Business Systems Delivery Area to Tickit.
- Life Administration Life Claims Area.

This ongoing registration programme improves process and management control and contributes to improved morale, communication and teamwork.

The tools of total quality have made a significant contribution to process improvement. They didn't want to make quality improvement 'tool-bound' and there were many examples where the only quality improvement action taken to solve a problem was people talking to each other to agree requirements. During the Way of Life awareness training, however, every member of staff was taught how to use various tools and techniques in their quality improvement activity. They were also given a simple four-stage problem-solving process to follow, which was designed to solve problems permanently. This four-stage process was called DICE. The process is:

1 *Define problem:* There are six questions to be answered, which include defining the problem in a non-judgemental way, assessing its impact on the business and setting a success measure.
2 *Immediate fix:* The message was: 'Do not pass on errors to your customer'. If some short-term action can be taken it should be, unless it tampers with the process.
3 *Corrective action on root cause:* Problem-solving tools are used to establish the root cause of problems and corrective action is taken to eliminate the root cause.
4 *Evaluation:* After the action has been taken, a period of evaluation follows to ensure that the root cause of the problem has been identified and eliminated. Benefit analysis also takes place within this stage.

The structured approach to problem-solving is the basis of a combined tool which they have called the QICPAC, which stands for Quality Improvement Cycle (Prudential Assurance Company).

Prudential fully understand that the control of processes is a key element in TQM. Service excellence can only be delivered through capable processes so a programme of work (project PRISM) began to establish the best practice processes. A team of analysts worked with staff to chart all the existing procedures within Life Administration Following initial charting, brainstorming and critical analysis sessions were held to agree best practices across all areas. These procedures were then implemented. Life Administration has estimated that project PRISM will deliver productivity improvements of up to £2m, and improve the speed and accuracy of many key processes.

Customer satisfaction

As the quality objectives are also the business objectives, the measurement systems for quality improvement at a Life Administration-wide level are similar. There are some additional measurement systems which record quality improvement progress on a local scale and the effectiveness of the quality improvement process itself is evaluated annually by way of an independent review.

The three customer KBIs and the way they are measured are summarized below:

Customer KBIs: *benefits to customers*	*Main Measurement*
1 Attitude	Measured by quarterly customer satisfaction surveys. One-month service-level agreement reviews (SLAs)
2 Speed	Measured by monthly sampling at departmental level
3 Accuracy	Measured by monthly sampling at departmental level

Attitude

Internal customers

These customers are other departments within Life Administration. The main method used to monitor customer satisfaction is by reviewing the supplier's performance against established service-level agreements, or SLAs for short. Monthly reviews are conducted to discuss performance. Some areas also conduct internal customer satisfaction surveys.

The field staff also fall into this category. A comprehensive quarterly customer satisfaction survey is conducted to assess the level of service Life Administration is giving across various aspects of the business. There are three mainline administration areas: Industrial Branch area, which has offices in Reading and Belfast; Ordinary Branch area, and Personal Pensions area. Within these line areas, measurement is made against their performance on new business, servicing and claims. Performance is also monitored through SLAs. This is done in a similar way to that described above.

External customers–policy-holders

External customers are dealt with when servicing their contracts and paying their death claims or maturities. Most contact is by mail, although there is some telephone contact. Customer satisfaction is measured in three ways. All line departments keep a log of complaints. Great effort is put into resolving these complaints to the satisfaction of the policy-holder. Analysis is undertaken to look for trends to that preventive action can be taken.

A second way to monitor customer satisfaction is in the form of songs of praise. These are letters which record a customer's appreciation of the service they have provided, since they have taken the trouble to write and thank the company. The number of 'songs of praise' received is measured.

Benchmarks are also established for the industry by commissioning work through market research agencies.

Speed and accuracy

Staff, independent of the areas being measured, select samples from the high business volumes to measure both speed and accuracy. Sampling techniques are used for the audits as they are the most effective given the volumes and current system technology. A significant achievement was the introduction, in a pilot area, of a new system-based measurement system for speed. The system, based on a database called ACUMEN, counts all work that passes through the pensions new-business area. Both volume and elapsed time are measured and feedback is given to the area the following day. This allows for immediate analysis and corrective action when failures occur.

Table C4.2 *Life Administration speed and accuracy performance*

	Year 1	Year 2	Mid-year 3	Dec. year 3
Speed 5 days	92%	97%	95%	89%
Speed 10/8 days	93%	99%	99%	97%
Accuracy	99%	99%	98%	98%

Speed: percentage claims processed within the specified time period.
Accuracy: percentage correct on completion of each stage of process.

An important aspect of this new system is the detail of the data. Whereas the current sampling systems record elapsed time from receipt of a proposal to the issue of a policy, the ACUMEN-based system breaks down the process and provides data at the various stages, i.e. proposal date to receipt in Reading, proposal receipt to acceptance and proposal acceptance to issue of policy. Such detail reduces the process scope in the case of failure and makes for more effective corrective action.

The results for speed and accuracy are shown in Table C4.2. Customer satisfaction results are shown in Figure C4.6. In the case of the speed figures, the first year secondary target was 10 days and in the second year it was 8 days.

The slight deterioration in the speed measures was due to two main reasons:

1 The volume of work exceeded the forecast volume.
2 A major internal customer, the field staff, went through a restructuring exercise to improve service and productivity during the last quarter of Year 2. This had a major knock-on effect on Life Administration in that there was a major increase in

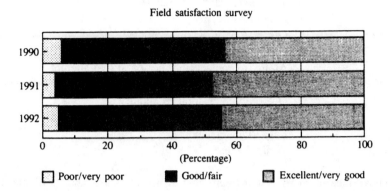

Figure C4.6 *Life administration customer satisfaction results*

enquiries from the field staff during this period of uncertainty and a resulting decrease in the quality of the inputs supplied to Life Administration.

The field satisfaction survey shows a tightening of customer expectations due to improved service.

Recent developments

The performance measures described above were part of a philosophy that attempted to achieve the best possible performance. The word 'possible' was open to interpretation and Life Administration have now realized that they need to strive for superior performance in all their business areas. They also questioned whether they measure the right thing and a Quality Initiative Team reviewed the whole measurement question as part of the Customer Experience Measures project. This project was set up under the direction of the Head of Life Administration to provide more meaningful and reliable customer-focused management information.

The first phase of the project identified the key business transactions, then key activities and recommended a system of core measurements to be applied to each of the key transactions. The three core measurements are detailed below:

Core measurement	Measure
1 Speed	Average speed of each response time to perform complete transaction
2 Accuracy	Correctness on despatch of each stage of process
3 Interaction	Attitude
	Helpfulness
	Respect to the customer

> Politeness
> Keeping promises
> Telephone technique/manner
> Care and sincerity
> Ownership
> Contactability
> Ability to contact right person at first attempt
> Telephone answered promptly
> One reply to customer's enquiry
> Documentation
> Easy to understand
> Well-presented

The above measurement system represents a mix of 'hard' and 'soft' measures. Market research highlighted the need to develop a set of 'soft' measures to complement the traditional harder measures. Handling a death claim requires sensitivity and this should be measured. Many of the new measures (e.g. speed), represent true end-to-end measurement. Previously, in measuring the time to get a policy to the customer, work that couldn't be processed for any reason was excluded for measurement purposes (e.g. forms incorrectly completed by customer). This has changed under the new system and 'time to perform complete transaction' represents a true end-to-end measure of the process cycle time.

The second phase of the Customer Experience Measures project took the analysis of the measures and key transactions a step further to identify what customer measures could be put in place, and the techniques that could be used to provide the measurements. Four measurement techniques were proposed:

1 Speed audits for the speed measures.
2 Accuracy audits for the accuracy measures and the interaction (documentation) measures.
3 Telephone audits for the interaction (attitude, contractability and documentation)
4 Customer surveys for the interaction (attitude) measures.

The objective of the phase 2 report was to gain approval to pilot the proposed measures for partial implementation in January year 4. A time-scaled action plan was developed to implement the new system during the first half of that year.

People satisfaction

The 'people' KBI is morale and this is monitored by surveys. An annual attitude survey is conducted across all Life Administration. The results are analysed in terms of a communication index, morale index, training index and service index. The results of the last survey are shown opposite:

Index		*Target*
Communication	54	50
Morale	56	50
Training	55	50
Service	66	50

The Way of Life reviews, considered in the leadership section, also provide extensive information about aspects of people satisfaction.

Impact on society

As a provider of a service, the Prudential is not directly involved in activities impacting upon the environment and ecology as is, say, a chemical company. However, the company's management is conscious of the 'green' movement and its obligations to play an active role in this area. There is no written environmental policy; however, Life Administration actively promotes certain environmentally friendly practices. For example, all suppliers are made aware of the company's preference to use recycled or environmentally friendly products. 'Green' products are always chosen for stationery, etc. The company also operates comprehensive systems to promote recycling of paper and some plastic products.

The company works with local councils to promote environmental issues. This involves setting targets for space, heating and lighting consumption; general and proper waste reduction, reuse and recycling; incentives for reduced vehicle use through car sharing, etc. The move to new office premises in Reading resulted in considerable energy savings.

The Prudential is actively involved in many community activities at both a national and local level. These activities include support to charities and the involvement in education and training activities in the community. A recent innovation has been the launch of the Prudential community investment programme, outline details of which are given in Appendix B. Prudential employees are actively involved in the organization and running of many activities on the community.

Some examples of this activity are listed below:

- £20 000 was donated to local hospitals, schools and the community of Reading in general.
- A large donation of £10 000 was made to the Delwood Cancer Unit in Reading.
- Many members of staff also engage in other activities to support the local community. These include:

(a) Young Enterprise Scheme, where employees give up their own time to go and help schoolchildren develop business acumen.
(b) Various sponsored charity events.
(c) Several employees are members of the BBONT club, which stands for Berkshire, Buckinghamshire, Oxfordshire National Trust Club, where volunteers go out to help the environment.

Business results

The business results for the first three years of the TQM programme are shown in Appendix C4.A. Non-financial measures include the KBI productivity. This is measured by 4-weekly productivity measurement and budget monitoring.

Initial productivity measures in most operation areas used the British Standards (BS) method. Areas counted work volumes, which were scaled by unit times to give a theoretical workload. This workload was compared with the actual utilization time, which led to the calculation of the BS figure. Work on productivity has allowed them to put more accurate productivity measures in place across all operation areas. Calculations of accurate standard times for all processes now allows pinpointing of problem areas.

Significant productivity gains were made. For example, the median productivity for the Ordinary Branch area improved from 76.8 to 99.6% during a one-year period.

Table C4.3 *Life Administration cycle time comparisons*

(a) Productivity – new business average time per case

	Life Assurance	*Pension*
May Year 2	40 min	56 min
Aug Year 2	43 min	52 min
Jan Year 3	37 min	48 min
May Year 3	30 min	38 min
Jan Year 2	58 min	57 min
Aug Year 3	28 min	37 min

(b) Productivity – claims: average time per case

Aug Year 2	19 min
Aug Year 3	16 min

Productivity improvements are also reflected in the dramatic reduction in cycle times for many key business activities (Table C4.3).

In addition to these productivity improvements, there have also been savings of £5m in operation costs.

Conclusion

The Prudential Life Administration Group's approach to TQM is a comprehensive example of the involvement of people in process improvement in a service environment. The programme is actively led by management and has delivered significant improvement to customer service in many areas of the business. This in turn has improved the overall effectiveness and efficiency of the business. Maintaining this momentum and quality focus is a challenge but events such as quality weeks help everyone celebrate their successes and stimulate the search for new improvement opportunities.

Although this case has only looked at a small part of the Prudential Group, it is typical of the TQM approach across the whole company. The Prudential Board is committed to customer service and adding customer value.

Acknowledgements

The authors would like to acknowledge the invaluable help of the following people in the preparation of this case:

Mr K. Alliston, Prudential Assurance Company Ltd.
Dr S. Tanner, Prudential Assurance Company Ltd.
Mr R. Walker, Industry Motivation Ltd.
Ms S. Dawson, John McDonald Associates.
Mr J. McDonald, John McDonald Associates.
Mr R. Jones, Universal Sound Principles.
Mr G. Binney, Ashridge Management College.

Appendix C4.A Business results

Home Service Division
Year 3 Results

Getting fit for the future

Yesterday Prudential Corporation announced its Year 3 results. This report deals with Home Service's contribution to those results. A report on the overall results will be issued later.

Year 3 was a difficult year. The recession continued and consumer confidence remained low. At the same time competition became more intense, both within the Direct Sales sector and outside. Despite this, we achieved a creditable sales performance and have made a good start on further restructuring our business to achieve our twin aims of increasing sales and reducing costs.

At the half year I reported on the start of Field Management Restructuring, the reorganization of our sales management into five teams of Regional Managers and 180 Branch Managers. The programme has now been successfully rolled out and we have moved to the next stage, the reorganization of the support structure for Branches.

The Divisional Office restructuring was announced in November. The plans involve replacing the 12 Divisional Offices with a Branch Service Centre at Bristol and the establishment of five Regional Business Development Units.

The next stage is the introduction of changes to the way we operate in the Field. Consultation with staff on "Fit for the Future" outline proposals continued throughout the latter half of Year 3 and we have used this feedback to shape our proposals. In February of Year 4 we began negotiations with the NUIW on the overall structure and the likely changes in terms and conditions.

While the salesforce has been going through these changes, Head Office has also been undergoing reorganization. The majority of Head Office functions announced their headcount reduction targets during November and these plans have been implemented in early Year 4. The most significant of these is within Home Service Systems, where staff numbers have been reduced from 660 to 450.

In December we announced our decision to transfer our Commercial business to Provincial. Specialist Commercial staff transferred to Provincial in January, but we will continue to accept renewal business until 1 May.

I am grateful to staff for their commitment and hard work at a time of considerable change. Without your support, the achievements of Year 3 would not have been possible. I cannot promise that Year 4 will be any easier, but with your continued help I know that we can achieve our vision of delivering best customer value and becoming the biggest and the best in the business.

Managing Director
24 March, Year 4

Home service premiums and profit (£m)

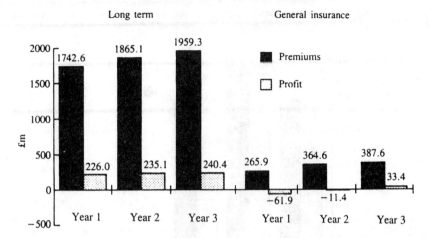

- Total Home Service profits of £273.8 m were 22.4% up on Year 2.
- The increase is principally due to the very welcome turnaround in the General Business result.
- Long-term premiums were 5% above Year 2 levels, helped by a 10% increase in sales of Home Service single premium products.
- The rise in General Insurance premiums is a result of increases in premium rates.
- The policy-holders' share of total profits distributed for Year 3 was £1400 m. A man aged 30 paying £30 per month into a 10-year savings with-profit plan started 10 years ago will receive £6296 on 1 May Year 4 – an equivalent rate of return of 10.8%.

Home Service Division
Life new business sales

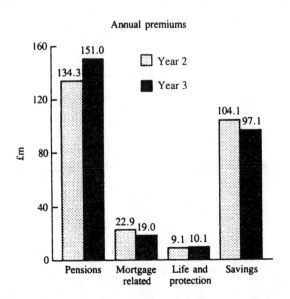

Annual premiums

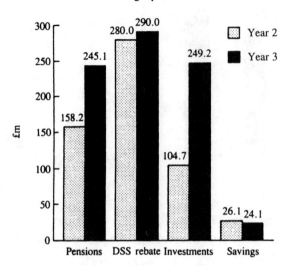

Single premiums

- The highlights of the year was the strong sales of single-premium products. Single premiums, excluding DSS rebate, were 79.4% above Year 2 supported by high sales of Prudence Bond and Pension Transfer business. Launched late in Year 2, Prudence Bond sales in Year 3 totalled £181 m.
- The DSS rebate figure is the amount of premiums receivable for the Year 2/3 tax year, and largely relates to business sold in previous years. New DSS business sold in Year 3 totalled £11 m.
- Annual premium sales have improved by 2.6% from the low level of Year 2, with pension sales making the strongest contribution.
- Our sales target is an increase in Ordinary Branch product sales (measured as annual premium + 1/10 single premium) of 50% over the Year 2 level. We achieved a 16% increase in Year 3.

Home Service Division
General insurance results – Year 3

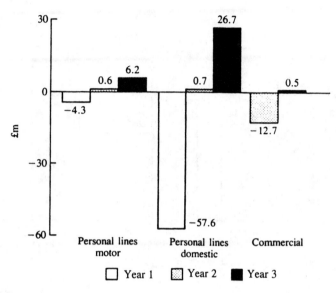

Personal lines

- The significant improvement in Personal Lines profit results from better claims experience and premium rate increases. This has reduced the claims ratio from 73.3 to 63.3%.
- Weather-related claims were 14.2% down on Year 2. However, domestic theft claims increased by 8.9%.
- The decline of our in-force policy base has continued, with year-end-in-force policies for both motor and domestic lower than in Year 2. The overall fall in our policy base by 9.8% has been offset by the increase in average premiums, so that gross written premiums were 7.1% higher than in Year 2.

Commercial

- The Commercial account benefited slightly from the consequences of the sale to Provincial; however, the improvement over Year 2 is very welcome. The result would have been seen as marginal had we been continuing in the business.

Home Service Division
Expenses

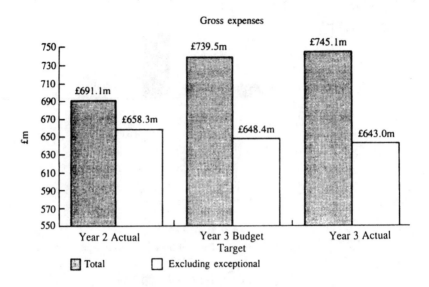

Gross expenses

- Gross expenses are calculated before deducting Systems income from other divisions, service charges, costs allocated to claims and deferral of acquisition expenses on general business. They also include Group overheads. So gross expenses are greater than those reported in Team Brief, which are net of these amounts.
- Exceptional items include expenditure on Field Management Restructuring, the Divisional Office Review, Scenario 3, the relocation of the Data Centre, the redundancy programmes, Genesis and Commercial disposal costs.
- Of the target expense reduction of £100 m, the major key Action Plans implemented by the end of Year 3 will contribute £36m per annum (Field Management Restructuring – £16 m; Genesis – £10 m; Divisional Office Review – £7 m; Data Centre Relocation – £3 m).
- The restructuring of Home Service Systems implemented in early Year 4 will contribute a further £4 m savings per annum.
- Our expense levels are also benefiting from lower interest rates, which have reduced the cost of the staff mortgage subsidy by £11 m.

Appendix C4.B Prudential community investment programme

Management briefing
Information for senior management of Prudential Corporation

Prudential will announce the first details of its community investment programme on May 28 Year 4. Over the next five years, the Corporation will be supporting those in the UK who care for sick, elderly or disabled dependants in their own home, through a national programme known as the Prudential Carers' Initiative.

Prudential will work in partnership wth two voluntary organizations in the development of its Carers' Initiative: The Princess Royal Trust for Carers and Crossroads, the UK's leading voluntary agency in the provision of respite care in the home.

The project will be run by Corporate Communications, which in the past has responded to appeals from various charities and community organizations in the UK.

Following a review of the role of its community support, the Prudential board approved a programme for the next five years which will focus on two issues only – carers and safer communities.

The overall objectives has been set:

To establish Prudential as an innovative and effective participant in addressing the key social issues affecting the community. This will be achieved through long-term and dedicated support for research, prevention, education and community care programmes directed towards specific target areas.

The first step in the programme, to be announced by Mick Newmarch on May 28, is the Prudential Carers' Initiative.

Mick Newmarch, who is a trustee of the Princess Royal Trust, is keen that Prudential takes the lead in raising public awareness of carers' needs and of the contribution they make to society.

In particular, he hopes that other companies will be persuaded to look at how they too can help to improve community care.

A strategy to promote the Initiative and involve business areas is now being devised.

Carers are those who, in their own home, look after a parent, child or family friend, dependent on the carer because of age, health or disability.

The partnership between Prudential and the two voluntary organizations has two main objectives:

- To further develop the network of carer centres in the UK through The Princess Royal Trust for Carers.
- To enhance the quality of respite care schemes through Crossroads in the same locations.

The Princess Royal Trust for Carers

The Trust is a fund-raising charity, established by HRH The Princess Royal, specifically to benefit carers.

It has a vision of society in which carers are properly valued and supported by government and community, so enabling them to share and fulfil their caring role as effectively and as happily as possible.

The mission of the Trust is to:

- Raise public awareness of carers' needs and of the contribution they make to society
- Provide information counselling and support to carers.

Key objectives of the Trust are also to identify hidden carers in the community and address the problems of carers in employment.

The trust aims to establish carer centres in every local authority area throughout the UK, and is able to lever funds from local authorities to do so. Since the first centre was opened by HRH The Princess Royal in January Year 4, another nine have been established.

Crossroads

Crossroads is the UK's leading voluntary agency in the provision of respite care in the home.

It offers help for carers who need a regular dependable break from their task, in order to have some time of their own.

Since it was established twenty years ago, Crossroads has set up more than 200 schemes located within Social Service local authority districts, funded by local statutory services.

Crossroads has four main objectives:

- To relieve stress in families or people responsible for caring
- To avoid admission to hospital or residential care of people in care, should the household be unable to look after them
- To supplement and complement existing statutory services
- To maintain a high standard of care.

The Prudential carers' initiative

This newly formed partnership will establish new carer centres and develop respite care services in the same locations.

The carer centres will meet many of the needs already identified by carers themselves: particularly respite care, access to information, and the opportunity to meet with others in similar situations and overcome feelings of isolation.

They will provide a service to all carers, regardless of the condition of the dependant – such as physical disability, mental handicap or illness, terminal illness or senility.

They will also provide support, advice and guidance from easily accessible town centre sites, staffed by a manager and a small team of volunteers.

Preliminary discussions are taking place in Sutton, Mid Glamorgan, Newry and Mourne, North Tyneside, Lincs, Essex, Sefton, Sheffield, Hammersmith and Fulham, Bristol and Reading.

The aim of a Management Briefing is to inform managers in advance of public announcements, allowing them to plan further communication to their own staff at their discretion.

Discussion questions

1 Discuss the preparations required for the negotiation of a one-year contract with a major raw material suppplier.

2 Imagine that you are the chief executive or equivalent in an organization of your own choice, and that you plan to introduce the concept of Just-in-Time (JIT) into the organization.
(a) Prepare a briefing of your senior managers, which should include your assessment of the aims, objectives and benefits to be gained from the implementation.
(b) Outline the steps you would take to implement JIT, and explain how you would attempt to ensure its success.

3 You are the manager of a busy insurance office. Last year's abnormal winter gales led to an exceptionally high level of insurance claims for house damage caused by strong winds, and you had considerable problems in coping with the greatly increased work load. The result was excessively long delays in both acknowledging and settling customers' claims.
Your area manager has asked you to outline a plan for dealing with such a situation should it arise again. The plan should identify what actions you would take to deal with the work, and what, if anything, should be done now to enable you to take those actions should the need arise.
What proposals would you make, and why?

4 Explain the basic philosophy behind quality systems such as the BS EN ISO 9000 (BS 5750) series. How can an effective quality system contribute to continuous improvement in an international banking operation?

5 What role does a quality management system, based on BS EN ISO 9000 series, have in TQM? How should an organization such as Rolls-Royce view such a standard?

6 Explain what is meant by independent third part certification to a standard such as BS EN ISO 9000 , and discuss the merits of such a scheme for an organization.

7 Compare and contrast the role of quality systems in the following organizations:

(a) a private hospital;
(b) a medium-sized engineering company;
(c) a branch of a clearing bank.

8 List the nine main categories of the European Quality Award criteria. How may such criteria be used as the basis for a TQM self-assessment process?

9 Self-assessment using the European Quality Award (EQA) criteria enables an organization to systematically review its business processes and results. Briefly describe the (EQA) criteria and discuss the main self-assessment methods.

10 Self-appraisal or assessment against the European Quality Award (EQA) can be used by organizations to monitor the progress of their TQM programmes.

(a) Briefly describe the EQA criteria and explain the steps that an organization would have to follow to carry out a self-assessment.
(b) How could self-assessment against the EQA be used in a large multi-site organization to drive continuous improvement?

Case study assignments

C3 CarnaudMetal Box

Evaluate the quality system approach adopted by CMB in relation to their TQM processes.

Discuss the links between the work on SPC and the quality system at CMB.

Will the next steps, discussed briefly at the end of the case, sustain the momentum of TQM; what additional areas should be considered?

C4 Prudential Assurance

Using the framework of the European Quality Award – the nine headings under which the case is presented – assess the organization's progress towards total quality. Under each category state the strengths and the areas for improvement.

Part Three

TQM – The Tools and the Improvement Cycle

How doth the little busy bee
Improve each shining hour
And gather honey all the day
From every opening Flower?

Isaac Watts, 1674-1748, from 'Against idleness and mischief'

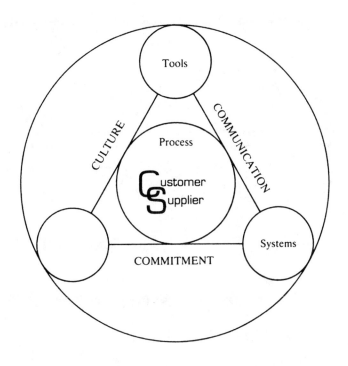

Measurement of quality

7.1 Measurement and the improvement cycle

Traditionally, performance measures and indicators have been derived from cost-accounting information, often based on outdated and arbitrary principles. These provide little motivation to support attempts to introduce TQM and, in some cases, actually inhibit continuous improvement because they are unable to map process performance. In the organization that is to survive over a long term, performance must begin to be measured by the improvements seen by the customer.

In the cycle of never ending improvement, measurement plays an important role in:

- Identifying opportunities for improvement (quality costing).
- Comparing performance against internal standards (process control and improvement).
- Comparing performance against external standards (benchmarking).

Measures are used in *process control*, e.g. control charts (see Chapter 8), and in *performance improvement*, e.g. quality improvement teams (see Chapters 10 and 11), so they should give information about how well processes and people are doing and motivate them to perform better in the future.

The author has seen many examples of so-called performance measurement systems that frustrated improvements efforts. Various problems include systems that:

1 Produce irrelevant or misleading information.
2 Track performance in single, isolated dimensions.
3 Generate financial measures too late, e.g. quarterly, for mid-course corrections or remedial action.
4 Do not take account of the customer perspective, both internal and external.
5 Distort management's understanding of how effective the organization has been in implementing its strategy.
6 Provide behaviour that *undermines* the achievement of the strategic objectives.

Typical harmful summary measures of local performance are purchase price, machine or plant efficiencies, direct labour costs, and ratios of direct to indirect labour. These are incompatible with quality-improvement measures such as process and throughput times, delivery performance, inventory reductions, and increases in flexibility, which are first and foremost *non-financial*. Financial summaries provide valuable information of course, but they should not be used for control. Effective decision-making requires direct physical measures for operational feedback and improvement.

One example of a 'measure' with these shortcomings is return on investment (ROI). ROI can be computed only after profits have been totalled for a given period. It was designed therefore as a single-period, long-term measure, but it is increasingly being used as a short-term one. Perhaps this is because most executive bonus 'packages' in the West are based on short-term measures. ROI tells us what happened, not what is happening or what will happen, and, for complex and detailed projects, ROI is inaccurate and irrelevant.

Many managers have a poor or incomplete understanding of their processes and products or services, and, looking for an alternative stimulus, become interested in financial indicators. The use of ROI, for example, for evaluating strategic requirements and performance can lead to a discriminatory allocation of resources. In many ways the financial indicators used in many businesses have remained static while the environment in which they operate has changed dramatically.

Traditionally, the measures used have not been linked to the processes where the value-adding activities take place. What has been missing is improvement measures that provide feedback to people in all areas of business operations. Of course TQM stresses the need to start with the process for fulfilling customer needs.

The critical elements of a good performance measurement and management effort look like any other list associated with total quality management:

- Leadership and commitment.
- Full employee involvement.
- Good planning.
- Sound implementation strategy.
- Measurement and evaluation.
- Control and improvement.
- Achieving and maintaining standards of excellence.

The Deming cycle of continuous improvement – PLAN DO CHECK ACT – clearly requires measurement to drive it, and yet it is a useful design aid for the measurement system itself:

PLAN: establish performance objectives and standards.
DO: measure actual performance.
CHECK: compare actual performance with the objectives and standards – determine the gap.
ACT: take the necessary actions to close the gap and make the necessary improvements.

Before we use performance measurement in the improvement cycle, however, we should attempt to answer four basic questions:

1   Why measure?
2   What to measure?
3   Where to measure?
4   How to measure?

Why measure?

It has been said often that it is not possible to manage what cannot be measured. Whether this is strictly true or not, there are clear arguments for measuring. In a quality-driven, never ending improvement environment, the following are some of the main reasons *why measurement is needed* and why it plays a key role in quality and productivity improvement.

- To ensure customer requirements *have* been met.
- To be able to set sensible *objectives* and comply with them.
- To provide *standards* for establishing comparisons.
- To provide *visibility* and provide a 'score-board' for people to *monito*r their own performance levels.
- To highlight *quality problems* and determine which areas require *priority attention*.
- To give an indication of the *costs of poor quality*.
- To justify the *use of resources*.
- To provide *feedback* for driving the improvement effort.

It is also important to know the impact of TQM on improvements in business performance, on sustaining current performance, and perhaps on reducing any decline in performance.

What to measure?

In the business of process improvement, process understanding, definition, measurement, and management are tied inextricably together. In order to assess and evaluate performance accurately, appropriate measurement must be designed, developed and maintained by people who *own* the processes concerned. They may find it necessary to measure effectiveness, efficiency, quality, impact, and productivity. In these areas there are many types of measurement, including direct output or input figures, the cost of poor quality, economic data, comments and complaints from customers, information from customer or employee surveys, etc., generally continuous variable measures (such as time) or discrete attribute measures (such as absentees).

No one can provide a generic list of what should be measured but, once it has been decided what measures are appropriate, they may be converted into indicators. These include ratios, scales, rankings, and financial and time-based indicators. Whichever measures and indicators are used by the process owners, they must reflect the true performance of the process in customer/supplier terms, and emphasize continuous improvement. Time-related measures and indicators have great value.

Where to measure?

If true measures of the effectiveness of TQM are to be obtained, there are three components that must be examined – the human, technical and business components.

The human component is clearly of major importance and the key tests are that, wherever measures are used, they must be:

1 Understood by all the people being measured.
2 Accepted by the individuals concerned.
3 Compatible with the rewards and recognition systems.
4 Designed to offer minimal opportunity for manipulation.

Technically, the measures must be the ones that truly represent the controllable aspects of the processes, rather than simple output measures that cannot be related to process management. They must also be correct, precise and accurate.

The business component requires that the measures are objective, timely, and result-oriented, and above all they must mean something to those working in and around the process, *including the customers.*

How to measure?

Measurement, as any other management system, requires the stages of design, analysis, development, evaluation, implementation and review. The system must be designed to measure *progress*, otherwise it will not engage the improvement cycle. Progress is important in five main areas: effectiveness, efficiency, productivity, quality, and impact.

Effectiveness

Effectiveness may be defined as the percentage actual output over the expected output:

$$\text{Effectiveness} = \frac{\text{Actual output}}{\text{Expected output}} \times 100 \text{ per cent}$$

Hence effectiveness looks at the *output* side of the process and is about the implementation of the objectives – doing what you said you would do. Effectiveness measures should reflect whether the organization, group or process owner(s) are achieving the desired results, accomplishing the right things. Measures of this may include:

• Quality, e.g. a grade of product, or a level of service.
• Quantity, e.g. tonnes, lots, bedrooms cleaned, accounts opened.
• Timeliness, e.g. speed of response, product lead times, cycle time.
• Cost/price, e.g. unit costs.

Efficiency

Efficiency is concerned with the percentage resources actually used over the resources that were planned to be used:

$$\text{Efficiency} = \frac{\text{Resources actually used}}{\text{Resources planned to be used}} \times 100 \text{ per cent}$$

Clearly, this is a process *input* issue and measures performance of the process system management. It is, of course, possible to use resources 'efficiently' while being *ineffective*, so performance efficiency improvement must be related to certain output objectives.

All process inputs may be subjected to efficiency measurement, so we may use labour/staff efficiency, equipment efficiency (or utilization), material efficiency, information efficiency, etc. Inventory data and throughput times are often used in efficiency and productivity ratios.

Productivity

Productivity measures should be designed to relate the process outputs to its inputs:

$$\text{Productivity} = \frac{\text{Outputs}}{\text{Inputs}}$$

and this may be quoted as expected or actual productivity:

$$\text{Expected productivity} = \frac{\text{Expected output}}{\text{Resources expected to be consumed}}$$

$$\text{Actual productivity} = \frac{\text{Actual output}}{\text{Resources actually consumed}}$$

There is a vast literature on productivity and its measurement, but simple ratios such as tonnes per man-hour (expected and actual), pages of word-processing per operator-day, and many others like this are in use. Productivity measures may be developed for each input or a combination of inputs, e.g. sales/all employee costs.

Quality

This has been defined elsewhere of course (see Chapter 1). The *non-quality* related measures include the simple counts of defect or error rates (perhaps in parts per million), percentage outside specification or Cp/Cpk values, deliveries not on time, or more generally as the costs of poor quality. When the positive costs of prevention of poor quality are included, these provide a balanced measure of the costs of quality.

The quality measures should also indicate positively whether we are doing a good job in terms of customer satisfaction, implementing the objectives, and whether the designs, systems, and solutions to problems are meeting the requirements. These really are voice-of-the-customer measures

Impact

Impact measures should lead to key performance indicators for the business or organization, including monitoring improvement over time. Value-added management (VAM) requires the identification and elimination of all non-value-adding wastes, including time. Value added is simply the volume of sales (or other measure of 'turnover') minus the total input costs, and provides a good direct measure of the impact of the improvement process on the performance of the business. A related ratio, percentage return on value added (ROVA):

$$\text{ROVA} = \frac{\text{Net profits before tax}}{\text{Value added}} \times 100 \text{ per cent}$$

is another financial indicator that may be used.

Other measures or indicators of impact on the business are *growth* in sales, assets, numbers of passengers/students, etc., and *asset-utilization* measures such as return on investment (ROI) or capital employed (ROCE), earnings per share, etc.

Some of the impact measures may be converted to people productivity ratios, e.g.:

$$\frac{\text{Value added}}{\text{Number of employees (or employee costs)}}$$

Activity-based costing (ABC) is an information system that maintains and processes data on an organization's activities and cost objectives. It is based on the activities performed being identified and the costs being traced to them. ABC uses various 'cost drivers' to trace the cost of activities to the cost of the products or services. The activity and cost-driver concepts are the heart of ABC. Cost drivers reflect the demands placed on activities by products, services or other cost targets. Activities are processes or procedures that cause work and thereby consume resources. This clearly measures impact, both on and by the organization.

7.2   The implementation of performance measurement systems

It has already been established that a good measurement system will start with the customer and measure the right things. The value of any measure clearly needs to be compared with the cost of producing it. There will be appropriate measures for different parts of the organization, but everywhere they must relate process performance to the needs of the process customer. All critical parts of the process must be measured, and it is often better to start with simple measures and improve them.

There must be a recognition of the need to distinguish between different measures for different purposes. For example, an operator may measure time, various process parameters, and amounts, while at the management level measuring costs and delivery timeliness may be more appropriate.

Participation in the development of measures enhances their understanding and acceptance. Process-owners can assist in defining the required performance measures, provided that senior managers have communicated their mission clearly, defined the critical success factors, and identified the critical processes (see Chapter 13).

If all employees participate, and own the measurement processes, there will be lower resistance to the system, and a positive commitment towards future changes will be engaged. This will derive from the 'volunteered accountability', which will in turn make the individual contribution more visible. Involvement in measurement also strengthens the links in the customer–supplier chains and gives quality improvement teams much clearer objectives. This should lead to greater short-term and long-term productivity gains.

There are a number of possible reasons why measurement systems fail:

1 They do not define performance operationally.
2 They do not relate performance to the process.
3 The boundaries of the process are not defined.
4 The measures are misunderstood or misused or measure the wrong things.
5 There is no distinction between control and improvement.
6 There is a fear of exposing poor and good performance.
7 It is seen as an extra burden in terms of time and reporting.
8 There is a perception of reduced autonomy.
9 Too many measurements are focused internally and too few are focused externally.
10 There is a fear of the introduction of tighter management controls.

These and other problems are frequently due to poor planning at the implementation stage or a failure to assess current systems of measurement. Before the introduction of a total quality-based performance measurement system, an audit of the existing systems should be carried out. Its purpose is to establish the effectiveness of existing measures, their compatibility with the quality drive, their relationship with the processes concerned, and their closeness to the objectives of meeting customer requirements. The audit should also highlight areas where performance has not been measured previously, and indicate the degree of understanding and participation of the employees in the existing systems and the actions that result.

Generic questions that may be asked during the audit include:

- Is there a performance measurement system in use?
- Has it been effectively communicated throughout the organization?
- Is it systematic?
- Is it efficient?
- Is it well understood?
- Is it applied?
- Is it linked to the mission and objectives of the organization?
- Is there a regular review and update?

- Is action taken to improve performance following the measurement?
- Are the people who own the processes engaged in measuring their own performance?
- Have employees been properly trained to conduct the measurement?

Following such an audit, there are twelve basic steps for the introduction of TQM-based performance measurement. Half of these are planning steps and the other half implementation.

Planning

1 Identify the purpose of conducting measurement, i.e. is it for:
   (a) Reporting, e.g. ROI reported to shareholders.
   (b) Controlling, e.g. using process data on control charts.
   (c) Improving, e.g. monitoring the results of a quality improvement team project.
2 Choose the right balance between individual measures (activity- or task-related) and group measures (process- and sub-process-related) and make sure they reflect process performance.
3 Plan to measure all the key elements of performance, not just one, e.g. time, cost, and product quality variables may all be important.
4 Ensure that the measures will reflect the voice of the internal/external customers.
5 Carefully select measures that will be used to establish standards of performance.
6 Allow time for the learning process during the introduction of a new measurement system.

Implementation

7 Ensure full participation during the introductory period and allow the system to mould through participation.
8 Carry out cost/benefit analysis on the data generation, and ensure measures that have high 'leverage' are selected.
9 Make the effort to spread the measurement system as widely as possible, since effective decision-making will be based on measures from *all* areas of the business operation.
10 Use *surrogate* measures for subjective areas where quantification is difficult, e.g. improvements in morale may be 'measured' by reductions in absenteeism or staff turnover rates.
11 Design the measurement systems to be as flexible as possible, to allow for changes in strategic direction and continual review.
12 Ensure that the measures reflect the quality drive by showing small incremental achievements that match the never ending improvement approach.

In summary the measurement system must be designed, planned and implemented to reflect customer requirements, give visibility to the processes and the progress made, communicate the total quality effort and engage the never ending improvement cycle. So it must itself be periodically reviewed.

7.3   Benchmarking

Product, service and process improvements can take place only in relation to established standards, and the improvements then being incorporated into the new standards. *Benchmarking*, one of the most transferable aspects of Rank Xerox's approach to total quality management, and thought to have originated in Japan, measures an organization's operations, products and services against those of its competitors in a ruthless fashion. It is a means by which targets, priorities and operations that will lead to competitive advantage can be established.

Benchmarking is the continuous process of measuring products, services and processes against those of industry leaders or the toughest competitors. This results in a search for best practice, those that will lead to superior performance, through measuring performance, continuously implementing change, and emulating the best.

There may be many reasons for carrying out benchmarking. Some of them are set against various objectives in Table 7.1. The links between benchmarking and TQM are clear – establishing objectives based on industry best practice should directly contribute to better meeting of the internal and external customer requirements.

There are four basic types of benchmarking:

Internal – a comparison of internal operations.
Competitive – specific competitor to competitor comparisons for a product or function of interest.
Functional – comparisons to similar functions within the same broad industry or to industry leaders.
Generic – comparisons of business processes that are very similar, regardless of the industry.

Table 7.1 *Reasons for benchmarking*

Objectives	Without benchmarking	With benchmarking
Becoming competitive	• Internally focused • Evolutionary change	• Understanding of competitiveness • Ideas from proven practices
Industry best practices	• Few solutions • Frantic catch up activity	• Many options • Superior performance
Defining customer requirements	• Based on history or gut feeling • Perception	• Market reality • Objective evaluation
Establishing effective goals and objectives	• Lacking external focus • Reactive	• Credible, unarguable • Proactive
Developing true measures of productivity	• Pursuing pet projects • Strength and weaknesses not understood • Route of least resistance	• Solving real problems • Understanding outputs • Based on industry best practices

The evolution of benchmarking in an organization is likely to progress through four focuses. Initially attention will be concentrated on competitive products or services, including, for example, design, development and operational features. This should develop into a focus on industry best practices and may include, for example, aspects of distribution or service. The real breakthrough is when the organization focuses on all aspects of the total business performance, across all functions and aspects, and addresses current *and projected* performance gaps. This should lead to the final focus on true continuous improvement.

At its simplest competitive benchmarking, the most common form, requires every department to examine itself against its counterpart in the best competing companies. This includes a scrutiny of all aspects of their activities. Benchmarks that may be important for *customer satisfaction*, for example, might include:

- Product or service consistency.
- Correct and on-time delivery.
- Speed of response or new product development.
- Correct billing.

For *impact* the benchmarks may be:

- Waste, rejects or errors.
- Inventory levels/work in progress.
- Costs of operation.
- Staff turnover.

The task is to work out what has to be done to improve on the competition's performance in each of the chosen areas.

At regular (say, weekly) meetings, managers should discuss the results off the competitive benchmarking, and on a daily basis departmental managers should discuss quality problems with staff. One afternoon may be set aside for the benchmark meetings, followed by a 'walkabout', when the manager observes the activities actually taking place and compares them mentally with the competitors' operations.

The process has fifteen stages, and these are all focused on trying to *measure* comparisons of competitiveness:

PLAN	Select department(s) or process group(s) for benchmarking.
	Identify best competitor, perhaps using customer feed-back or industry observers.
	Identify benchmarks.
	Bring together the appropriate team.
	Decide information and data-collection methodology (do not forget desk research!)
	Prepare for any visits and interact with target organizations.
	Use data-collection methodology.
ANALYSE	Compare the organization and its 'competitors', using the benchmark data.
	Catalogue the information and create a 'competency centre'.

Understand the 'enabling processes' as well as the performance measures.

DEVELOP   Set new performance level objectives/standards.
              Develop action plans to achieve goals and integrate into the organization.

IMPROVE   Implement specific actions and integrate them into the business processes.

REVIEW   Monitor the results and improvements.
              Review the benchmarks and the ongoing relationship with the target organization.

Benchmarking is very important in the administrative areas, since it continuously measures services and practices against the equivalent operation in the toughest direct competitors or organizations renowned as leaders in the areas, even if they are in the same organization. An example of quantitative benchmarks in absenteeism is given in Table 7.2.

Technologies and conditions vary between different industries and markets, but the basic concepts of measurement and benchmarking are of general validity. The objective should be to produce products and services that conform to the requirements of the customer in a never ending improvement environment. The way to accomplish this is to use the continuous improvement cycle in all the operating departments – nobody should be exempt. Measurement and benchmarking are not separate sciences or unique theories of quality management, but rather strategic approaches to getting the best out of people, processes, products, plant, and programmes.

Table 7.2 *Quantitative benchmarking in absenteeism*

Organization's absence level (%)	Productivity opportunity
Under 3	This level matches an aggressive benchmark that has been achieved in 'excellent' organizations.
3-4	This level may be viewed within the organization as a good performance – representing a moderate productivity opportunity improvement.
5-8	This level is tolerated by many organizations but represents a major improvement opportunity.
9-10	This level indicates that a serious absenteeism problem exists.
Over 10	This level of absenteeism is totally unacceptable.

7.4 Costs of quality

Manufacturing a quality product, providing a quality service, or doing a quality job – one with a high degree of customer satisfaction – is not enough. The cost of achieving these goals must be carefully managed, so that the long-term effect of quality costs on the business or organization is a desirable one. These costs are a true measure of the quality effort. A competitive product or service based on a balance between quality and cost factors is the principal goal of responsible management. The objective is best accomplished with the aid of competent analysis of the costs of quality (COQ).

The analysis of quality related costs is a significant management tool that provides:

- A method of assessing the effectiveness of the management of quality.
- A means of determining problem areas, opportunities, savings, and action priorities.

The costs of quality are no different from any other costs. Like the costs of maintenance, design, sales, production/operations, and other activities, they can be budgeted, measured and analysed.

Having specified the quality of design, the operating units have the task of matching it. The necessary activities will incur costs that may be separated into prevention costs, appraisal costs and failure costs, the so-called P-A-F model first presented by Feigenbaum. Failure costs can be further split into those resulting from internal and external failure.

Prevention costs

These are associated with the design, implementation and maintenance of the total quality management system. Prevention costs are planned and are incurred before actual operation. Prevention includes:

Product or service requirements

The determination of requirements and the setting of corresponding specifications (which also takes account of process capability) for incoming materials, processes, intermediates, finished products and services.

Quality planning

The creation of quality, reliability, and operational, production, supervision, process control, inspection and other special plans, e.g. pre-production trials, required to achieve the quality objective.

Quality assurance

The creation and maintenance of the quality system.

Inspection equipment

The design, development and/or purchase of equipment for use in inspection work.

Training

The development, preparation and maintenance of training programmes for operators, supervisors, staff, and managers both to achieve and maintain capability.

Miscellaneous

Clerical, travel, supply, shipping, communications and other general office management activities associated with quality.

Resources devoted to prevention give rise to the '*costs of doing it right the first time*'.

Appraisal costs

These costs are associated with the supplier's and customer's evaluation of purchased materials, processes, intermediates, products and services to assure conformance with the specified requirements. Appraisal includes:

Verification

Checking of incoming material, process set-up, first-offs, running processes, intermediates and final products, including product or service performance appraisal against agreed specifications.

Quality audits

To check that the quality system is functioning satisfactorily.

Inspection equipment

The calibration and maintenance of equipment used in all inspection activities.

Vendor rating

The assessment and approval of all suppliers, of both products and services.

Appraisal activities result in the '*costs of checking it is right*'.

Internal failure costs

These costs occur when the results of work fail to reach designed quality standards and are detected before transfer to the customer takes place. Internal failure includes the following:

Waste

The activities associated with doing unnecessary work or holding stocks as the result of errors, poor organization or poor communications, the wrong materials, etc.

Scrap

Defective product, material or stationery that cannot be repaired, used or sold.

Rework or rectification

The correction of defective material or errors to meet the requirements.

Re-inspection

The re-examination of products or work that have been rectified.

Downgrading

A product that is usable but does not meet specifications may be downgraded and sold as 'second quality' at a low price.

Failure analysis

The activity required to establish the causes of internal product or service failure.

External failure costs

These costs occur when products or services fail to reach design quality standards but are not detected until after transfer to the consumer. External failure includes:

Repair and servicing

Either of returned products or those in the field.

Warranty claims

Failed products that are replaced or services re-performed under some form of guarantee.

Complaints

All work and costs associated with handling and servicing of customers' complaints.

Returns

The handling and investigation of rejected or recalled products or materials, including transport costs.

Liability

The result of product or service liability litigation and other claims, which may include a change of contract.

Loss of goodwill

The impact on reputation and image, which impinges directly on future prospects for sales.

External and internal failures produce the *'costs of getting it wrong'*.

Order re-entry, retyping, unnecessary travel and telephone calls, conflict, are just a few examples of the wastage or failure costs often excluded. Every organization must be aware of the costs of getting it wrong, and management needs to obtain some idea how much failure is costing each year.

Clearly, this classification of cost elements may be used to interrogate any internal transformation process. Using the internal customer requirements concept as the standard for failure, these cost assessments can be made wherever information, data, materials, service or artefacts are transferred from one person or one department to another. It is the 'internal' costs of lack of quality that lead to the claim that approximately one-third of *all* our efforts are wasted.

The relationship between the quality related costs of prevention, appraisal, and failure and increasing quality awareness and improvement in the organization is shown in Figure 7.1. Where the quality awareness is low the total quality related costs are high,

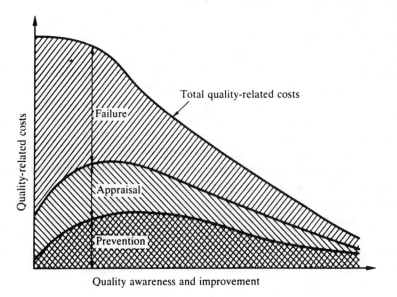

Figure 7.1 *Increasing quality awareness and improvement activities. Source: British Standard BS6143, 1991*

the failure costs predominating. As awareness of the cost to the organization of failure gets off the ground, through initial investment in training, an increase in appraisal costs usually results. As the increased appraisal leads to investigations and further awareness, further investment in prevention is made to improve design features, processes and systems. As the preventive action takes effect, the failure *and* appraisal costs fall and the total costs reduce.

The first presentations of the P–A–F model suggested that there may be an optimum operating level at which the combined costs are at the minimum. The author, however, has not yet found one organization in which the total costs have risen following investment in prevention.

7.5 The process model for quality costing

The P–A–F model for quality costing has a number of drawbacks. In TQM, prevention of problems, defects, errors, waste, etc., is one of the prime functions, but it can be argued that everything a well managed organization does is directed at preventing quality problems. This makes separation of *prevention costs* very difficult. There are clearly a range of prevention activities in any manufacturing or service organization that are integral to ensuring quality but may never be included in the schedule of quality related costs.

It is probably impossible and unnecessary to categorize costs into the three categories of P–A–F. For example, a design review may be considered a prevention cost, an appraisal cost, or even a failure cost, depending on how and where it is used in the process. Another criticism of the P–A–F model is that it focuses attention on cost reduction and plays down, or in some cases even ignores, the positive contribution made to price and sales volume by improved quality.

The most serious criticism of the original P–A–F model presented by Feigenbaum and used in, for example, British Standard 6143 (1981) 'Guide to the determination and use of quality related costs', is that it implies an acceptable 'optimum' quality level above which there is a trade-off between investment in prevention and failure costs. Clearly, this is not in tune with the never ending improvement philosophy of TQM. The key focus of TQM is on process improvement, and a cost categorization scheme that does not consider process costs, such as the P–A–F model, has limitations.

In a total quality related cost system that focuses on processes rather than products or services, the operating costs of generating customer satisfaction will be of prime importance. The so-called 'process cost model', now described in the revised BS6143 (1991) 'Guide to economics of quality', Part 1, sets out a method for applying quality costing to any process or service. It recognizes the importance of process ownership and measurement, and uses process modelling to simplify classification. The categories of the cost of quality (COQ) have been rationalized into the cost of conformance (COC) and the cost of non-conformance (CONC):

$$COQ = COC + CONC$$

The cost of conformance (COC) is the process cost of providing products or services to the required standards, by a given specified process in the most effective manner, i.e. the cost of the ideal process where every activity is carried out according to the requirements first time, every time. The cost of nonconformance (CONC) is the failure cost associated with a process not being operated to the requirements, or the cost due to variability in the process. Part 2 of BS6143 (1991) still deals with the P-A-F model, but without the 'optimum'/minimum cost theory (see Figure 7.1).

Process cost models can be used for any process within an organization and developed for the process by flowcharting. This will identify the key process steps and the parameters that are monitored in the process. The process cost elements should then be identified and recorded under the categories of product/service (outputs), and people, systems, plant or equipment, materials, environment, information (inputs). The COC and CONC for each stage of the process will comprise a list of all the parameters monitored.

Steps in process cost modelling

Process cost modelling is a methodology that lends itself to stepwise analysis, and the following are the key stages in building the model.

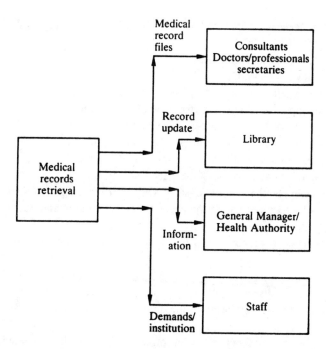

Figure 7.2 *Building the model: identify outputs and customers*

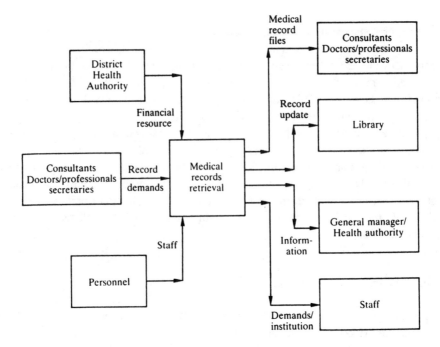

Figure 7.3 *Building the model: identify inputs and suppliers*

1 Choose a key process to be analysed, identify and name it, e.g. Retrieval of Medical Records (Acute Admissions).
2 Define the process and its boundaries.
3 Construct the process diagram:
   (a) Identify the outputs and customers (for example see Figure 7.2).
   (b) Identify the inputs and suppliers (for example see Figure 7.3).
   (c) Identify the controls and resources (for example see Figure 7.4).
4 Flowchart the process and identify the process owners (for example see Figure 7.5). Note, the process owners will form the improvement team.
5 Allocate the activities as COC or CONC (see Table 7.3).
6 Calculate or estimate the quality costs (COQ) at each stage (COC + CONC). Estimates may be required where the accounting system is unable to generate the necessary information.
7 Construct a process cost report (see Table 7.4). The report summary and results are given in Table 7.5.

There are three further steps carried out by the process owners – the improvement team – which take the process forward into the improvement stage:

8 Prioritize the failure costs and select the process stages for improvement through reduction in costs of non-comformance (CONC). This should indicate any require-

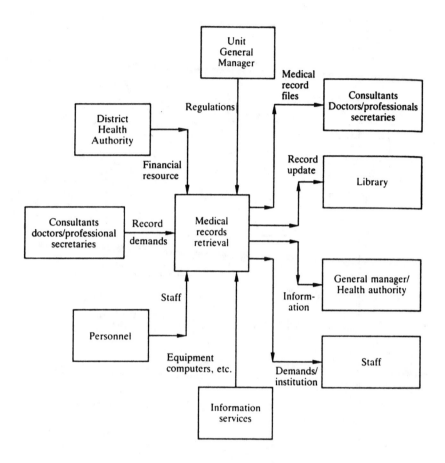

Figure 7.4 *Building the model: identify controls and resources*

ments for investment in prevention activities. An excessive cost of conformance (COC) may suggest the need for process redesign.

9 Review the flowchart to identify the scope for reductions in the cost of conformance. Attempts to reduce COC require a thorough process understanding, and a second flowchart of what the new process should be may help (see Chapter 4).

10 Monitor conformance and non-conformance costs on a regular basis, using the model and review for further improvements.

The process cost model approach must be seen as more than a simple tool to measure the financial implications of the gap between the actual and potential performance of a process. The emphasis given to the process, improving the understanding, and seeing in detail where the costs occur, should be an integral part of quality improvement.

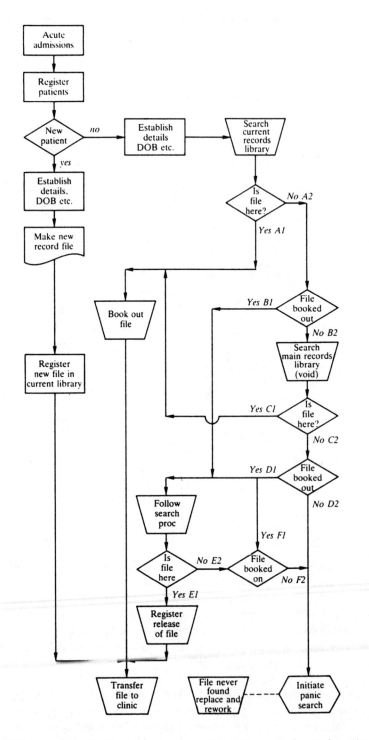

Figure 7.5 *Present practice flowchart for acute admissions, medical records retrieval*

Table 7.3 *Building the model: allocate activities as COC or CONC*

Key activities	COC	CONC
Search for files	Labour cost incurred finding a record while adhering to standard procedure	Labour cost incurred finding a record while unable to adhere to standard procedure
Make up new files	New patient files	Patients whose original files cannot be located
Rework		Cost of labour and materials for all rework files/records never found as a direct consequence of . . .
Duplication		Cost incurred in duplicating existing files

Table 7.4 *Building the model: process cost report*

Process cost report
Process: medical records retrieval (acute admissions)
Process owner: various
Time allocation: 4 days (96 hrs)

Process COC	Process CONC	Cost details Act	Synth	Definition	Source	
	Labour cost incurred finding records	# ref. sample		Cost of time required to find missing records	Medical records	£98
	Cost incurred making up replacement files		#	Labour and material costs multiplied by number of files replaced	Medical records	£40
	Rework		#	Labour and material cost of all rework	Medical records	£50
	Duplication		#		Medical records	£9

Table 7.5 *Process cost model: report summary*

Labour cost

       13.75 hrs x £5.80/hr = £80

       £80 x overhead and contribution factor 22%

       = £98

Replacement costs

       No of files unfound 9

       Cost to replace each file £4.50

       Overall cost £40

Rework costs

       2 x Pathology reports to be retyped £50

Duplication costs

       No of files duplicated 2

       Cost per file £4.50

       Overall cost £9

TOTAL COST £197

RESULTS

Acute admissions operated 24 hrs/day 365 days/year

This project established a cost of nonconformance of approx. £197

This equates to £197 x 365/4 = £17,976

or two personnel fully employed for 12 months

Acknowledgement

The author is grateful to his colleagues Dr Mohamed Zairi and Dr Les Porter, Lecturers at the European Centre for TQM, for their significant contribution to this chapter.

Chapter highlights

Measurement and the improvement cycle

- Traditional performance measures based on cost-accounting information provide little to support TQM, because they do not map process performance and improvements seen by the customer.
- Measurement is important in identifying opportunities, and comparing performance internally and externally. Measures, typically non-financial, are used in process control and performance improvement.
- Some financial indicators, such as ROI, are often inaccurate, irrelevant and too late to be used as measures for performance improvement.
- The Deming cycle of PLAN DO CHECK ACT is a useful design aid for

measurement systems, but firstly four basic questions about measurement should be asked, i.e. why, what, where, and how.

- In answering the question 'how to measure?' progress is important in five main areas: effectiveness, efficiency, productivity, quality, and impact.
- Activity-based costing (ABC) is based on the activities performed being identified and costs traced to them. ABC uses cost drivers, which reflect the demands placed on activities.

The implementation of performance measurement systems

- The value of any measure must be compared with the cost of producing it. All critical parts of the process must be measured, but it is often better to start with the simple measures and improve them.
- Process-owners should take part in defining the performance measures, which must reflect customer requirements.
- Prior to introducing TQM measurement, an audit of existing systems should be carried out to establish their effectiveness, compatibility, relationship and closeness to the customer.
- Following the audit, there are twelve basic steps for implementation, six of which are planning steps.

Benchmarking

- Benchmarking measures an organization's operations, products, and services against those of its competitors. It will establish targets, priorities, and operations, leading to competitive advantage.
- There are four basic types of benchmarking: internal, competitive, functional, and generic. The evolution of benchmarking in an organization is likely to progress through four focuses towards continuous improvement.
- The implementation of benchmarking has fifteen stages, which are categorized into plan, analyse, develop, improve, and review.

Costs of quality

- A competitive product or service based on a balance between quality and cost factors is the principal goal of responsible management.
- The analysis of quality related costs provide a method of assessing the effectiveness of the management of quality and of determining problem areas, opportunities, savings, and action priorities.
- Total quality costs may be categorized into prevention, appraisal, internal failure, and external failure costs, the P–A–F model.
- Prevention costs are associated with doing it right the first time, appraisal costs with checking it is right, and failure costs with getting it wrong.

- When quality awareness in an organization is low, the total quality related costs are high, the failure costs predominating. After an initial rise in costs, mainly through the investment in training and appraisal, increasing investment in prevention causes failure, appraisal and total costs to fall.

The process model for quality costing

- The P–A–F model for quality costing has a number of drawbacks, mainly due to estimating the prevention costs, and its association with an 'optimized' or minimum total cost.
- An alternative – the process cost model – rationalizes costs of quality (COQ) into the cost of conformance (COC) and the cost of non-conformance (CONC). COQ = COC + CONC at each process stage.
- Process cost modelling calls for choice of a process and its definition; construction of a process diagram; identification of outputs and customers, inputs and suppliers, controls and resources; flowcharting the process and identifying owners; allocating activities as COC or CONC; and calculating the costs. A process cost report with summaries and results is produced.
- The failure costs or CONC should be prioritized for improvements.

8

Tools and techniques for quality improvement

8.1 A systematic approach

In the never-ending quest for improvement in the ways processes are operated, numbers and information will form the basis for understanding, decisions and actions; and a thorough data gathering, recording and presentation system is essential.

In addition to the basic elements of a quality system that provide a framework for recording, there exists a set of methods the Japanese quality guru Ishikawa has called the seven basic tools. These should be used to interpret and derive the maximum use from data. The simple methods listed below, of which there are clearly more than seven, will offer any organization means of collecting, presenting, and analysing most of its data:

- Process flowcharting – what is done?
- Check sheets/tally charts – how often is it done?
- Histograms – what do overall variations look like?
- Scatter diagrams – what are the relationships between factors?
- Stratification – how is the data made up?
- Pareto analysis – which are the big problems?
- Cause and effect analysis and Brainstorming (including CEDAC, NGT, and the five whys) – what causes the problems?
- Force-field analysis – what will obstruct or help the change or solution?
- Emphasis curve – which are the most important factors?
- Control charts – which variations to control and how?

Sometimes more sophisticated techniques, such as analysis of variance, regression analysis, and design of experiments, need to be employed.

The effective use of the tools requires their application by the people who actually work on the processes. Their commitment to this will be possible only if they are assured that management cares about improving quality. Managers must show they are serious by establishing a systematic approach and providing the training and implementation support required.

Improvements cannot be achieved without specific opportunities, commonly called problems, being identified or recognized. A focus on improvement opportunities leads to the creation of teams whose membership is determined by their work on and detailed knowledge of the process, and their ability to take improvement action. The teams must then be provided with good leadership and the right tools to tackle the job.

The systematic approach (Figure 8.1) should lead to the use of factual information, collected and presented by means of proven techniques, to open a channel of communications not available to the many organizations that do not follow this or a similar approach to problem solving and improvement. Continuous improvements in the quality of products, services, and processes can often be obtained without major capital investment, if an organization marshals its resources, through an understanding and breakdown of its processes in this way.

By using reliable methods, creating a favourable environment for team based problem solving, and continuing to improve using systematic techniques, the never-ending improvement helix (see Chapter 2) will be engaged. This approach demands the real time management of data, and actions on processes and inputs, not outputs. It will require a change in the language of many organizations from percentage defects, percentage 'prime' product, and number of errors, to *process capability*. The climate must change from the traditional approach of 'If it meets the specification, there are no problems and no further improvements are necessary'. The driving force for this will be the need for better internal and external customer satisfaction levels, which will lead to the continuous improvement question, 'Could we do the job better?'

8.2   Some basic tools and techniques

Understanding processes so that they can be improved by means of the systematic approach requires knowledge of a simple kit of tools or techniques. What follows is a brief description of each technique, but a full description and further examples of some of them may be found in references 1 and 2 (p. 216).

Process flowcharting

The use of this technique, which is described in Chapter 4, ensures a full understanding of the inputs and flow of the process. Without that understanding, it is not possible to draw the correct flowchart of the process. In flowcharting it is important to remember that in all but the smallest tasks no single person is able to complete a chart without help from others. This makes flowcharting a powerful team forming exercise.

Check sheets or tally charts

A check sheet is a tool for data gathering, and a logical point to start in most process control or problem solving efforts. It is particularly useful for recording direct observations and helping to gather in facts rather than opinions about the process. In the recording process it is essential to understand the difference between data and numbers.

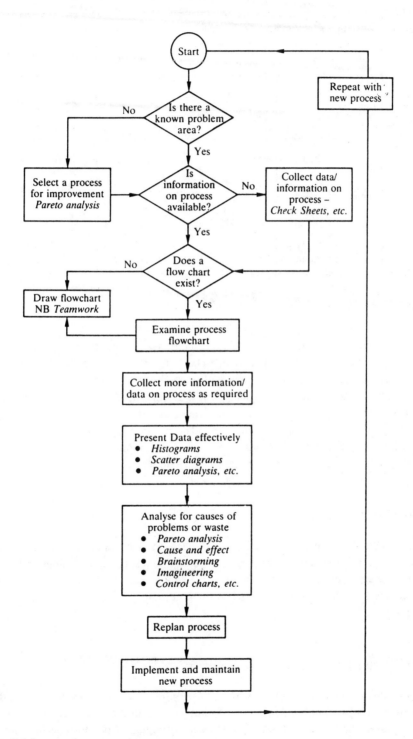

Figure 8.1 *Strategy for process improvement*

Observer *F. Oldsman* Computer No. *148*		Date *26 June*	
Number of observations 95		Total	Percentage
Computer in use	⊔⊔⊤ ⊔⊔⊤ ⊔⊔⊤ ⊔⊔⊤ ⊔⊔⊤ ⊔⊔⊤ ⊔⊔⊤ ⊔⊔⊤ ⊔⊔⊤ ⊔⊔⊤ ⊔⊔⊤	55	57.9
Computer idle	Repairs ⊔⊔⊤	5	5.3
	No work ⊔⊔⊤ ⊔⊔⊤ ll	12	12.6
	Operator absent ⊔⊔⊤ ⊔⊔⊤	10	10.5
	System failure ⊔⊔⊤ ⊔⊔⊤ lll	13	13.7

Figure 8.2 *Activity sampling record in an office*

Data are pieces of information, including numerical information, that are useful in solving problems, or provide knowledge about the state of a process. Numbers alone often represent meaningless measurements or counts, which tend to confuse rather than to enlighten. Numerical data on quality will arise either from counting or measurement.

The use of simple check sheets or tally charts aids the collection of data of the right type, in the right form, at the right time. The objectives of the data collection will determine the design of the record sheet used. An example of a tally chart is shown in Figure 8.2. This gives rise to a frequency distribution.

Histograms

Histograms show, in a very clear pictorial way, the frequency with which a certain value or group of values occurs. They can be used to display both attribute and variable data, and are an effective means of letting the people who operate the process know the results of their efforts. Data gathered on truck turnround times is drawn as a histogram in Figure 8.3.

Scatter diagrams

Depending on the technology, it is frequently useful to establish the association, if any, between two parameters or factors. A technique to begin such an analysis is a simple X-Y plot of the two sets of data. The resulting grouping of points on scatter diagrams (e.g. Figure 8.4) will reveal whether or not a strong or weak, positive or negative,

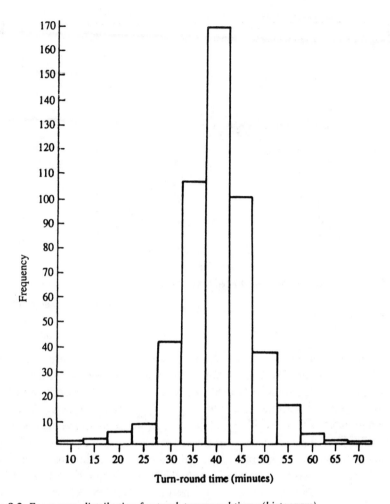

Figure 8.3 *Frequency distribution for truck turnround times (histogram)*

correlation exists between the parameters. The diagrams are simple to construct and easy to interpret, and the absence of correlation can be as revealing as finding that a relationship exists.

Stratification

Stratification is simply dividing a set of data into meaningful groups. It can be used to great effect in combination with other techniques, including histograms and scatter diagrams. If, for example, three shift teams are responsible for the output described by the histogram (a) in Figure 8.5, 'stratifying' the data into the shift groups might produce histograms (b), (c) and (d), and indicate process adjustments that were taking place at shift change overs.

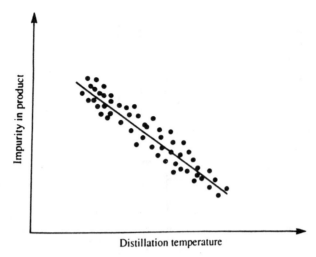

Figure 8.4 *Scatter diagram showing a negative correlation between two variables*

Pareto analysis

If the symptoms or causes of defective output or some other 'effect' are identified and recorded, it will be possible to determine what percentage can be attributed to any cause, and the probable results will be that the bulk (typically 80 per cent) of the errors, waste, or 'effects', derive from a few of the causes (typically 20 per cent). For example, Figure 8.6 shows a *ranked frequency distribution* of incidents in the distribution of a certain product. To improve the performance of the distribution process, therefore, the major incidents (broken bags/drums, truck scheduling, temperature problems) should be tackled first. An analysis of data to identify the major problems is known as *Pareto analysis*, after the Italian economist who realized that approx 90 per cent of the wealth in his country was owned by approx 10 per cent of the people. Without an analysis of this sort, it is far too easy to devote resources to addressing one symptom only because its cause seems immediately apparent.

Cause and effect analysis and brainstorming

A useful way of mapping the inputs that affect quality is the *cause and effect diagram*, also known as the Ishikawa diagram (after its originator) or the fishbone diagam (after its appearance, Figure 8.7). The effect or incident being investigated is shown at the end of a horizontal arrow. Potential causes are then shown as labelled arrows entering the main cause arrow. Each arrow may have other arrows entering it as the principal factors or causes are reduced to their sub-causes, and sub-sub-causes by *brainstorming*.

Brainstorming is a technique used to generate a large number of ideas quickly, and may be used in a variety of situations. Each member of a group, in turn, may be invited to put forward ideas concerning a problem under consideration. Wild ideas are safe to

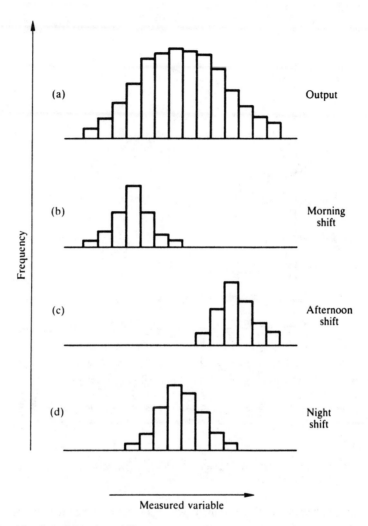

Figure 8.5 *Stratification of data into shift teams*

offer, as criticism or ridicule is not permitted during a brainstorming session. The people taking part do so with equal status to ensure this. The main objective is to create an atmosphere of enthusiam and originality. All ideas offered are recorded for subsequent analysis. The process is continued until all the conceivable causes have been included. The proportion of non-conforming output attributable to each cause, for example, is then measured or estimated, and a simple Pareto analysis identifies the causes that are most worth investigating.

A useful variant on the technique is negative brainstorming and cause/effect analysis. Here the group brainstorms all the things that would need to be done to ensure a negative outcome. For example, in the implementation of TQM, it might be useful for the senior management team to brainstorm what would be needed to make sure TQM

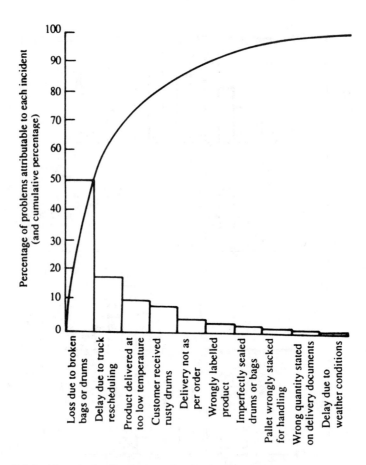

Figure 8.6 *Incidents in the distribution of a chemical product*

was not implemented. Having identified in this way the potential road blocks, it is easier to dismantle them.

CEDAC

A variation on the cause and effect approach, which was developed at Sumitomo Electric and now is claimed to be used by major Japanese corporations across the world, is the cause and effect diagram with addition of cards (CEDAC).

The effect side of a CEDAC chart is a quantified description of the problem, with an agreed and visual quantified target and continually updated results on the progress of achieving it. The cause side of the CEDAC chart uses two different coloured cards for writing facts and ideas. This ensures that the facts are collected and organized before solutions are devised. The basic diagram for CEDAC has the classic fishbone appearance.

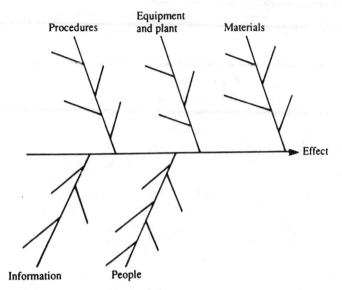

Figure 8.7 *The cause-and-effect, Ishikawa or fishbone diagram*

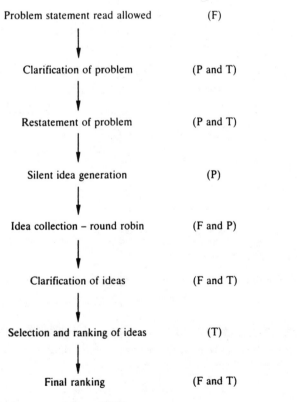

Figure 8.8 *Nominal group technique (NGT)*

Nominal group technique (NGT)

The nominal group technique (NGT) is a particular form of team brainstorming used to prevent domination by particular individuals. It has specific application for multi-level, multi-disciplined teams, where communication boundaries are potentially problematic.

In NGT a carefully prepared written statement of the problem to be tackled is read out by the facilitator (F). Clarification is obtained by questions and answers, and then the individual participants (P) are asked to restate the problem in their own words. The group then discusses the problem until its formulation can be satisfactorily expressed by the team (T). The method is set out in Figure 8.8. NGT results in a set of ranked ideas that are close to a team consensus view, obtained without domination by one or two individuals.

Even greater discipline may be brought to brainstorming by the use of 'Soft systems methodology (SSM)', developed by Peter Checkland.[3] The component stages of SSM are gaining a 'rich understanding' through 'finding out', input/output diagrams, root definition (which includes the so-called CATWOE analysis: customers, 'actors', transformations, 'world-view', owners, environment), conceptualization, comparison, and recommendation.

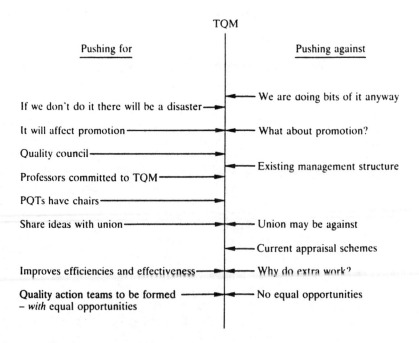

Figure 8.9 *Force-field analysis*

Force field analysis

Force field analysis is a technique used to identify the forces that either obstruct or help a change that needs to be made. It is similar to negative brainstorming-cause/effect analysis and helps to plan how to overcome the barriers to change or improvement. It may also provide a measure of the difficulty in achieving the change.

The process begins with a team describing the desired change or improvement, and defining and objectives or solution. Having prepared the basic force field diagram, it identifies the favourable/positive/driving forces and the unfavourable/negative/ restraining forces, by brainstorming. These forces are placed in opposition on the diagram and, if possible, rated for their potential influence on the ease of implementation. The results are evaluated. Then comes the preparation of an action plan to overcome some of the restraining forces, and increase the driving forces. Figure 8.9 shows a force field analysis produced by a senior management team considering the implementation of TQM in its organization.

The emphasis curve

This is a technique for ranking a number of factors, each of which cannot be readily quantified in terms of cost, frequency of occurrence, etc., in priority order. It is almost impossible for the human brain to make a judgement of the relative importance of more than three or four non-quantifiable factors. It is, however, relatively easy to judge which is the most important of two factors, using some predetermined criteria. The emphasis curve technique uses this fact by comparing only two factors at any one time. The procedural steps for using the emphasis curve chart (matrix) are given by Oakland (1993).[4]

Control charts

A control chart is a form of traffic signal whose operation is based on evidence from the small samples taken at random during a process. A green light is given when the process should be allowed to run. All too often processes are 'adjusted' on the basis of a single measurement, check or inspection, a practice that can make a process much more variable than it is already. The equivalent of an amber light appears when trouble is possibly imminent. The red light shows that there is practically no doubt that the process has changed in some way and that it must be investigated and corrected to prevent production of defective material or information. Clearly, such a scheme can be introduced only when the process is 'in control'. Since samples taken are usually small, there are risks of errors, but these are small, calculated risks and not blind ones. The risk calculations are based on various frequency distributions.

These charts should be made easy to understand and interpret and they can become, with experience, sensitive diagnostic tools to be used by operating staff and first-line supervision to prevent errors or defective output being produced. Time and effort spent to explain the working of the charts to all concerned are never wasted.

The most frequently used control charts are simple run charts, where the data is plotted on a graph against time or sample number. There are different types of control charts for variables and attribute data: for variables mean ($\overline{X}$) and range (**R**) charts are used together; number defective or **np** charts and proportion defective or **p** charts are the most common ones for attributes. Other charts found in use are moving average and range charts, number of defects (**c** and **u**) charts, and cumulative sum (cusum) charts. The latter offer very powerful management tools for the detection of trends or changes in attributes and variable data.

The cusum chart is a graph that takes a little longer to draw than the conventional control chart, but gives a lot more information. It is particularly useful for plotting the evolution of processes, because it presents data in a way that enables the eye to separate true changes from a background of random variation. Cusum charts can detect small changes in data very quickly, and may be used for the control of variables and attributes. In essence, a reference or 'target value' is subtracted from each successive sample observation, and the result accumulated. Values of this cumulative sum are plotted, and 'trend lines' may be drawn on the resulting graphs. If they are approximately horizontal, the value of the variable is about the same as the target value. A downward slope shows a value less than the target, and an upward slope a value greater. The technique is very useful, for example, in comparing sales forecast with actual sales figures.

Figure 8.10 shows a comparison of an ordinary run chart and a cusum chart that have been plotted from the same data – errors in samples of 100 invoices. The change, which is immediately obvious on the cusum chart, is difficult to detect on the conventional control chart.

The range of type and use of control charts is now very wide, and within the present text it is not possible to indicate more than the basic principles underlying such charts.[5]

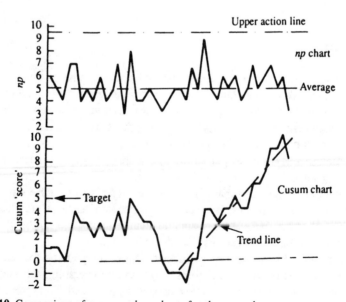

Figure 8.10 *Comparison of cusum and np charts for the same data*

8.3   Failure mode, effect and criticality analysis (FMECA)

It is possible to analyse products, services and processes to determine possible modes of failure and their effects on the performance of the product or operation of the process or service system. Failure mode and effect analysis (FMEA) is the study of potential failures to determine their effects. If the results of an FMEA are ranked in order of seriousness, then the word CRITICALITY is added to give FMECA. The primary objective of a FMECA is to determine the features of product design, production or operation and distribution that are critical to the various modes of failure, in order to reduce failure. It uses all the available experience and expertise, from marketing, design, technology, purchasing, production/operation, distribution, service, etc., to identify the importance levels or criticality of potential problems and stimulate action to reduce these levels. FMECA should be a major consideration at the design stage of a product or service (see Chapter 3).

The elements of a complete FMECA are:

- *Failure mode* – the anticipated conditions of operation are used as the background to study the most probable failure mode, location and mechanism of the product or system and its components.
- *Failure effect* – the potential failures are studied to determine their probable effects on the performance of the whole product, process, or service, and the effects of the various components on each other.
- *Failure criticality* – the potential failures on the various parts of the product or service system are examined to determine the severity of each failure effect in terms of lowering of performance, safety hazard, total loss of function, etc.

FMECA may be applied to any stage of design, development, production/ operation or use, but since its main aim is to prevent failure, it is most suitably applied at the design stage to identify and eliminate causes. With more complex product or service systems, it may be appropriate to consider these as smaller units or sub-systems, each one being the subject of a separate FMECA.

Special FMECA pro-formas are available and they set out the steps of the analysis as follows:

1   Identify the product or system components, or process function.
2   List all possible failure modes of each component.
3   Set down the effects that each mode of failure would have on the function of the product or system.
4   List all the possible causes of each failure mode.
5   Assess numerically the failure modes on a scale from 1 to 10. Experience and reliability data should be used, together with judgement, to determine the values, on a scale 1-10, for:
    P the probability of each failure mode occurring (1 = low, 10 = high).
    S the seriousness or criticality of the failure (1 = low, 10 = high).
    D the difficulty of detecting the failure before the product or service is used by the consumer (1 = easy, 10 = very difficult). See Table 8.2.

6 Calculate the product of the ratings, C = P x S x D, known as the criticality index or risk priority number (RPN) for each failure mode. This indicates the relative priority of each mode in the failure prevention activities.
7 Indicate briefly the corrective action required and, if possible, which department or person is responsible and the expected completion date.

Table 8.2 *Probability and seriousness of failure and difficulty of detection*

Value	1	2	3	4	5	6	7	8	9	10
P	low chance of occurrence ———————————————— almost certain to occur									
S	not serious, minor nuisance ——————————— total failure, safety hazard									
D	easily detected ————————————————————— unlikely to be detected									

When the criticality index has been calculated, the failures may be ranked accordingly. It is usually advisable, therefore, to determine the value of C for each failure mode before completing the last columns. In this way the action required against each item can be judged in the light of the ranked severity and the resources available.

Moments of truth

(MoT) is a concept that has much in common with FMEA. The idea was created by Jan Carlzon,[6] CEO of Scandinavian Airlines (SAS) and was made popular by Albrecht and Zemke.[7] An MoT is the moment in time when a customer first comes into contact with the people, systems, procedures, or products of an organization, which leads to the customer making a judgement about the quality of the organization's services or products.

In MoT analysis the points of potential dissatisfaction are identified proactively, beginning with the assembly of process flow chart type diagrams. Every small step taken by a customer in his/her dealings with the organization's people, products, or services is recorded. It may be dificult or impossible to identify all the MoTs, but the systematic approach should lead to a minimalization of the number and severity of unexpected failures, and this provides the link with FMEA.

8.4   Statistical process control (SPC)

The responsibility for quality in any transformation process must lie with the operators of that process. To fulfil this responsibility, however, people must be provided with the tools necessary to:

- Know whether the process is capable of meeting the requirements.
- Know whether the process is meeting the requirements at any point in time.
- Make correct adjustment to the process or its inputs when it is not meeting the requirements.

The techniques of statistical process control (SPC) will greatly assist in these stages. To begin to monitor and analyse any process, it is necessary first of all to identify what the process is, and what the inputs and outputs are. Many processes are easily understood and relate to known procedures, e.g. drilling a hole, compressing tablets, filling cans with paint, polymerizing a chemical using catalysts. Others are less easily identifiable, e.g. servicing a customer, delivering a lecture, storing a product in a warehouse, inputting to a computer. In many situations it can be extremely difficult to define the process. For example, if the process is inputting data into a computer terminal, it is vital to know if the scope of the process includes obtaining and refining the data, as well as inputting. Process definition is so important because the inputs and outputs change with the scope of the process.

Once the process is specified, the inputs and suppliers, outputs and customers can also be defined, together with the requirements at each of the interfaces. The most difficult areas in which to do this are in non-manufacturing organizations or parts of organizations, but careful use of the questioning method, introduced in Chapter 1, should release the necessary information. Examples of outputs in non-manufacturing include training courses or programmes, typed letters, statements of intent (following a decision process), invoices, share certificates, deliveries of consignments, reports, serviced motor cars, purchase orders, wage slips, forecasts, material requirements plans, legal contracts, design change documents, clean offices, recruited trainees, and advertisements. The list is endless. Some processes may produce primary and secondary outputs, such as a telephone call answered *and* a message delivered.

If the requirements are not clarified or quantified, they are often assumed or estimated. Even if this does not lead to direct complaints, it will lead to waste – lost time, confusion – and perhaps lost customers. It is salutary for some suppliers of internal customers to realize that the latter can sometimes find new suppliers if their true requirements are not properly identified and/or repeatedly not met.

Inputs to processes include:

1 Equipment, tools, or plant required.
2 Materials – including paper.
3 Information – including the specification for the outputs.
4 Methods or procedures – including instructions.
5 People (and the inputs they provide, such as skills, training, knowledge, etc.).
6 Records.

Again this is not an exhaustive list.

Prevention of failure in any transformation is possible only if the process definition, flow, inputs, and outputs are properly documented and agreed. The documentation of procedures will allow reliable data about the process itself to be collected, analysis to be performed, and action to be taken to improve the process and prevent failure or non-conformance with the requirements. The target in the operation of any process is the total avoidance of failure. If the idea of no failures or error free work is not adopted, at least as a target, then it certainly will never be achieved.

All processes can be monitored and brought 'under control' by gathering and using data – to measure the performance of the process and provide the feedback required for corrective action, where necessary. Statistical process control (SPC) methods, backed by management commitment and good organization, provide objective means of *controlling* quality in any transformation process, whether used in the manufacture of artefacts, the provision of services, or the transfer of information.

SPC is not only a tool kit, it is a strategy for reducing variability, the cause of most quality problems: variation in products, in times of deliveries, in ways of doing things, in materials, in people's attitudes, in equipment and its use, in maintenance practices, in everything. Control by itself is not sufficient. Total quality management requires that the processes should be improved continually by reducing variability. This is brought about by studying all aspects of the process, using the basic question: 'Could we do this job more consistently and on target?' The answer drives the search for improvements. This significant feature of SPC means that it is not constrained to measuring conformance, and that it is intended to lead to action on processes that are operating within the 'specification' to minimize variability.

Process control is essential, and SPC forms a vital part of the TQM strategy. Incapable and inconsistent processes render the best design impotent and make supplier quality assurance irrelevant. Whatever process is being operated, it must be reliable and consistent. SPC can be used to achieve this objective.

In the application of SPC there is often an emphasis on techniques rather than on the implied wider managerial strategies. It is worth repeating that SPC is not only about plotting charts on the walls of a plant or office, it must become part of the company-wide adoption of TQM and act as the focal point of never-ending improvement. Changing an organization's environment into one in which SPC can operate properly may take several years rather than months. For many companies SPC will bring a new approach, a new 'philosophy', but the importance of the statistical techniques should not be disguised. Simple presentation of data using diagrams, graphs, and charts should become the means of communication concerning the state of control of processes. It is on this understanding that improvements will be based.

The SPC system

A systematic study of any process through answering the questions:

> Are we capable of doing the job correctly?
> Do we continue to do the job correctly?
> Have we done the job correctly?
> Could we do the job more consistently and on target?[8]

provides knowledge of the *process capability* and the sources of non-conforming outputs. This information can then be fed back quickly to marketing, design, and the 'technology' functions. Knowledge of the current state of a process also enables a more balanced judgement of equipment, both with regard to the tasks within its capability and its rational utilization.

Statistical process control procedures exist because there is variation in the characteristics of all material, articles, services, and people. The inherent variability in each transformation process causes the output from it to vary over a period of time. If this variability is considerable, it is impossible to predict the value of a characteristic of any single item or at any point in time. Using statistical methods, however, it is possible to take meagre knowledge of the output and turn it into meaningful statements that may then be used to describe the process itself. Hence, statistically based process control procedures are designed to divert attention from individual pieces of data and focus it on the process as a whole. SPC techniques may be used to measure and control the degree of variation of any purchased materials, services, processes, and products, and to compare this, if required, to previously agreed specifications. In essence, SPC techniques select a representative, simple, random sample from the 'population', which can be an input to or an output from a process. From an analysis of the sample it is possible to make decisions regarding the current performance of the process.

8.5   Quality improvement techniques in non-manufacturing

Organizations that embrace the TQM concepts should recognize the value of SPC techniques in areas such as sales, purchasing, invoicing, finance, distribution, training, and in the service sector generally. These are outside the traditional areas for SPC use, but SPC needs to be seen as an organization-wide approach to reducing variation with the specific techniques integrated into a programme of change throughout. A Pareto analysis, a histogram, a flowchart, or a control chart is a vehicle for communication. Data are data and, whether the numbers represent defects or invoice errors, weights or delivery times, or the information relates to machine settings, process variables, prices, quantities, discounts, sales or supply points, is irrelevant – the techniques can always be used.

In the author's experience, some of the most exciting applications of SPC have emerged from organizations and departments which, when first introduced to the methods, could see little relevance in them to their own activities. Following appropriate training, however, they have learned how to, for example:

- *Pareto analyse* errors on invoices to customers and industry injury data.
- *Brainstorm and cause and effect analyse* reasons for late payment and poor purchase invoice matching.
- *Histogram* defects in invoice matching and arrival of trucks at certain times during the day.
- *Control chart* the weekly demand of a product.

Distribution staff have used control charts to monitor the proportion of late deliveries, and Pareto analysis and force field analysis to look at complaints about the distribution system. Word processor operators have been seen using cause and effect analysis, NGT and histograms to represent errors in the output from their service. Moving average and cusum charts have immense potential for improving processes in the marketing area.

Those organizations that have made most progress in implementing continuous improvement have recognized at an early stage that SPC is for the whole organization. Restricting it to traditional manufacturing or operational activities means that a window of opportunity for improvement has been closed. Applying the methods and techniques outside manufacturing will make it easier, not harder, to gain maximum benefit from an SPC programme.

Sales, marketing and customer-service are areas often resistant to SPC training on the basis that it is difficult to apply. Personnel in these vital functions need to be educated in SPC methods for two reasons:

1   They need to understand the way the manufacturing or service producing processes in their organizations work. This will enable them to have more meaningful dialogues with customers about the whole product/service/delivery system capability and control. It will also enable them to influence customers' thinking about specifications and create a competitive advantage from improving process capabilities.
2   They will be able to improve the marketing processes and activities. A significant part of the sales and marketing effort is clearly associated with building relationships, which are best built on facts (data) and not opinions. There are also opportunities to use SPC techniques directly in such areas as forecasting demand levels and market requirements, monitoring market penetration, marketing control, and product development, all of which must be viewed as processes.

SPC has considerable applications for non-manufacturing organizations, including universities! Data and information on patients in hospitals, students in universities, polytechnics, colleges and schools, people who pay (and do not pay) tax, draw social security benefit, shop at Sainsbury's or Macy's, are available in abundance. If the information were to be used in a systematic way, and all operations treated as processes, far better decisions could be made concerning past, present, and future performances of some service sectors.

Chapter highlights

A systematic approach

- Numbers and information will form the basis for understanding, decisions, and actions in never ending improvement.
- A set of simple tools is needed to interpret fully and derive maximum use from data. More sophisticated techniques may need to be employed occasionally.
- The effective use of the tools requires the commitment of the people who work on the processes. This in turn needs management support and the provision of training.

Some basic tools and techniques

- The basic tools and the questions answered are:

Process flow charting	– what is done?
Check/tally charts	– how often is it done?
Histograms	– what do variations look like?
Scatter diagrams	– what are the relationships between factors?
Stratification	– how is the data made up?
Pareto analysis	– which are the big problems?
Cause and effect analysis and brainstorming (also CEDAC and NGT)	– what causes the problem?
Force-field analysis	– what will obstruct or help the change or solution?
Emphasis curve	– which are the most important factors?
Control charts (including cusum)	– which variations to control and how?

Failure mode, effect and criticality analysis (FMECA)

- FMEA is the study of potential product, service, or process failures and their effects. When the results are ranked in order of criticality, the technique is called FMECA. Its aim is to reduce the probablity of failure.
- The elements of a complete FMECA are to study failure mode, effect, and criticality. It may be applied at any stage of design, development, production/operation, or use.
- Moments of truth (MoT) is a similar concept to FMEA. It is the moment in time when a customer first comes into contact with an organization, leading to a judgement about quality.

Statistical process control

- People operating a process must know whether it is capable of meeting the requirements, know whether it is actually doing so at any time, and make correct adjustments when it is not. SPC techniques will help here.
- Before using SPC, it is necessary to identify what the process is, what the inputs/outputs are, and how the suppliers and customers and their requirements are defined. The most difficult areas for this can be in non-manufacturing.
- All processes can be monitored and brought 'under control' by gathering and using data. SPC methods, with management commitment, provide objective means of controlling quality in any transformation process.
- SPC is not only a toolkit, it is a strategy for reducing variability, part of never ending improvement. This is achieved by answering the following questions:

  Are we capable of doing the job correctly?
  Do we continue to do the job correctly?
  Have we done the job correctly?
  Could we do the job more consistently and on target?

This provides knowledge of process capability.

Quality improvement techniques in non-manufacturing

- SPC techniques have value in the service sector and in the non-manufacturing areas, such as marketing and sales, purchasing, invoicing, finance, distribution, training and personnel.

References

1   John Oakland, Total Quality Management, 2nd edition, Butterworth-Heinemann, Oxford, 1993.
2   John Oakland and Roy Followell, *Statistical Process Control*, 2nd edition, Butterworth-Heinemann, Oxford, 1990.
3   Peter Checkland, *Soft Systems Methodology in Action*, Wiley, 1990.
4   See Oakland and Followell, *op. cit.*
5   *Ibid.*
6   Jan Carlzon, *Moments of Truth*, Harper & Row, 1987.
7   Albrecht, K. and Zemke, R., *Service America! – doing business in the new economy*, Dow Jones-Irwin, Homewood, Ill. (USA), 1985.
8   This system for process capability and control is based on Frank Price's very practical framework for thinking about quality in manufacturing:

Can we make it OK?
Are we making it OK?
Have we made it OK?
Could we make it better?

which he presented in this excellent book *Right First Time*.

Some additional techniques for process improvement

9.1 Seven new tools for quality design

Seven new tools may be used as part of quality function deployment (see Chapter 3) to improve the innovation processes. These do not replace the basic systematic tools described previously in Chapter 8, neither are they extensions of these. The new tools are systems and documentation methods used to achieve success in design by identifying objectives and intermediate steps in the finest detail. The seven new tools are:

1 Affinity diagram.
2 Interrelationship digraph.
3 Tree diagram.

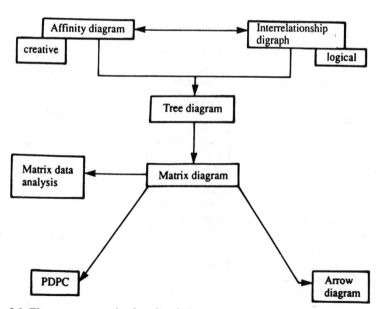

Figure 9.1 *The seven new tools of quality design*

4   Matrix diagram or quality table.
5   Matrix data analysis.
6   Process decision programme chart (PDPC).
7   Arrow diagram.

The tools are interrelated, as shown in Figure 9.1. The promotion and use of the tools by the QFD Team should obtain better designs in less time. They are summarized below and described in more detail in reference 1.

1   Affinity diagram

This is used to gather large amounts of language data (ideas, issues opinions) and organizes them into groupings based on the natural relationship between the items. In other words, it is a form of brainstorming. The affinity diagram is not recommended when a problem is simple or requires a very quick solution.

The output of the exercise is a compilation of a maximum number of ideas under a limited number of major headings (see, for example, Figure 9.2). This data can then be used with other tools to define areas for attack. One of these tools is the interrelationship digraph.

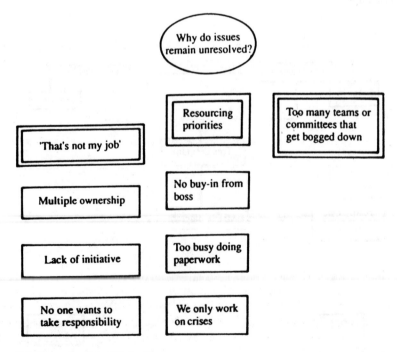

Figure 9.2 *Example of an affinity diagram*

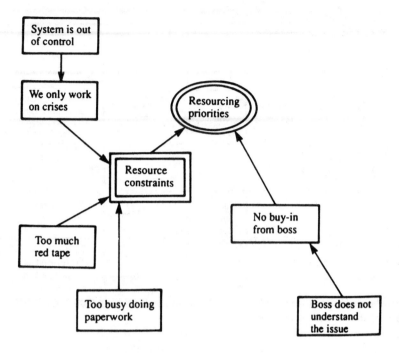

Figure 9.3 *Example of the interrelationship digraph*

2 Interrelationship digraph

This tool is designed to take a central idea, issue or problem, and map out the logical or sequential links among related factors. While this still requires a very creative process, the interrelationship digraph begins to draw the logical connections that surface in the affinity diagram.

The interrelationship digraph is adaptable to both specific operational issues and general organizational questions. For example, a classic use of this tool at Toyota focused on all the factors behind the establishment of a 'billboard system' as part of their JIT programme. On the other hand, it has also been used to deal with issues underlying the problem of getting top management support for TQM.

Figure 9.3 gives an example of a simple interrelationship digraph.

3 Systems flow/tree diagram

The systems flow/tree diagram (usually referred to as a tree diagram) is used to systematically map out the full range of activities that must be accomplished in order to reach a desired goal. It may also be used to identify all the factors contributing to a problem under consideration. Major factors identified by an interrelationship digraph can be used as inputs for a tree diagram. One of the strengths of this method is that it forces the user to examine the logical and chronological link between tasks. This assists

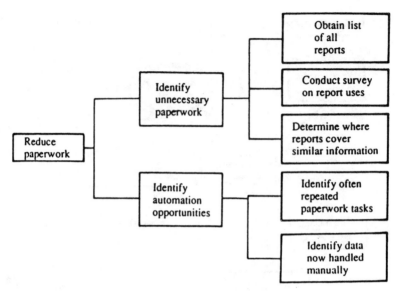

Figure 9.4 *An example of the tree diagram*

in preventing a natural tendency to jump directly from goal or problem statement to solution (Ready . . . Fire . . . Aim!).

An example is shown in Figure 9.4.

4 Matrix diagrams

The matrix diagram is the heart of the seven new tools and the house of quality described in Chapter 3. The purpose of the matrix diagram is to outline the interrelationships and correlations between tasks, functions or characteristics, and to show their relative importance. There are many versions of the matrix diagram, but the most widely used is a simple L-shaped matrix known as the *quality table*.

Quality table

In a *quality table* customer demands (the whats) are analysed with respect to substitute quality characterisics (the hows), e.g. Figure 9.5. Correlations between the two are categorized as strong, moderate and possible. The customer demands shown on the left of the matrix are determined in co-operation with the customer. This effort requires a kind of a verbal 'ping-pong' with the customer to be truly effective: ask the customer what he wants, write it down, show it to him and ask him if that is what he meant, then revise and repeat the process as necessary. This should be done in a joint meeting with the customer, if at all possible. It is often of value to use a tree diagram to give structure to this effort.

Substitute quality characteristics

	MFR	Ash	Importance	Current	Best competitor	Plan	IR	SP	RQW
No film-breaks	○ 17	▲ 6	4	4	4	4	1	○	5.6
High rates	◉ 23		3	3	4	4	1.3		4.6
Low gauge variability	◉ 37	▲ 7	4	3	4	4	1.3	○	7.3

Customer demands

◉ Strong correlation
○ Some correlation
▲ Possible correlation

IR Improvement ratio

SP Sales point

RQW Relative quality weight

Figure 9.5 *An example of the matrix diagram (quality table)*

The right side of the chart is often used to compare current performance to competitors' performance, company plan, and potential sales points with reference to the customer demands. Weights are given to these items to obtain a 'relative quality weight', which can be used to identify the key customer demands. The relative quality weight is then used with the correlations identified on the matrix to determine the key quality characteristics.

A modification that is added to create the house of quality table is a second matrix that explores the correlations between the quality characteristics. This is done so that errors caused by the manipulation of variables in a one-at-a-time fashion can be avoided. This also gives indications of where designed experiments would be of use in the design process. In the training required for use of this technique, several hours should be dedicated to a detailed explanation of the steps in the construction of a quality table, and the system to be used to compare numerically the various items.

T-shaped matrix diagram

The T-shaped matrix is nothing more than the combination of two L-shaped matrix diagrams. It is based on the premise that two separate sets of items are related to a third set. Therefore A items are somehow related to both B and C items.

5   Matrix data analysis

Matrix data analysis is used to take data displayed in a matrix diagram and arrange them so that they can be more easily viewed and show the strength of the relationship between variables. It is used most often in marketing and product research. The concept

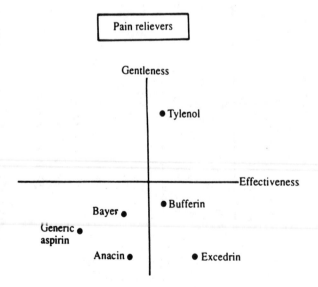

Figure 9.6 *An example of matrix data analysis*

behind matrix data analysis is fairly simple, but its execution (including data gathering) can be complex.

A good idea of the uses and value of the construction of a chart for matrix data analysis may be shown in a simple example in which types of pain relievers are compared based on gentleness and effectiveness (Figure 9.6). This information could be used together with some type of demographic analysis to develop a marketing plan. Based on the information, advertising and product introduction could be effectively tailored for specific areas. New product development could also be carried out to attack specific niches in markets that would be profitable.

6   Process decision programme chart

A process decision programme chart (PDPC) is used to map out each event and contingency that can occur when progressing from a problem statement to its solution. The PDPC is used to anticipate the unexpected and plan for it. It includes plans for counter-measures on deviations. The PDPC is related to a failure mode and effect

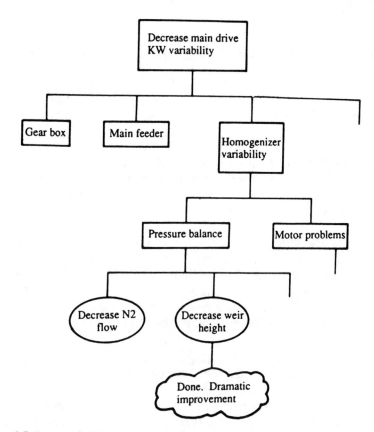

Figure 9.7 *Process decision programme chart*

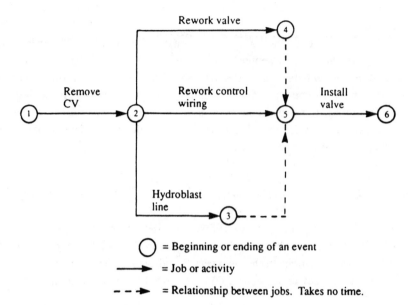

Figure 9.8 *The arrow diagram*

analysis and its structure is similar to that of a tree diagram. An example of the PDPC is shown in Figure 9.7.

7   Arrow diagram

The arrow diagram is used to plan or schedule a task. To use it, one must know the sub-task sequence and duration. This tool is essentially the same as the standard Gantt chart. Although it is a simple and well known tool for planning work, it is surprising how often it is ignored. The arrow diagram is useful in analysing a repetitive job in order to make it more efficient (see Figure 9.8).

What has been described in this section is a system for improving the design of products, processes, and services by means of seven new tools, sometimes called the quality function deployment tools. For the most part the seven tools are neither new nor revolutionary, but rather a compilation and modification of some tools that have been around for a long time. The tools do not replace statistical methods or other tools, but they are meant to be used together as part of the design process.

9.2   Taguchi methods for process improvement

Genichi Taguchi is a noted Japanese engineering specialist who has advanced 'quality engineering' as a technology to reduce costs and improve quality simultaneously. The popularity of Taguchi methods today testifies to the merit of his philosophies on quality. The basic elements of Taguchi's ideas, which have been extended here to all aspects of product, service and process quality, may be considered under four main headings.

1   Total loss function

An important aspect of the quality of a product or service is the total loss to society that it generates. Taguchi's definition of product quality as 'the loss imparted to society from the time a product is shipped', is rather strange, since the word *loss* denotes the very opposite of what is normally conveyed by using the word *quality*. The essence of his definition is that the smaller the loss generated by a product or service from the time it is transferred to the customer, the more desirable it is.

The main advantage of this idea is that it encourages a new way of thinking about investment in quality improvement projects, which become attractive when the resulting savings to customers are greater than the cost of improvements.

Taguchi claims with some justification that any variation about a target value for a product or process parameter causes loss to the customer. The loss may be some simple inconvenience, but it can represent actual cash losses, owing to rework or badly fitting parts, and it may well appear as loss of customer goodwill and eventually market share. The loss (or cost) increases exponentially as the parameter value moves away from the target, and is at a minimum when the product or service is at the target value.

2   Design of products, services and processes

In any product or service development three stages may be identified: product or service design, process design, and production or operations. Each of these overlapping stages has many steps, the output of one often being the input to others. The output/input transfer points between steps clearly affect the quality and cost of the final product or service. The complexity of many modern products and services demands that the crucial role of design be recognized. Indeed the performance of the quality products from the Japanese automotive, banking, camera, and machine tool industries can be traced to the robustness of their product and process designs.

The prevention of problems in using products or services under varying operating and environmental conditions must be built in at the design stage. Equally, the costs during production or operation are determined very much by the actual manufacturing or operating process. Controls, including SPC methods, added to processes to reduce imperfections at the operational stage are expensive, and the need for controls *and* the production of non-conformance can be reduced by correct initial designs of the process itself.

Taguchi distinguishes between *off-line* and *on-line* quality control methods, 'quality control' being used here in the very broad sense to include quality planning, analysis and improvement. Off-line QC uses technical aids in the *design* of products and processes, whereas on-line methods are technical aids for controlling quality and costs in the *production* of products or services. Too often the off-line QC methods focus on evaluation rather than improvement. The belief by some people (often based on experience!) that it is unwise to buy a new model of a motor car 'until the problems have been sorted out' testifies to the fact that insufficient attention is given to improvement at the product and process design stages. In other words, the bugs should be removed *before* not after product launch. This may be achieved in some organizations by replacing detailed quality and reliability evaluation methods with approximate estimates, and using the liberated resources to make improvements.

3   Reduction of variation

The objective of a continuous quality improvement programme is to reduce the variation of key products performance characteristics about their target values. The widespread practice of setting specifications in terms of simple upper and lower limits conveys the wrong idea that the customer is satisfied with all values inside the specification band, but is suddenly not satisfied when a value slips outside one of the limits. The practice of stating specifications as tolerance intervals only can lead manufacturers to produce and despatch goods whose parameters are just inside the specification band. Owing to the interdependence of many parameters of component parts and assemblies, this is likely to lead to quality problems.

The target value should be stated and specified as the ideal, with known variability about the mean. For those performance characteristics that cannot be measured on the continuous scale, the next best thing is an ordered categorical scale such as excellent, very good, good, fair, unsatisfactory, very poor, rather than the binary classification of 'good' or 'bad' that provides meagre information with which the variation reduction process can operate.

Taguchi has introduced a three-step approach to assigning nominal values and tolerances for product and process parameters:

(a) System design – the application of scientific engineering and technical knowledge to produce a basic functional prototype design. This requires a fundamental understanding of the needs of the customer *and* the production environment.
(b) Parameter design – the identification of the settings of product or process parameters that reduce the sensitivity of the designs to sources of variation. This requires a study of the whole process system design to achieve the most robust operational settings, in terms of tolerance to ranges of the input variables. This is similar to the experiments needed to identify the plant varieties that can tolerate variations in weather conditions, soil and handling. Manual processes that can tolerate the ranges of dimensions of the human body provide another example.
(c) Tolerance design – the determination of tolerances around the nominal settings identified by parameter design. This requires a trade-off between the customer's loss due to performance variation and the increase in production or operational costs.

4   Statistically planned experiments

Taguchi has pointed out that statistically planned experiments should be used to identify the settings of product and process parameters that will reduce variation in performance. He classifies the variables that affect the performance into two categories: design parameters and sources of 'noise'. As we have seen earlier, the nominal settings of the *design parameters* define the specification for the product or process. The *sources of noise* are all the variables that cause the performance characteristics to deviate from the target values. The *key* noise factors are those that represent the major sources of variability, and these should be identified and included in the experiments to design the parameters at which the effect of the noise factors on the performance is minimum. This is done by systematically varying the design parameter settings and comparing the effect of the noise factors for each experimental run.

Statistically planned experimentss may be used to identify:

(a) The design parameters that have a large influence on the product or performance characteristic.
(b) The design parameters that have no influence on the performance characteristics (the tolerances of these parameters may be relaxed).
(c) The settings of design parameters at which the effect of the sources of noise on the performance characteristic is minimal.
(d) The settings of design parameters that will reduce cost without adversely affecting quality.[2]

Taguchi methods have stimulated a great deal of interest in the application of statistically planned experiments to product and process designs. The use of 'design of experiments' to improve industrial products and processes is not new – Tippett used these techniques in the textile industry more than 50 years ago. What Taguchi has done, however, is to acquaint us with the scope of these techniques in off-line quality control.

Taguchi's methods, like all others, should not be used in isolation, but be an integral part of continuous improvement.

9.3   Adding the tools to the TQM model

Having looked at some of the many tools and techniques of measurement and improvement, we see that the generic term 'tools' may be added, as the second hard management necessity, to the TQM model (Figure 9.9). The systems manage the processes, and the tools are used to progress further round the improvement cycle by creating better customer–supplier relationships, both externally and internally. They provide the means for analysis, correlation and prediction of what *action* to take on the systems.

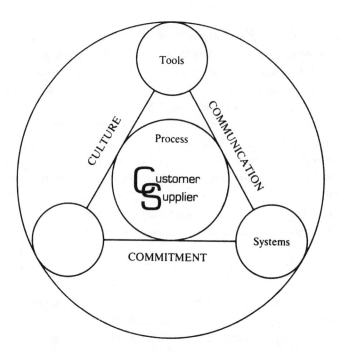

Figure 9.9 *Total quality management model – the basic tools*

Chapter highlights

Seven new tools for quality design

- Seven new tools may be used as part of quality function deployment (QFD, see Chapter 3) to improve the innovation processes. These are systems and documentation methods for identifying objectives and intermediate steps in the finest detail.
- The seven new tools are: affinity diagram, interrelationship digraph, tree diagram, matrix diagrams or quality table, matrix data anaysis, process decision programme chart (PDPC), and arrow diagram.
- The tools are interrelated and their promotion and use should lead to better designs in less time. They work best when people from all parts of an organization are using them. Some of the tools can be used in problem solving activities not related to design.

Taguchi methods for process improvement

- Genichi Taguchi has advanced 'quality engineering' as a technology to reduce costs and make improvements.
- Taguchi's approach may be classified under four headings; total loss function;

design of products, services and processes; reduction in variation; and statistically planned experiments.
- Taguchi methods, like all others, should not be used in isolation, but as an integral part of continuous improvement.

Adding the tools to the TQM model

A second hard management necessity – the tools – may be added, with the systems, to the TQM model to progress further round the never-ending improvement cycle.

References

1 John S. Oakland, *Total Quality Management*, 2nd edition, Butterworth-Heinemann, Oxford, 1993.
2 Roland Caulcutt, *Statistics in Research and Development*, 2nd edition, Chapman and Hall, London, 1991.

Case studies

C5

Measuring improvement through total quality: the Shorts experience

Introduction

Shorts Brothers launched their Total Quality programme several years ago. Since then all personnel have received quality improvement training and over 1300 quality improvement projects have been completed, with estimated benefits exceeding £46m per year. The company's efforts have received national recognition, with Shorts winning both the British Quality Award and the Northern Ireland Quality Award.

These results were achieved in spite of the uncertainties of privatization and the disruption caused by a fundamental reorganization of the company. This case describes the major initiative within Shorts, the measured performance improvements to date, and future plans for the Total Quality programme.

The Shorts experience shows that performance improvement through Total Quality requires the commitment and involvement of personnel at all levels. Furthermore, sustained quality improvement is achieved only when it clearly supports the business objectives as perceived at different levels throughout the company.

Shorts Brothers PLC are the largest industrial employers in Northern Ireland, with some 8400 personnel. The company has been engaged in the aviation business for over 90 years and its activities include the design and manufacture of civil and military aircraft, major components for other aerospace companies and close air defence weapon systems. Shorts are part of Bombardier Inc., a Canadian-based international corporation engaged in the design, manufacture and marketing of transportation equipment, aerospace and motorized consumer goods. These products are sold worldwide into increasingly demanding and competitive markets.

During the 1980s, increasingly fierce competition highlighted the importance of and the need to reduce the 'cost of poor quality' within the company. The search for new methods led the company to investigate TQM and Shorts needed an approach that would be meaningful to every aspect of its business, including clerical, commercial, design and manufacturing areas. In view of previous experiences, the chosen method would also have to provide a sound basis for identifying the most important opportunities for improvement and for defining the true cause of a problem before attempting to resolve it.

A review of the quality improvement literature, and of the approaches adopted by some of their customers, suggested the most appropriate methodology to meet their requirement. The company recognized the need for initial training to be consultant-led in order to provide credibility and a breadth of experience which did not exist within the company at that time. They chose, therefore, a consultancy which could help implement the chosen approach and gained Board-level approval for the programme. Detailed planning started immediately.

A team consisting of Shorts personnel and consultants was formed to devise an implementation programme for the Total Quality activities. The team defined the organizational structure needed to direct continuous improvement throughout the company. This consisted of a Company Quality Council, two Divisional Councils and 18 Functional Quality Teams (FQTs). The planning team also specified the initial membership of each of these groups, ensuring the involvement of senior management in each team.

The Company Quality Council is chaired by the President and comprises Vice-presidents from each Division who provide overall leadership and direction for the programme. The Divisional Councils are chaired by their respective Vice-presidents who, with senior management, meet to set objectives and monitor progress in their respective divisions. The Functional Teams are chaired by a senior manager and comprise departmental managers who lead Total Quality in their functions.

A Total Quality Centre was established to act as a focal point for training and support, and to take the leading role in assisting the Company Council develop a Total Quality strategy. It was staffed by six full-time secondees from a wide range of company departments who would serve 12-14 months, acting as planner, trainer, facilitator and coordinator.

The planning phase lasted less than 2 months. In hindsight it might have been beneficial to have spent more time analysing the objectives since the focus was almost solely on training and techniques. If more attention had been given to solving the everyday problems faced by team members, Shorts may have had a more widespread uptake in the first few months. However, they had a structure in place to manage the programme, and the training of the teams became the first priority.

The training programme

The company fully understood the need for top-level understanding, commitment and involvement in the programme. Thus the training programme was very definitely a 'top-down' process. It began with the President and his Management Committee and moved systematically through the company until all personel were trained.

Quality Council and FQT Training

The first training session consisted of a 3-day off-site workshop for the members of the Company Quality Council. It was followed by 12 similar workshops for the other

Quality Councils and FQTs. Over 200 Vice-presidents and Senior Managers were involved in the training.

Each workshop covered the theory, practice and tools of quality improvement. On the final day of training, each group elected a chairperson and secretary, set an agenda and held their first meeting to discuss opportunities and priorities for improvement. These meetings continued on a weekly or biweekly basis after the workshops.

Project Team Leaders

Each project team has a Team Leader to guide and control the team's efforts. All Team Leaders attended a 4-day off-site course on tools, techniques, leadership and presentation skills. These courses were scheduled concurrently with the training for Councils and Functional Teams so that Team Leaders were available to lead nominated projects. Approximately 50 courses have been held, providing a pool of over 750 trained leaders. The initial training courses were consultant-led with increasing involvement of Total Quality Centre personnel. Since then all courses have been run by Shorts staff, forming a successful and visible part of Shorts ownership of the process. Team Leader training is an ongoing task which is currently provided on a point-of-need basis.

Management and senior executives

The remainder of Senior Management and Senior Executives attended a 1-day on-site training session. These were highly interactive and focused on the need for Total Quality. Practical exercises were also introduced to familiarize the participants with the basic quality tools.

A total of 70 courses were held involving 1000 personel. Participants were very enthusiastic and, despite some initial anticipated cynical reactions, the majority of people left the session eager to put their new-found knowledge into practice.

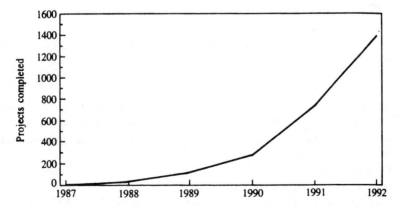

Figure C5.1 *Projects completed*

Senior technical, admin and supervisory staff

A further 40 1-day sessions were held to cover 700 personnel. The enthusiastic input from shopfloor supervisors was very encouraging, although concern over the imminent privatization and possible redundancies was becoming apparent. This was partially compensated for by the increasing number of completed improvement projects throughout the company (Figure C5.1).

Privatization – obstacle or respite?

During the third year of the programme the company underwent a major reorganization in which the existing three divisions were transformed into five largely autonomous Business Units and the Corporate functions. This fundamental change in structure resulted in the relocation of personnel and was the precursor to privatization.

It was fortunate that the previous training phase had been completed before the full effect of the reorganization had been felt. Quality improvement ceased almost completely as the Total Quality organizational structure became obsolete. However, the resulting 2-month pause allowed the company to examine progress so far and to design a new organizational structure which focused more intently on the Business Unit objectives. Commercial awareness and acccountability have since increased and reduction of quality costs has taken on new strategic importance.

Thus, Total Quality was relaunched with a new relevance to the company's goals. The revised organizational structure now consists of five Divisional Quality Councils, and a Corporate Quality Council, supported by 36 FQTs. Once this structure was in place it was possible to reallocate the existing 100 Total Quality projects, some of which had lost their teams during the reorganization. Total Quality was now restored to life and Shorts embarked on the most ambitious training phase yet – to educate the remainder of the workforce.

1900 down, 7100 to go!

In preparing to train the workforce, the company was very aware of potential barriers to progress, e.g. trade union resistance, the fear of redundancies, and the false impression that this was a managers' programme since the training so far had been for senior staff.

Trade union resistance was avoided by involving them in discussions about the aims of the programme and by giving shop stewards the opportunity of participating in the training in advance of their members. This resulted in the trade union giving the programme their full support.

At this stage, Shorts changed the format of the training sessions. They realized that, if training was to be interesting and relevant to non-managerial staff, it had to be sharply focused on the particular opportunities in their work areas. The solution was to involve local managers in delivering the training. To maximize the impact of this training phase, they completed the training of one Business Unit before starting another. This allowed the Business Unit goals to be integrated with the training material and also enabled them to perform brainstorming in a real situation with each group.

Training of all personnel was completed, after some 400 training sessions, in which 20000 brainstorm ideas were generated. A high level of awareness was created amongst the workforce and a great majority of people were enthusiastic about the programme.

Because of the focus on training and the fact that some of the earliest improvement projects were chosen more as training exercises than as attempts to improve the business, there was a growing feeling that Total Quality was 'interesting' but nothing to do with 'real' work. At this stage the Total Quality Centre staff, who attended both Council and FQT meetings, gently steered each meeting towards activities that were more relevant to the business objectives. This approach resulted in an increased focus on meaningful projects.

Total Quality projects – a means of reducing costs

For many historical reasons Shorts had not proved to be a profitable business for at least the 5 years before privatization. Indeed, the financial performance was steadily deteriorating, despite the fact that order books had never looked more healthy.

It was decided that the Total Quality programme should be used to identify areas where better management would result in cost reduction. After their training, the Quality Councils and FQTs met regularly with a prime objective of identifying the most significant opportunities for improvement in their areas. Each team created a list of possible projects by brainstorming, through an analysis of their quality costs and by focusing on the customer–supplier interfaces within their own department. In essence this meant finding areas where large financial savings could be made by improving a process, getting things right first time, improving efficiency, motivating people, improving technological capabilities, and so on.

The potential savings of each project were estimated, as was the cost of each project, and those with the greatest return were given priority. In many cases these projects spawned smaller, more manageable projects. Projects also resulted from the extensive brainstorm lists generated by the non-managerial staff during their training sessions. During these sessions it was stressed that the Total Quality programme was not only trying to save money but was also a useful and important vehicle with which to transform the company culture. This meant not only listening to ideas but acting on them.

Having chosen a project, a suitable Team Leader was selected from the pool of already trained personnel. A project team, consisting of on average four to six people with an interest in the problem, was then assembled. Their role was to analyse the problem and suggest a plan of remedial action. This was then presented to the relevant Council or FQT for authorization.

One major difficulty learned with project teams was providing them with enough time to complete the project. It was vital that adequate priority was given to Total Quality activities, that the team was empowered to make decisions; and that progress was monitored to ensure that blocks to progress were removed. Without this, teams could become demoralized and flounder.

Experience at Shorts has shown that, across the 1300 projects completed, the majority of teams have enjoyed their involvement and found continuous improvement both challenging and rewarding. Team members have been 'amazed' at the progress made in the novel 'no-blame' environment of their meetings and have developed a greater respect for their colleagues from other departments.

Recent developments with the programme

The company continually reviews the effectiveness of its approach to ensure that the programme continues to support the needs of the business. Recently the suporting role of the Total Quality Centre has become focused on the divisional needs by the provision of a dedicated member of staff. The divisional representative now plays a pivotal role by providing timely, accurate information on performance against Total Quality Plans, acting as a source of ideas for improvement techniques and providing examples of best practice in other companies.

The company has also begun to benchmark in an effort to discover best practices and to compare its performance against selected metrics. A wide range of areas are being benchmarked and medium- and long-term targets are being set based on these activities.

No Total Quality programme is complete if it does not address the supplier issue. The company is currently attempting to reduce the supply base and to build long-term partnerships with a number of preferred suppliers. Shorts staff now liaise closely with suppliers, providing support and a range of training services such as quality improvement workshops, symposia and seminars. Suppliers are invited to send delegates to the Team Leader Training courses and are encouraged to participate in joint improvement teams in an effort to encourage them to embrace Total Quality.

Shorts have also begun to incorporate advanced quality techniques into the programme. The Manufacturing Division has recently introduced a Process Review Programme aimed at systematically improving their manufacturing processes. The programme is based on Statistical Design of Experiments and is aimed at reducing variation and eliminating defects at resource. They have also begun to establish a proactive approach to business process improvement and process optimization which will be deployed throughout the company.

Performance improvements to date

Business results: financial measures

From the outset the company realized that the Total Quality programme would only survive if it could provide tangible benefits for the company. At the end of the first year, during which time the emphasis had been on training, only one project had been completed, with a saving of less than £30 000 per year. Five and a half years on, after

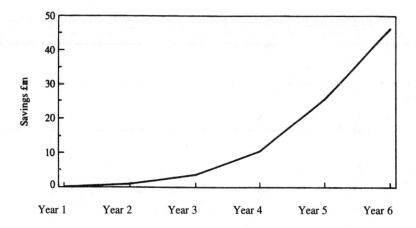

Figure C5.2 *Savings in millions of pounds*

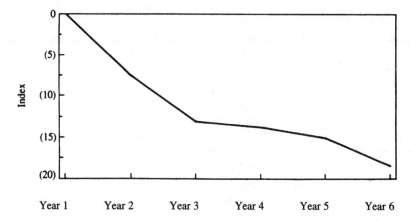

Figure C5.3 *Reductions in quality costs as a percentage of turnover*

a fundamental shift towards projects support, Shorts have completed over 1300 projects, with an estimated benefit of over £46m per year (Figures C5.1-C5.3).

It must be stated, however, that success is not simply measured by the magnitude of the savings. The important factor is that the savings, no matter how small, continue to mount up.

Company turnover has more than doubled since the start of total quality. Although the order book has expanded, the company has not had to increase the number of employees over the period, resulting in turnover per employee more than doubling.

Business results: non-financial measures

The Total Quality programme has resulted in a number of other benefits. Process improvements enabled Shorts to deliver 59 wing sets in Year 5, representing a 50%

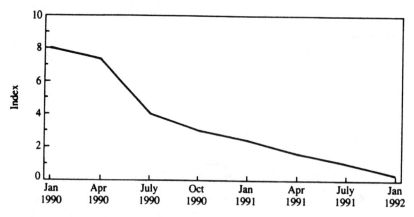

Figure C5.4 *Company shortages Years 4-6*

increase from Year 4. The work-hours required to produce a complete wing set have been reduced by 50%, leading to a doubling of efficiency levels. Overtime has been reduced by 10% in the same period and the learning curve is better than anything previously achieved on similar contracts in Shorts' history.

The level of shortages within the assembly areas had caused numerous delays and diversions for many years in Shorts. Through reducing non-conformances, and other contributors to the problem, shortages have reduced by a factor of more than 25 over a period of less than 2 years (Figure C5.4) Focusing on improving the accuracy of the management information systems has enabled them to achieve previously unheard-of accuracy levels for inventory, typically between 98 and 100% (Figure C5.5). In addition, all areas of the company have vigorously pursued stock value reductions, with achievements of 40% or more being typical.

Improvements in production control and master scheduling systems have enabled

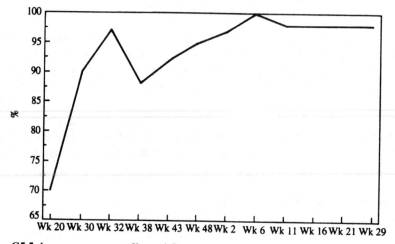

Figure C5.5 *Inventory accuracy Years 4-5*

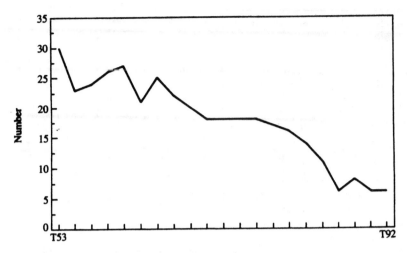

Figure C5.6 *Concession reductions*

Shorts to plan activities more accurately. When combined with manufacturing leadtime reductions (some sheet metal parts have had leadtimes reduced from 4 weeks to 4 days) and assembly hour reductions of up to 34%, Shorts have been able to meet delivery schedules and other key milestones ahead of programme.

People satisfaction

The Total Quality programme has generated many changes whose value would be difficult to measure in monetary terms, e.g. improved service levels and improved industrial–academic liaison. A major benefit is that all employees are now aware of the competitive threats facing Shorts and the benefits presented by Total Quality. Through the training process they are capable of applying simple problem-solving tools in their day-to-day work. They also understand the concept of the internal and external customer and realize the necessity of satisfying their needs if the company is to become a leader in each sector of its business.

Perhaps the biggest change is that of attitude. Not only has the workforce attitude changed, but that of the middle and senior managers as well. Although this culture change is by no means complete, there is objective evidence that the company is moving in the desired direction, e.g. over 4200 management and staff are involved in improvement activities at any one time. The company believes that through sustaining this commitment and working as a team it will continue to effect the required cultural change.

Customer satisfaction

Shorts fully appreciate that to survive and prosper, it is necessary to guarantee customer

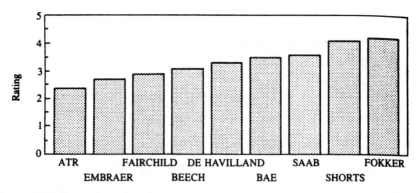

Figure C5.7 *Perceptions of product support: manufacturers of turboprop aircraft*
Source: Commuter Regional Aircraft News

satisfaction. They have focused on the chain of events from the supplier, through internal customers and suppliers, to the end-customer in an attempt to ensure they meet customer requirements.

They begin by agreeing customer requirements during the bid phase of the programme. These are regularly reviewed through customer conferences and involve customer representatives in the multidisciplinary design-build teams. This approach has enabled the company to reduce engineering change levels and product development cycle time by up to 44%. In addition, customer complaints, on one programme alone, have reduced by a factor of 10 over a 2-year period, and there has been a dramatic reduction in the number of concessions (Figure C5.6).

Customer satisfaction teams have developed key performance indicators that, when combined with industry standard measures, enable Shorts to compare themselves with competitors. Using these mechanisms to identify where to improve is beginning to show results, e.g. Shorts product support activities were recently rated second among the manufacturers of turboprop aircraft by *Commuter Regional Airline News* (Figure C5.7). The Sherpa Combined Logistics Support Group were given an overall rating of 'outstanding' (the highest rating attainable) for each year of service with the US Airforce in Germany. In addition, Super Sherpa achieved 99% despatch reliability, and Starburst missile system was 100% operational during the Gulf Crisis; the company received many letters of commendation praising its efforts.

Shorts have also won nine Boeing Pride in Excellence Awards and were the first company in Europe, and only the second in the world, to be approved to the new Advanced Quality Standard D1-9000. Currently Shorts is the only company to gain Boeing D1-9000 reapproval.

Impact on society

The Total Quality programme has brought indirect gains in terms of enhanced company image as a result of publicizing the programme. Some may say that TQM is simply a marketing issue, but at Shorts they realize it is a competitive and survival issue.

Members of Shorts staff have had the opportunity to attend and present papers at international conferences This both publicizes the fact that Shorts are involved in TQM and gives the staff the chance to discover what other companies are doing and how their approach may help. This has already proved beneficial, e.g. the first Total Quality Plan was developed as a result of attendance at a US conference. This was one of the most significant developments of the programme as there now exists a series of clearly defined and challenging divisional and company goals forming parts of the Company Business Plan. This has resolved the conflict of 'real work' versus TQM activities.

Other benefits include the winning of an LTK National Training Award for the Total Quality training programme, the British Quality Award and the Northern Ireland Quality Award. These reflect the widespread support and commitment from all personnel to the Total Quality programme.

Lessons learned

Shorts Total Quality programme has survived during the most turbulent period of the company's history. The results so far are encouraging but they feel they still have a great deal to do, especially in transforming the organization to world-class status.

Five and a half years into the programme, Shorts management can look back and assess how things were done, how they could have been done better, what were the problems encountered, and the lessons learned:

- The Company's Chief Executive must be absolutely committed to TQM if there is to be even the slightest chance of sustained success. Shorts President has provided visible suport to the programme and has played a key role in its implementation.
- The Shorts Total Quality team feel that they failed to publicize Total Quality successes on a wide-enough scale. Until recently, employees were generally unaware of Total Quality success stories outside their immediate work area. This led to a belief that TQM was not happening and was just another of those good ideas that never reached fruition. They now realize that employee achievements and contributions must be recognized. They also need to be aware that the programme is working and that things are changing. Shorts have recently introduced a quarterly magazine which informs everyone of progress. Dedicated displays, the company newspaper, divisional newsletters and team meetings are also used to publicize Total Quality activities.
- Total Quality, like any other business activity, is a dynamic process which must be regularly reviewed to maintain its success and relevance to company goals.
- The more effort put into the planning phase of a TQM programme, the greater the likelihood of success. Plans must be practical and reasonable, with sufficient resources and commitment to implement them. It is comparatively simpler to rally support for a TQM programme than it is to maintain that support when operational problems occur or interest fades. Nothing short of sustained commitment will provide the necessary results.
- The top-down approach to training appears to be the best method of creating sustained improvement within a large organization, even if it does slow the message

reaching every level in the company. The need to devolve responsibility and accountability cannot be overemphasized; employees at every level want to get involved and have a major contribution to make.

- Total Quality makes good business sense. Shorts estimate that the benefits to date exceed the total programme cost, including training, by a factor of 13.

The future

The Total Quality Plan was reviewed recently and endorsed by the President and Company Quality Council. The plan prioritized the following areas for attention for the following year.

Strategic framework

The company will incorporate a strategic Total Quality framework into their Total Quality Plans, based on the European Model for Total Quality Management. This will help to integrate the various major initiatives currently underway of planned. Further performance measures, which will assess the effectiveness of the Total Quality Strategy, will be established and monitored and a self-assessment of each division will be undertaken using the elements of the strategic framework.

People involvement

Shorts management plan to raise employee involvement level to 60% through the provision of suitable training, involvement in Total Quality projects and the suggestion scheme.

Benchmarking

Each division will develop its respective benchmarking methodologies and action plans based on its findings, to ensure the achievement of company-wide world-class business practices.

Customer focus

The customer focus teams for each division will further develop relevant satisfaction metrics, thus identifying further opportunities for improvement.

Concluding remarks

- To date, the results are encouraging, both financially and in the way the company deals with its people, but the management know they have more to do before Shorts

become a Total Quality company.
- If the company claims that people are its greatest asset, it must mean it and show it. Long-term survival depends largely on the ability to harness the knowledge and enthusiasm of the entire workforce. Total Quality is the vehicle for achieving this aim at Shorts.
- It is clear that the Total Quality programme has played, and will continue to play, a vital part in the transformation of Shorts. To build on what they already have achieved will require the continuing support of personnel at all levels. Only through this support do the management feel they can progress towards Total Quality.

Acknowledgement

This is from a case study by Desmond A. Bell.

C6

Problem-solving and the use of improvement tools and techniques at Hills Industries

Introduction

Hills Industries is a wholly owned subsidiary of a South Australian public listed company, has a turnover of £3m and 110 employees. It has been based in Caerphilly (10-15 miles north of Cardiff) for about 20 years. Hills manufacture rotary clothes dryers, various outdoor and indoor drying devices and a range of garden and industrial sprayers.

When Managing Director Mark Canny arrived from Australia some years ago to head the British subsidiary, he found its management hierarchical in style, with senior managers involved in decisions which should be delegated to subordinates. As a young Australian brought up in the automative component industry, and exposed to Japanese quality demands and management philosophy, he wanted to change to a more informal, team-based approach.

At the same time Mark was required to introduce the parent company's system of material requirements planning (MRP) and saw the quality assurance standard BS5750 (ISO9000 series) as a market necessity for the future.

This case study concentrates, however, on the manufacture of sprayers and the use of tools/techniques for quality improvement. At Hills, the manufacturing process for sprayers commences with the production of a bottle which is blow-moulded from high-density polyethylene. The bottle is then printed and placed on to a conveyor belt where various components and subassemblies are added to the bottle. The subassemblies are produced on the side of the flow line; the components come partly from in-house manufacture in other sections (for example, injection mouldings) and also come from outside suppliers.

Quality problems

There is a very great sensitivity within Hills to the quality of the sprayers produced. This sensitivity originates mainly from the very adverse results of the production of poor-quality sprayers 7-8 years ago. At that time Hills developed a new range of products which they released on to the market before a satisfactory testing programme had been completed. The products were visually very appealing and sold very well. Unfortunately, the customer dissatisfaction with poorly performing products was so bad that the products returned in great quantity. The upshot of this was that Hills suffered a significant loss of market share. That market share has never been completely regained and the story remains a part of the company folklore.

Last year, Hills decided that certification to BS5750 would become a market-place necessity for them within the next 2 years. Certification was already a precondition for trade in a number of other industries. After vigorous management debate, Hills decided to embark on a TQM programme, with BS5750 certification being simply a milestone in that process. Some 6-8 months after commencing the programme, Hills suffered a burst of sprayer returns. Although they did not yet have a system for recording returns, their sensitivity to sprayer quality meant that they picked up the problem very early. At this time, the engineering team and a number of senior management were heavily occupied in a major capital-spend programme in another part of the business. Accordingly, it was an ideal opportunity to make use of the philosophies of TQM, whereby the problem was given to a multidisciplinary team rather than to a group of engineers and/or a group of management.

The problem-solving approach

The team was assembled with great care and, of the five members of the team, three had day-to-day involvement with the manufacturing process; the other two members were from engineering and sales management.

The first step was to take the team through a training programme on scientific problem-solving. The original training of the sprayer team was conducted by an outside consultant who was helping Hills with its TQM programme. It is very common for a group of people to see a problem and, before even clearly defining what the problem is, jump to conclusions as to what the solution should be. To avoid this happening the training focused on a mechanism for solving problems which was a step-by-step process. This process ensured that the problem-solvers carefully researched the problem and collected the facts before beginning the process of devising various possible solutions. The training focused on brainstorming, fishbone diagrams, Pareto analysis, process flow diagrams, histograms and tally sheets, amongst other techniques. The team was then given a clear definition of the problem which the management wanted solved and they then set about the task.

After collecting an amount of information, the team decided that the production process should be stopped completely and that all line operators should be involved in a thorough analysis of the products in the finished goods store. The team made this proposal to management, the management accepted the proposal and the line stoppage was put into effect. The line was stopped for a total of 20 days. This was a very important sign to the workforce that the company was serious about quality

The team was now working hand-in-hand with all of the members of the production unit. They produced a process flow diagram and made judgements about those parts of the process which were under control and those parts which needed further investigation. They also carefully examined every sprayer in the finished goods stock and kept tally charts of the faults which they found. These results were then put on to a Pareto chart so that the actions could be prioritized. The charts were produced by hand and were very simple. Their view was that there was no need for computer-aided devices in this area.

The operators were given the autority to stop the line when they found a problem of any sort with the process. This authority has not been abused. When it has been used, the reasons have always been justified and very sensible. The company management felt that the front-line operators must have greater involvement in finding solutions to day-to-day problems and then, of course, implementing those agreed solutions.

Tackling major issues

The largest problem by far was the apparent random occurrence of an overly long internal dip tube (this tube carries the fluid from inside the sprayer to the delivery lance in the spraying process and excessively long tubes caused blocking at the base of the sprayer). The team visited the supplier of the tube. Working with the supplier they discovered that the supplier did not recognize that the length of the tube would have a material effect on the performance of the sprayer. Hills had not previously recognized this either and had never discussed it with their supplier. Accordingly, the supplier had always treated the length definition as a minimum requirement and, accordingly, supplied the cut-off lengths as a longer piece. Once Hills had discussed this problem with the supplier, they were very willing and able to comply with Hills' real needs of the component.

The second problem on the Pareto chart related to snapping pump handles. These handles were made of an ABS compound and the finished component needed to have a compromise of strength and flexibility. Following what they had learned from their dip tube experience, Hills contacted the supplier of the pump handles. It transpired that the supplier of the pump handles had been unable to obtain the normal grade of ABS used in the process. The supplier instead purchased a more expensive grade of ABS compound assuming that if it was more expensive, it must be better. As it transpired, the more expensive grade of ABS had superior strength characteristics but less flexibility. Hence this new grade of ABS produced a component which failed under various conditions. The corrective action in this case was of course very straightforward.

Buoyed by these two successes, the team moved on to look at the ongoing process of sprayer production. They grouped their findings and recommendations into three categories.

1   Process control
2   Incoming supplies
3   Operator training

The team made a presentation to management and requested help in resolving the issues they had highlighted.

In terms of operator training, there were two issues that could be very easily addressed. Firstly, the supervisor constructed a simple chart showing which operators had been trained to work on which sections of the assembly process. This chart highlighted the need for further training to fill the gaps. Once this training was complete, the operators were more easily able to move from one position to another, therefore increasing their interest and enthusiasm in the job which, of course, translates into better-quality performance.

Secondly, the operators recommended that there should be simple diagrammatic work instructions at each workstation. These work instructions would mean that an operator moving to a new workstation would be able to have an instant refresher course on the job which was to be done at that station. The team co-opted a member of the engineering staff to produce these diagrams and asked the maintenance section to install large boards at each workstation in order to display the diagrams. When the boards were installed (as per the team's design) it was suddenly realized that the effect was to leave operators feeling quite isolated. They were now unable to see the majority of the flow line and were unable to see their fellow workers. If these boards had been installed as a management idea, the effect would have been to create a confrontation. Because the boards were installed to operator specification, however, ownership of the mistake was accepted and the boards were modified to enable them to display the work instructions while also allowing good visibility for the operators.

Since this early work, the improvement process has continued in the sprayer section. It must be noted, however, that sometimes the process does not flow smoothly and early gains are sometimes partially lost. The improvement process requires constant reinforcing, work and input from all those involved. Some of the reversals suffered have been quite large and have led to periods of low morale but, because there are memories of the success achieved, this situation has always been able to be turned around.

The use of Statistical Process Control (SPC) at Hills Industries

There were two different examples of SPC at Hills Industries which are worthy of consideration:

1   *Where they did not use SPC:* As a step in the manufacture of pressure sprayers, a unit called a pressure relief valve (PRV) is assembled. This valve works by releasing air from the sprayer if the pressure within the vessel becomes too high. The PRV consists of a rod which moves inside a cylinder with an 'O' ring around the rod to produce the seal. At the upper end of the cylinder there is a step. If the 'O' ring passes the step, the gas is released.

   Given the safety-critical nature of the PRV, the subassembly was 100% tested on the production line, using a 'go/no-go' gauge. The company did not, however, keep any data on either percentage rates of failure or, more specifically, measures of the pressure at which individual batches of PRVs released.

   Fortunately, the workforce had become quite aware of sprayer quality and were committed to improvement and a member of the workforce noticed that the number of reject PRVs was very high in a particular batch. The operator informed her supervisor and an investigation was undertaken.

   The investigation showed that, when a rod was at the lower size limit, the 'O' ring at the lower size limit, and the cylinder inside diameter at the upper size limit, the subassembly had minimal interference and effectively did not work. The major saving grace was that the fault was fail-safe – the PRV would release pressure far too early.

   Given this discovery, the company was able to change its specifications and tolerances for the components involved. Unfortunately, the company had gone through a number of years of producing faulty subassemblies, which were discarded, without learning that, although the individual parts were to specification, specifications alone were inappropriate.

2   *Where they did begin rudimentary charting of a process:* Absenteeism amongst the direct workforce had always been the 'stock/standard' reason (or excuse) for any failure to meet the production plans at Hills. The management believed that the company had high levels of absenteeism but were unwilling to take on extra staff to cover this because, if all direct workers arrived at work on a given day, then labour utilization would be low, i.e. there would not be enough work for them all.

   The Personnel Manager began to tackle this problem. Among her first activities was the keeping of a run-chart of the number of people absent each morning. After collecting the data for a short time, she saw a pattern and accordingly searched back through the records to examine a longer period of data. The run-chart showed that the absenteeism was in fact fairly stable – the fluctuations from the mean were not very large. Accordingly the company could quite confidently take on extra staff to cover expected, ongoing absenteeism without any real risk of being overstaffed on particular days. Additionally the management were able to compare themselves with other companies in the area. They discovered that their absenteeism rates were, in fact, very modest when compared to other factories nearby.

   The information which Hills Industries gleaned from the simple runchart enabled the management team to take some fundamental decisions about staffing levels and meaningful judgements about performance relative to local conditions.

The broad issues

The broad issues highlighted by the case are:

1   The tools and techniques are just that – they do not provide quality in themselves, and they rely on the environment in which they are used.
2   Tools and techniques fit into two broad categories:
    (a) Waste – problem-solving (to eliminate waste)
    (b) Random variation – SPC (to measure and control the variation)
    N.B.: 'Waste' and 'problem' have broad definitions and refer to any process which can be improved.
3   Achieving quality is an ongoing process which will never be complete – a journey, not a destination.

Being more specific

The specific lessons regarding problem-solving of the case are:

1   Hills Industries regarded themselves as lucky to notice the increase in product returns of sprayers – they did not (at that time) have a rigorous returned goods/customer complaints system in place, and the increase in returns was not so dramatic that it was noticed easily.
    The lesson the company learned was that it might not continue with this luck – a system/feedback mechanism was needed to tell the managers how customers felt about the products.
2   The time-honoured method for dealing with problems, such as product returns, was to call in the 'experts' (engineers and senior manager) – Hills were lucky that they were all too busy at the time!
3   The critical steps in the new approach were:
    (a) All of the people involved were given training in problem-solving.
    (b) The direct operators were very involved in the investigation progress.
    (c) The team was given a clear, unambiguous brief of what was required of them.
    (d) The management decision to accept the stopping of production sent a strong, clear message that solving this problem was being taken seriously.
4   The root causes of the problems turned out to be deceptively simple – moreover they were the result of good intentions and lack of communication.
5   As a result of being involved in the investigations and recommendations for improvement, the direct operators have a greater understanding of the process and a greater commitment to ongoing improvement.

The specific features/lessons of the Hills case, regarding the tools of quality improvement including SPC, are:

1 The use of a go/no-go test had hidden the real cause of problems for a long time.
2 Simply rejecting the rejects had meant that they had passed up an opportunity for improvement.
3 Hills' first steps with SPC have shown that they can become *proactive* rather than *reactive* with regard to quality in all areas of business activity.

Discussion questions

1 (a) Using the expression: 'if you don't measure you can't improve', discuss this in the context of TQM. Why is measurement important?
(b) What is the differnce between measuring for results and measuring for process improvement? Using your knowledge of process management, where do you think measurement should take place and how should it be conducted?

2 Discuss the important features of a performance measurement system based on a TQM approach? Suggest an implementation strategy for a performance measurement system in a progressive company which is applying TQM principles to its business processes.

3 It is often said that 'you can't control what you can't measure and you can't manage what you can't control'. Measurement is, therefore, considered to be at the heart of managing business processes, activities and tasks. What do you understand by improvement-based performance measurement? Why is it important? Suggest a strategy of introducing TQM-based performance measurement for an organization in the public sector.

4 Benchmarking is a new development in which most progressive organizations are interested. What do you understand by benchmarking? How does benchmarking link with performance measurement? Suggest a strategy for integrating benchmarking into a TQM programme.

5 (a) Some people would say that benchmarking is not different from competitor analysis and is a practice that organizations have always carried out. Do you agree with this? How would you define benchmarking and what are its key elements?
(b) Suggest a benchmarking approach for a progressive small company that has no previous knowledge or experience of doing this.

6 (a) What are the major limitations of the 'Prevention-Appraisal-Failure (PAF)' costing model? Why would the process cost model be a better alternative?
(b) Discuss the link between benchmarking and quality costing.
(c) Suggest an implementation plan for benchmarking in a large company in the communications sector which is highly committed to TQM.

7 A construction company is concerned about its record of completing projects on time. Considerable penalty costs are incurred if the company fails to meet the agreed contractual completion date. How would you investigate this problem and what methodology would you adopt?

8 English Aerospace is concerned about its poor delivery performance with the EA911. Considerable penalty costs are incurred if the company fails to meet agreed delivery dates.

As the company's TQM Manager you have been asked to investigate this problem using a systematic approach. Describe the methodology you would adopt.

9 The Marketing Department of a large chemical company is reviewing its sales forecasting activities. Over the last three years the sales forecasts have been grossly inaccurate. As a result, a Quality Improvement Team has been formed to look at this problem. Give a systematic account of how the 'systematic tools' of TQM could be used in this situation.

10 It has been suggested by Deming and Ishikawa that statistical techniques can be used by staff at all levels within an organization. Explain how such techniques can help:

(a) Senior managers to assess performance.
(b) Sales staff to demonstrate process capability to customers.
(c) Process teams to achieve quality improvement.

Case study assignments

C5 Shorts Brothers

Discuss the key TQM performance-based measures used by the company.

Evaluate the measures used and discuss other areas/measures which could be included.

Examine the lessons the company feel they have learned and the future issues, and offer advice for further advancement.

C6 Hills Industries

Consider the broad issues highlighted by the case and evaluate these in the light of your own analysis.

In which areas could the company have extended the use of appropriate tools and techniques and how would this have developed the total quality processes in the Company?

Discuss how further statistical process control techniques could be introduced into Hills and describe an implementation plan.

Part Four

TQM – The Organizational, Communication and Teamwork Requirements

Dust as we are, the immortal spirit grows
Like harmony in music; there is a dark
Inscrutable workmanship that reconciles
Discordant elements, makes them cling together
In one society.

William Wordsworth, 1770-1850

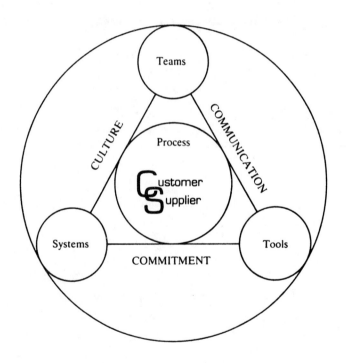

Organization for quality

10.1 The quality function and the quality director or manager

In many organizations management systems are viewed in terms of the internal dynamics between marketing, design, sales, production/operations, distribution, accounting, etc. A change is required from this to a larger system that encompasses and integrates the business interests of customers and suppliers. Management needs to develop an in-depth understanding of these relationships and how they may be used to cement the partnership concept. The quality function should be the organization's focal point in this respect, and should be equipped to gauge internal and external customers' expectations and degree of satisfaction. It should also identify quality deficiencies in all business functions, and promote improvements.

The role of the quality function is to make quality an inseparable aspect of every employee's performance and responsibility. The transition in many companies from quality departments with line functions will require careful planning, direction, and monitoring. Quality professionals have developed numerous techniques and skills, focused on product or service quality. In many cases there is a need to adapt these to broader applications. The first objectives for many 'quality managers' will be to gradually disengage themselves from line activities, which will then need to be dispersed throughout the appropriate operating departments. This should allow quality to evolve into a 'staff' department at a senior level, and to be concerned with the following throughout the organization:

- Encouraging and facilitating quality improvement.
- Monitoring and evaluating the progress of quality improvement.
- Promoting the 'partnership' in quality, in relations with customers and suppliers.
- Planning, managing, auditing, and reviewing quality systems.
- Planning and providing quality training and counselling or consultancy.
- Giving advice to management on:

(a) Establishment of quality systems and process control.
(b) Relevant statutory/legislation requirements with respect to quality.
(c) Quality improvement programmes necessary.
(d) Inclusion of quality elements in all job instructions and procedures.

Quality directors and managers have an initial task, however, to help those who control the means to implement this concept – the leaders of industry and commerce –

to really believe that quality must become an integral part of all the organization's operations.

The author has a vision of quality as a strategic business management function that will help organizations to change their cultures. To make this vision a reality, quality professionals must expand the application of quality concepts and techniques to all business processes and functions, and develop new forms of providing assurance of quality at every supplier–customer interface. They will need to know the entire cycle of products or services, from concept to the *ultimate* end user. An example of this was observed in the case of a company manufacturing pharmaceutical seals, whose customer expressed concern about excess aluminium projecting below and round a particular type of seal. This was considered a cosmetic defect by the immediate customer, the Health Service, but a safety hazard by a blind patient – the *customer's customer*. The prevention of this 'curling' of excess metal meant changing practices at the mill that rolled the aluminium – at the *supplier's supplier*. Clearly, the quality professional dealing with this problem needed to understand the supplier's problems and the ultimate customer's needs, in order to judge whether the product was indeed capable of meeting the requirements.

The shift in 'philosophy' will require considerable staff education in many organizations. Not only must people in other functions acquire quality related skills, but quality personnel must change old attitudes and acquire new skills – replacing the inspection, calibration, specification-writing mentality and knowledge of defect prevention, wide ranging quality systems design and audit. Clearly, the challenge for many quality professionals is not so much making changes in their organization as recognizing the changes required in themselves. It is more than an overnight job to change the attitudes of an inspection police force into those of a consultative, team-oriented improvement force. This emphasis on prevention and improvement-based systems elevates the role of quality professionals from a technical one to that of general management. A narrow departmental view of quality is totally out of place in an organization aspiring to TQM, and typical quality managers will need to widen their perspective and increase their knowledge to encompass all facets of the organization.

To introduce the concepts of operator self-inspection required for TQM will require not only a determination to implement change but sensitivity and skills in industrial relations. This will depend very much of course on the climate within the organization. Those whose management is truly concerned with co-operation and concerned for the people will engage strong employee support for the quality manager or director in his catalytic role in the quality improvement implementation process. Those with aggressive, confrontational management will create for the quality professional impossible difficulties in obtaining support from the 'rank and file'.

TQM appointments

Many organizations have realized the importance of the contribution a senior, qualified director of quality can make to the prevention strategy. Smaller organizations may well feel that the cost of employing a full-time quality manager is not justified, other than in certain very high risk areas. In these cases a member of the management team should be appointed to operate on a part-time basis, performing the quality management function in addition to his/her other duties. To obtain the best results from a quality director/manager, he/she should be given sufficient authority to take necessary action to secure the implementation of the organization's quality policy, and must have the personality to be able to communicate the message to all employees, including staff, management and directors. Occasionally the quality director/manager may require some guidance and help on specific technical quality matters, and one of the major attributes required is the knowledge and wherewithal to acquire the necessary information and assistance.

In large organizations, then, it may be necessary to make several specific appointments or to assign details to certain managers. The following actions may be deemed to be necessary.

Assign a TQM director, manager or co-ordinator

This person will be responsible for the planning and implementation of TQM. He or she will be chosen first for project management ability rather than detailed knowledge of quality assurance matters. Depending on the size and complexity of the organization, and its previous activities in quality management, the position may be either full or part-time, but it must report directly to the Chief Executive.

Appoint a quality management adviser

A professional expert on quality management will be required to advise on the 'technical' aspects of planning and implementing TQM. This is a consultancy role, and may be provided from within or without the organization, full or part-time. This person needs to be a persuader, philosopher, teacher, adviser, facilitator, reporter and motivator. He or she must clearly understand the organization, its processes and interfaces, be conversant with the key functional languages used in the business, and be comfortable operating at many organizational levels. On a more general level this person must fully understand and be an effective advocate and teacher of TQM, be flexible and become an efficient agent of change.

10.2   Councils, committees and teams

Devising and implementing total quality management for an organization takes considerable time and ability. It must be given the status of a senior executive project. The creation of cost effective quality improvement is difficult, because of the need for full integration with the organization's strategy, operating philosophy and management systems. It may require an extensive review and substantial revision of existing systems of management and ways of operating. Fundamental questions may have to be asked, such as 'Do the managers have the necessary authority, capability, and time to carry this through?'

Any review of existing management and operating systems will inevitably 'open many cans of worms' and uncover problems that have been successfully buried and

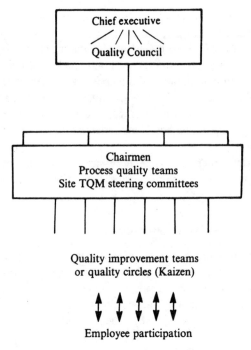

Figure 10.1 *Employee participation through the TQM structure*

smoothed over – perhaps for years. Authority must be given to those charged with following TQM through with actions that they consider necessary to achieve the goals. The commitment will be continually questioned and will be weakened, perhaps destroyed, by failure to delegate authoritatively.

The following steps are suggested in general terms. Clearly, different types of organization will have need to make adjustments to the detail, but the component parts are the basic requirements.

A disciplined and systematic approach to continuous improvement may be established in a quality council (Figure 10.1). The council should meet at least monthly to review strategy, implementation progress, and improvement. It should be chaired by the Chief Executive, who must attend every meeting – only death or serious illness should prevent him/her being there. Clearly, postponement may be necessary occasionally, but the council should not carry on meeting without the Chief Executive present. The council members should include the top management team and the chairmen of any 'site' TQM steering committees or process quality teams, depending on the size of the organization. The objectives of the council are to:

- Provide strategic direction on TQM for the organization.
- Establish plans for TQM on each 'site'.
- Set up and review the process quality teams that will own the key or critical business processes.
- Review and revise quality plans for implementation.

The process quality teams (PQTs) and any site TQM steering committees should also meet monthly, shortly before the council meetings. Every senior manager should be a member of at least one PQT. This system provides the 'top-down' support for employee participation in process management and development, through either a quality improvement team or a quality circle programme. It also ensures that the commitment to TQM at the top is communicated effectively through the organization.

The three-tier approach of quality council, process quality teams (PQTs) and quality improvement teams (QITs) allows the first to concentrate on quality strategy, rather than become a senior problem solving group. Progress is assured if the PQT chairmen are required to present a status report at each meeting.

The process quality teams or steering committees all control the QITs and have responsibility for:

- The selection of projects for the QITs.
- Providing an outline and scope for each project to give to the QITs.
- The appointment of team members and leaders.
- Monitoring and reviewing the progress and results from each QIT project.

As the focus of this work will be the selection of projects, some attention will need to be given to the sources of nominations. Projects may be suggested by:

(a) Council members representing their own departments, process quality teams, their suppliers or their customers, internal and external.
(b) Quality improvement teams.
(c) Quality circles (if in existence).
(d) Suppliers.
(e) Customers.

The PQT members must be given the responsibility and authority to represent their part of the organization in the process. The members must also feel that they represent the team to the rest of the organization. In this way the PQT will gain knowledge and respect and be seen to have the authority to act in the best interests of the organization, with respect to their process.

10.3 Quality improvement teams

A quality improvement team (QIT) is a group of people with the appropriate knowledge, skills, and experience who are brought together specifically by management to tackle and solve a particular problem, usually on a project basis. They are cross functional and often multi-disciplinary.

The 'task force' has long been a part of the culture of many organizations at the 'technology' and management levels. But quality improvement teams go a step further; they expand the traditional definition of 'process' to cover the entire production or operating system. This includes paperwork, communication and other units, operating procedures, and the process equipment itself. By taking this broader view, the teams can address new problems.

The actual running of quality improvement teams calls several factors into play:

- Team selection and leadership.
- Team objectives.
- Team meetings.
- Team assignments.
- Team dynamics.
- Team results and reviews.

Team selection and leadership

The most important element of a QIT is its members. People with knowledge and experience relevant to solving the problem are clearly required; however, there should be a limit of five to ten members to keep the team small enough to be manageable but allow a good exchange of ideas. Membership should include appropriate people from groups outside the operational and technical areas directly 'responsible' for the problem, if their presence is relevant or essential. In the selection of team members it is often useful to start with just one or two people concerned directly with the problem. If they try to draw flowcharts (see Chapter 4) of the relevant processes, the requirement to include other people, in order to understand the process and complete the charts, will aid the team selection. This method will also ensure that all those who can make a significant contribution to the improvement process are represented.

The team leader has a primary responsibility for team management and maintenance, and his/her selection and training is crucial to success. The leader need not be the highest ranking person in the team, but must be concerned about accomplishing the team objectives (this is sometimes described as 'task concern') and the needs of the members (often termed 'people concern'). Weakness in either of these areas will lessen the effectiveness of the team in solving problems. Team leadership training should be directed at correcting deficiencies in these crucial aspects.

Team objectives

At the beginning of any QIT project and at the start of every meeting the objectives should be stated as clearly as possible by the leader. This can take a simple form: 'This meeting is to continue the discussion from last Tuesday on the provision of current price data from salesmen to invoice preparation, and to generate suggestions for improvement in its quality'. Project and/or meeting objectives enable the team members to focus thoughts and efforts on the aims, which may need to be restated if the team becomes distracted by other issues.

Team meetings

An agenda should be prepared by the leader and distributed to each team member before every meeting. It should include the following information:

- Meeting place, time and how long it will be.
- A list of members (and co-opted members) expected to attend.
- Any preparatory assignments for individual members or groups.
- Any supporting material to be discussed at the meeting.

Early in a project the leader should orient the team members in terms of the approach, methods, and techniques they will use to solve the problem. This may require a review of the:

1 Systematic approach (Chapter 8).
2 Procedures and rules for using some of the basic tools, e.g. brainstorming – no judgement of initial ideas.
3 Role of the team in the continuous improvement process.
4 Authority of the team.

A team secretary should be appointed to take the minutes of meetings and distribute them to members as soon as possible after each meeting. The minutes should not be formal, but reflect decisions and carry a clear statement of the action plans, together with assignments of tasks. They may be handwritten initially, copied and given to team members at the end of the meeting, to be followed later by a more formal document that will be seen by any member of staff interested in knowing the outcome of the meeting. In this way the minutes form an important part of the communication system, supplying information to other teams or people needing to know what is going on.

Team assignments

It is never possible to solve problems by meetings alone. What must come out of those meetings is a series of action plans that assign specific tasks to team members. This is the responsibility of the team leader. Agreement must be reached regarding the responsibilities for individual assignments, together with the time scale, and this must be made clear in the minutes. Task assignments must be decided while the team is together and not by separate individuals in after meeting discussions.

Team dynamics

In any team activity the interactions between the members are vital to success. If solutions to problems are to be found, the meetings and ensuing assignments should assist and harness the creative thinking process. This is easier said than done, because many people have either not learned or been encouraged to be innovative. The team leader clearly has a role here to:

- Preparation and recommendation for problem solution.
- Management presentations.
- Quality circle administration.

A quality circle usually selects a project to work on through discussion within the circle. The leader then advises management of this choice and, assuming that no objections are raised, the circle proceeds with the work. Other suggestions for projects come from management, quality assurance staff, the maintenance department, various staff personnel, and other circles.

It is sometimes necessary for quality circles to contact experts in a particular field, e.g. engineers, quality experts, safety officers, maintenance personnel. This communication should be strongly encouraged, and the normal company channels should be used to invite specialists to attend meetings and offer advice. The experts may be considered to be 'consultants', the quality circle retaining responsibility for solving the particular problem. The overriding purpose of quality circles or Kaizen teams is to provide the powerful motivation of allowing people to take some part in deciding their own actions and futures.

10.5   Departmental purpose analysis

'Quality is everyone's business' is an often quoted cliché, but 'Everything is everyone's business', and so quality often becomes nobody's business. The responsibility for quality begins with the determination of the customer's quailty requirements and continues until the service or product is accepted by a satisfied customer. The department purpose analysis (DPA) technique, developed by IBM, helps to define the real purpose of each department, with the objective of improving performance and breaking down departmental barriers. It leads to an understanding and agreement on the key processes of each group. The department can then liaise with its immediate 'suppliers' and 'customers', often internally, to identify potential or actual problem areas and simultaneously carry out an analysis of what proportion of time is spent on the key activities. This begins the change from departmental to process management thinking.

Group discussions during the DPA process usually yield many good ideas for improvement, either eliminating wasteful activity or improving the quality of output from the department. Everyone becomes and should then remain aware of the prime purpose of the department, and the focus on efficiency and reducing waste usually carries through to all work activities. The manager of the department, who should run the exercise, must understand the DPA process and why it is necessary and important. He/she needs to be open minded towards change, and to encourage departmental staff to question whether all their activities add value to the product, service, or business. One of the greatest barriers to improvements through DPA is the 'but we've always done it that way' response.

Surplus page

Record data	– all processes can and should be measured.
	– all measurements should be recorded.
Use data	– if data are recorded and not used they will be abused.
Analyse data systematically	– data analysis should be carried out by means of the basic tools (Chapter 8).
Act on the results	– recording and analysis of data without action leads to frustration.

10.4   Quality circles or Kaizen teams

Kaizen is a philosophy of continuous improvement of all the employees in an organization, so that they perform their tasks a little better each day. It is a never-ending journey centred on the concept of starting anew each day with the principle that methods can always be improved. Using this approach, it is reported that Pratt and Whitney reduced reject rates on one process from 50 per cent to 4 per cent, and in 12 months eliminated overdue deliveries on a key sub-assembly.

Kaizen Teian is a Japanese system for generating and implementing employee ideas. Japanese suggestion schemes have helped companies to improve quality and productivity, and reduced prices to increase market share. They concentrate on participation and the rates of implementation, rather than on the 'quality' or value of the suggestion. The emphasis is on encouraging everyone to make improvements.

Kaizen Teian suggestions are usually small scale ones, in the worker's own area, and are easy and cheap to implement. Key points are that the rewards given are small, and implementation is rapid, which results in many small improvements that accumulate to massive total savings and improvements.

One of the most publicized aspects of the Japanese approach to quality has been quality circles or Kaizen teams. The quality circle may be defined as a group of workers doing similar work who meet:

- Voluntarily.
- Regularly.
- In normal working time.
- Under the leadership of their 'supervisor'.
- To identify, analyse, and solve work related problems.
- To recommend solutions to management.

Where possible quality circle members should implement the solutions themselves.

The quality circle concept first originated in Japan in the early 1960s, following a postwar reconstruction period during which the Japanese placed a great deal of emphasis on improving and perfecting their quality control techniques. As a direct result of work carried out to train foremen during that period, the first quality circles were conceived, and the first three circles registered with the Japanese Union of Scientists and Engineers (JUSE) in 1962. Since that time the growth rate has been phenomenal. The concept has spread to Taiwan, the USA and Europe, and circles in many countries have become successful. Many others have failed.

It is very easy to regard quality circles as the magic ointment to be rubbed on the affected spot, and unfortunately many managers in the West have seen them as a panacea for all ills. There are no panaceas, and to place this concept into perspective, Juran, who has been an important influence in Japan's improvement in quality, has stated that quality circles represent only 5–10 per cent of the canvas of the Japanese success. The rest is concerned with understanding quality, its related costs and the organization and techniques necessary for achieving customer satisfaction.

Given the right sort of commitment by top management, introduction, and environment in which to operate, quality circles can produce the 'shop floor' motivation to achieve quality performance at that level. Circles should develop out of an understanding and knowledge of quality on the part of senior management. They must not be introduced as a desperate attempt to do something about poor quality.

The structure of a quality circle organization

The unique feature about quality circles or Kaizen teams is that people are asked to join and not told to do so. Consequently, it is difficult to be specific about the structure of such a concept. It is, however, possible to identify four elements in a circle organization:

- Members.
- Leaders.
- Facilitators or co-ordinators.
- Management.

Members form the prime element of the programme. They will have been taught the basic problem solving and quality control techniques and, hence, possess the ability to identify and solve work related problems.

Leaders are usually the immediate supervisors or foremen of the members. They will have been trained to lead a circle and bear the responsibility of its success. A good leader, one who develops the abilities of the circle members, will benefit directly by receiving valuable assistance in tackling nagging problems.

Facilitators are the managers of the quality circle programmes. They, more than anyone else, will be responsible for the success of the concept, particularly within an organization. The facilitator must co-ordinate the meetings, the training and energies of the leaders and members, and form the link between the circles and the rest of the organization. Ideally the facilitator will be an innovative industrial teacher, capable of communicating with all levels and with all departments within the organization.

Management support and commitment are necessary to quality circles or, like any other concept, they will not succeed. Management must retain its prerogatives, particularly regarding acceptance or non-acceptance of recommendations from circles, but the quickest way to kill a programme is to ignore a proposal arising from it. One of the most difficult facts for management to accept, and yet one forming the cornerstone of the quality circle philosophy, is that the real 'experts' on performing a task are those who do it day after day.

Training quality circles

The training of circle/Kaizen leaders and members is the foundation of all successful programmes. The whole basis of the training operation is that the ideas must be easy to take in and be put across in a way that facilitates understanding. Simplicity must be the key word, with emphasis being given to the basic techniques. Essentially there are eight segments of training:

1 Introduction to quality circles.
2 Brainstorming.
3 Data gathering and histograms.
4 Cause and effect analysis.
5 Pareto analysis.
6 Sampling.
7 Control charts.
8 Presentation techniques.

Mangers should also be exposed to some training in the part they are required to play in the quality circle philosophy. A quality circle programme can only be effective if management believes in it and is supportive and, since changes in management style may be necessary, managers' training is essential.

Operation of quality circles/Kaizen teams

There are no formal rules governing the size of a quality circle/Kaizen team. Membership usually varies from three to fifteen people, with an average of seven to eight. It is worth remembering that, as the circle becomes larger than this, it becomes increasingly difficult for all members of the circle to participate.

Meetings must be held away from the work area, so that members are free from interruptions, and are mentally and physically at ease. The room should be arranged in a manner conductive to open discussion, and any situation that physically emphasizes the leader's position should be avoided.

Meeting length and frequency are variable, but new circles meet for approximately one hour once per week. Thereafter, when training is complete, many circles continue to meet weekly; others extend the interval to 2 or 3 weeks. To a large extent the nature of the problems selected will determine the interval between meetings, but this should never extend to more than 1 month, otherwise members will lose interest and the circle will cease to function.

Great care is needed to ensure that every meeting is productive, no matter how long it lasts or how frequently it is held. Any of the following activities may take place during a circle meeting:

● Training – initial or refresher.
● Problem identification.
● Problem analysis.

- Preparation and recommendation for problem solution.
- Management presentations.
- Quality circle administration.

A quality circle usually selects a project to work on through discussion within the circle. The leader then advises management of this choice and, assuming that no objections are raised, the circle proceeds with the work. Other suggestions for projects come from management, quality assurance staff, the maintenance department, various staff personnel, and other circles.

It is sometimes necessary for quality circles to contact experts in a particular field, e.g. engineers, quality experts, safety officers, maintenance personnel. This communication should be strongly encouraged, and the normal company channels should be used to invite specialists to attend meetings and offer advice. The experts may be considered to be 'consultants', the quality circle retaining responsibility for solving the particular problem. The overriding purpose of quality circles or Kaizen teams is to provide the powerful motivation of allowing people to take some part in deciding their own actions and futures.

10.5   Departmental purpose analysis

'Quality is everyone's business' is an often quoted cliché, but 'Everything is everyone's business', and so quality often becomes nobody's business. The responsibility for quality begins with the determination of the customer's quailty requirements and continues until the service or product is accepted by a satisfied customer. The department purpose analysis (DPA) technique, developed by IBM, helps to define the real purpose of each department, with the objective of improving performance and breaking down departmental barriers. It leads to an understanding and agreement on the key processes of each group. The department can then liaise with its immediate 'suppliers' and 'customers', often internally, to identify potential or actual problem areas and simultaneously carry out an analysis of what proportion of time is spent on the key activities. This begins the change from departmental to process management thinking.

Group discussions during the DPA process usually yield many good ideas for improvement, either eliminating wasteful activity or improving the quality of output from the department. Everyone becomes and should then remain aware of the prime purpose of the department, and the focus on efficiency and reducing waste usually carries through to all work activities. The manager of the department, who should run the exercise, must understand the DPA process and why it is necessary and important. He/she needs to be open minded towards change, and to encourage departmental staff to question whether all their activities add value to the product, service, or business. One of the greatest barriers to improvements through DPA is the 'but we've always done it that way' response.

The basic steps of DPA are:

1 Form the DPA group.
2 Brainstorm to list all the departmental tasks (see Chapter 8).
3 Agree which are the five main tasks.
4 Define the position and role of the departmental manager.
5 Review the main activities, and for each one identify the 'customer(s)' and 'supplier(s)'.
6 Consult the customer(s) and supplier(s) by means of a suitable questionnaire. This should be very similar to the list of questions suggested in Chapter 1 for interrogating any customer/supplier interface.
7 Review the customer/supplier survey results and brainstorm how improvements can be made.
8 Prioritize improvements to list those to be tackled first, and plan how.
9 Implement the improvement action plan, maintaining encouragement and support.
10 Review the progress made and repeat the DPA.

As with any new group activity, some successes are desirable early in the programme, if the department is to build confidence in its ability to make improvements and solve problems. For this reason DPA should confine itself, initially at least, to resolving issues that are within its control. It is unlikely, for example, that a sales team will be successful in getting a product redesigned in its first improvement project. Experience at IBM shows that, as confidence builds through continued management encouragement, the DPA groups will tackle increasingly difficult business processes and problems, with an increasing return of the investment in time.

Chapter highlights

The quality function and the quality director or manager

- The quality function should be the organization's focal point of the integration of the business interests of customers and suppliers into the internal dynamics of the organization.
- Its role is to encourage and facilitate quality improvement; monitor and evaluate progress; promote the quality chains; plan, manage, audit and review systems; plan and provide quality training, counselling and consultancy; and give advice to management.
- In larger organizations a quality director will contribute to the prevention strategy. Smaller organizations may appoint a member of the management team to this task on a part-time basis. An external TQM adviser is usually required.

Councils, committees and teams

- In devising and implementing TQM for an organization, it may be useful to ask first if the managers have the necessary authority, capability and time to carry it through.

- A disciplined and systematic approach to continuous improvement may be established in a quality council (QC), whose members are the senior management team.
- Reporting to the QC are the process quality teams (PQTs) or any site steering committees, which in turn control the quality improvement teams (QITs) and quality circles.

Quality improvement teams

- A QIT is a group brought together by management to tackle a particular problem on' a project basis. The running of QITs includes several team factors: selection and leadership, objectives, meetings, assignments, dynamics, results and reviews.

Quality circles or Kaizen teams

- Kaizen is a philosophy of small step continuous improvement, by all employees. In Kaizen teams the suggestions and rewards are small but the implementation is rapid.
- A quality circle or Kaizen team is a group of people who do similar work meeting voluntarily, regularly, in normal working time, to identify, analyse and solve work related problems, under the leadership of their supervisor. They make recommendations to management.

Departmental purpose analysis

- DPA helps to define the real purpose of each department, with the objective of improving performance and breaking down barriers. It leads to an understanding and agreement on the key processes of each group.
- The departmental manager runs the exercise and must understand DPA. The basic steps are form DPA group; list all departmental tasks; agree five main tasks; define position and role of manager; identify task customer(s) and supplier(s), and consult, review and brainstorm improvements; prioritize; implement plan; review progress and repeat DPA.

11

Culture change through teamwork for quality

11.1 The need for teamwork

The complexity of most of the processes that are operated in industry, commerce and the services places them beyond the control of any one individual. The only efficient way to tackle process improvement or problems is through the use of some form of teamwork. The use of the team approach to problem solving has many advantages over allowing individuals to work separately:

- A greater variety of complex problems may be tackled – those beyond the capability of any one individual or even one department – by the pooling of expertise and resources.
- Problems are exposed to a greater diversity of knowledge, skill, experience, and are solved more efficiently.
- The approach is more satisfying to team members, and boosts morale and ownership through participation in problem solving and decision making.
- Problems that cross departmental or functional boundaries can be dealt with more easily, and the potential/actual conflicts are more likely to be identified and solved.
- The recommendations are more likely to be implemented than individual suggestions, as the quality of decision making in *good teams*, is high.

Most of these factors rely on the premise that people are willing to support any effort in which they have taken part or helped to develop.

When properly managed and developed, teams improve the process of problem solving, producing results quickly and economically. Teamwork throughout any organization is an essential component of the implementation of TQM, for it builds trust, improves communications and develops interdependence. Much of what has been taught previously in management has led to a culture in the West of independence, with little sharing of ideas and information. Knowledge is very much like organic manure – if it is spread around it will fertilize and encourage growth, if it is kept closed in, it will eventually fester and rot.

Teamwork devoted to quality improvement changes the independence to interdependence through improved communications, trust and the free exchange of ideas, knowledge, data and information (Figure 11.1). The use of the face-to-face interaction method of communication, with a common goal, develops over time the sense of

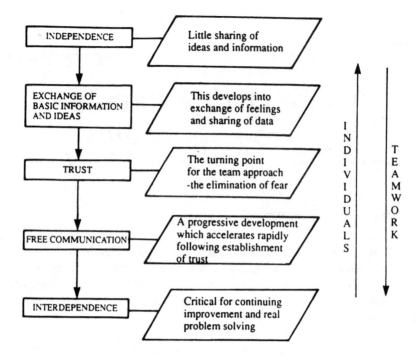

Figure 11.1 *Independence to interdependence through teamwork*

dependence on each other. This forms a key part of any quality improvement process, and provides a methodology for employee recognition and participation, through active encouragement in group activities.

Teamwork provides an environment in which people can grow and use all the resources effectively and efficiently to make continuous improvements. As individuals grow, the organization grows. It is worth pointing out, however, that employees will not be motivated towards continual improvement in the absence of:

- Commitment to quality for top management.
- The organizational quality 'climate'.
- A mechanism for enabling individual contributions to be effective.

All these are focused essentially at enabling people to feel, accept, and discharge responsibility. More than one organization has made this part of their quality strategy – to 'empower people to act'. If one hears from employees comments such as 'We know this is not the best way to do this job, but if that is the way management want us to do it, that is the way we will do it', then it is clear that the expertise existing at the point of operation has not been harnessed and the people do not feel responsible for the outcome of their actions. Responsibility and accountability foster pride, job satisfaction, and better work.

Empowerment to act is very easy to express conceptually, but it requires real effort and commitment on the part of all managers and supervisors to put into practice.

Recognition that only partially successful but good ideas or attempts are to be applauded and not criticized is a good way to start. Encouragement of ideas and suggestions from the workforce, particularly through their part in team or group activities, requires investment. The rewards are total commitment, both inside the organization and outside through the supplier and customer chains.

Teamwork for quality improvement has several components. It is driven by a strategy, needs a structure, and must be implemented thoughtfully and effectively. The strategy that drives the quality improvement teams at the various levels was outlined in Part 1, and will be dealt with in more detail in the final chapter of this book, but in essence it comprises:

- The mission of the organization.
- The critical success factors.
- The key processes.

The structure of having the top management team in a quality council, and the key processes being owned by process quality teams, which manage quality improvement projects through QITs and quality circles was detailed in Chapter 10, on the organizational requirements for quality. The remainder of this chapter will concentrate on teamwork and its implementation.

11.2 Teamwork and action-centred leadership

Over the years there has been much academic work on the psychology of teams and on the leadership of teams. Three points on which all authors are in agreement are that teams develop a personality and culture of their own, respond to leadership, and are motivated according to criteria usually applied to individuals.

Key figures in the field of human relations, like Douglas McGregor (Theories X & Y), Abraham Maslow (Hierarchy of Needs) and Fred Hertzberg (Motivators and Hygiene Factors), all changed their opinions on group dynamics over time as they came to realize that groups are not the democratic entity that everyone would like them to be, but respond to individual, strong, well directed leadership, both from without and within the group, just like individuals.

Adair

During the 1960s John Adair, senior lecturer in Military History and the Leadership Training Adviser at the Military Academy, Sandhurst and later assistant director of the Industrial Society, developed what he called the action-centred leadership model, based on his experiences at Sandhurst, where he had the responsibility to ensure that results in the cadet training did not fall below a certain standard. He had observed that some instructors frequently achieved well above average results, owing to their own natural ability with groups and their enthusiasm. He developed this further into a team model, which is the basis of the approach of the author and his colleagues to this subject.

In developing his model for teamwork and leadership, Adair brought out clearly that

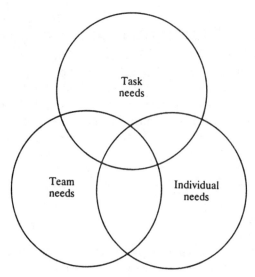

Figure 11.2 *Adair's model*

for any group or team, big or small, to respond to leadership, they need a clearly defined *task*, and the response and achievement of that task are interrelated to the needs of the *team* and the separate needs of the *individual members* of the team (Figure 11.2).

The value of the overlapping circles is that it emphasizes the unity of leadership and the interdependence and multifunctional reaction to single decisions affecting any of the three areas.

Leadership tasks

Drawing upon the discipline of social psychology, Adair developed and applied to training the functional view of leadership. The essence of this he distilled into the three interrelated but distinctive requirements of a leader. These are to define and achieve the job or task, to build up and co-ordinate a team to do this, and to develop and satisfy the individuals within the team (Figure 11.3).

1   *Task needs*. The difference between a team and a random crowd is that a team has some common purpose, goal or objective, e.g. a football team. If a work team does not achieve the required results or meaningful results, it will become frustrated. Organizations have to make a profit, to provide a service, or even to survive. So anyone who manages others has to achieve results; in production, marketing, selling or whatever. Achieving objectives is a major criterion of success.

2   *Team needs*. To achieve these objectives, the group needs to be held together. People need to be working in a co-ordinated fashion in the same direction. Team work will ensure that the team's contribution is greater than the sum of its parts. Conflict within the team must be used effectively; arguments can lead to ideas or to tension and lack of co-operation.

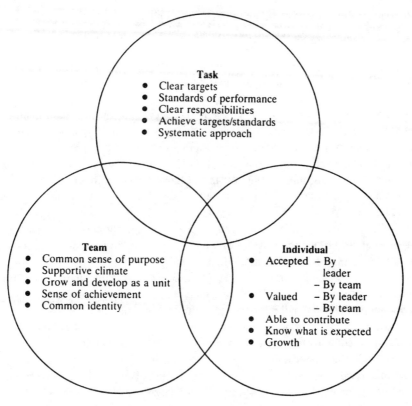

Figure 11.3 *The leadership needs*

3   *Individual needs*. Within working groups, individuals also have their own set of needs. They need to know what their responsibilities are, how they will be needed, how well they are performing. They need an opportunity to show their potential, take on responsibility and receive recognition for good work.

The task, team and individual functions for the leader are as follows:

(a) *Task functions*   Defining the task
                    Making a plan.
                    Allocating work and resources.
                    Controlling quality and tempo of work.
                    Checking performance against the plan.
                    Adjusting the plan.

(b) *Team functions*   Setting standards.
                    Maintaining discipline.
                    Building team spirit.
                    Encouraging, motivating, giving a sense of purpose.
                    Appointing sub-leaders.
                    Ensuring communication within the group.
                    Training the group.

(c) *Individual functions*   Attending to personal problems.
Praising individuals.
Giving status.
Recognizing and using individual abilities.
Training the individual.

The team leader's or facilitator's task is to concentrate on the small central area where all three circles overlap. In a business that is introducing TQM this is the 'action to change' area, where the leaders are attempting to manage the change from *business as usual*, through total quality management, to *TQM equals business as usual*, using the cross-functional quality improvement teams at the strategic interface.

In the action area the facilitator's or leader's task is similar to the task outlined by John Adair. It is to try to satisfy all three areas of need by achieving the task, building the team, and satisfying individual needs. If a leader concentrates on the task, e.g. in going all out for production schedules, while neglecting the training, encouragement and motivation of the team and individuals, (s)he may do very well in the short term. Eventually, however, the team members will give less effort than they are capable of. Similarly, a leader who concentrates only on creating team spirit, while neglecting the task and the individuals, will not receive maximum contribution from the people. They may enjoy working in the team but they will lack the real sense of achievement that comes from accomplishing a task to the utmost of the collective ability.

So the leader/facilitator must try to achieve a balance by acting in all three areas of overlapping need. It is always wise to work out a list of required functions within the context of any given situation, based on a general agreement on the essentials. Here is Adair's original Sandhurst list, on which one's own adaptation may be based:

- *Planning*, e.g. seeking all available information.
  Defining group task, purpose or goal.
  Making a workable plan (in right decision-making framework).
- *Initiating*, e.g. briefing group on the aims and the plan.
  Explaining why aim or plan is necessary.
  Allocating tasks to group members.
  Setting group standards.
- *Controlling*, e.g. maintaining group standards.
  Influencing tempo.
  Ensuring all actions are taken towards objectives.
  Keeping discussion relevant.
  Prodding group to action/decision.
- *Supporting*, e.g. expressing acceptance of persons and their contribution.
  Encouraging group/individuals.
  Disciplining group/individuals.
  Creating team spirit.
  Relieving tension with humour.
  Reconciling disagreements or getting others to explore them.
- *Informing*, e.g. clarifying task and plan.
  Giving new information to the group,

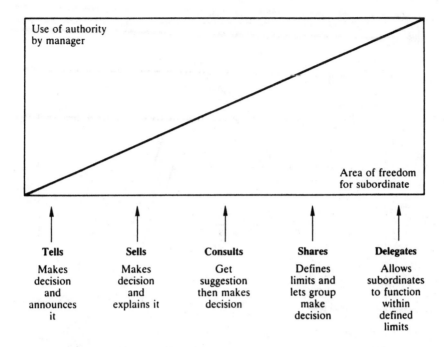

Figure 11.4 *Continuum of leadership behaviour*

i.e. keeping them 'in the picture'.
Receiving information from group.
Summarizing suggestions and ideas coherently.
- *Evaluating*, e.g. checking feasibility of an idea.
Testing the consequences of a proposed solution.
Evaluating group performance.
Helping the group to evaluate its own performance against standards.

Situational leadership

In dealing with the task, the team, and with any individual in the team, a style of leadership appropriate to the situation must be adopted. The teams and the individuals within them will, to some extent, start 'cold', but they will develop and grow in both strength and experience. The interface with the leader must also change with the change in the team, according to the Tannenbaum and Schmidt model (Figure 11.4).[1]

Initially a very directive approach may be appropriate, giving clear instructions to meet agreed goals. Gradually, as the teams become more experienced and have some success, the facilitating team leader will move through coaching and support to less directing and eventually a less supporting and less directive approach – as the more interdependent style permeates the whole organization.

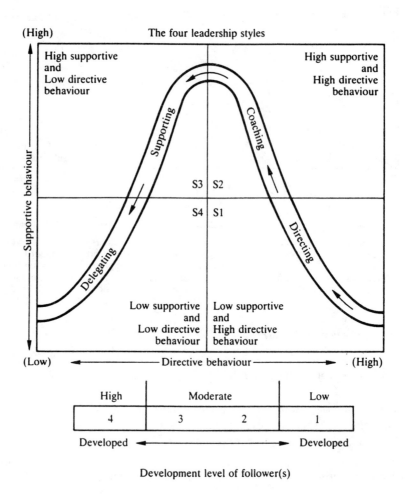

(High)   The four leadership styles

High supportive
and
Low directive
behaviour

High supportive
and
High directive
behaviour

S3 | S2
S4 | S1

Low supportive
and
Low directive
behaviour

Low supportive
and
High directive
behaviour

(Low) ◄──────── Directive behaviour ────────► (High)

High	Moderate		Low
4	3	2	1

Developed ◄──────────────────────► Developed

Development level of follower(s)

Figure 11.5 *Situational leadership – progressive empowerment through TQM*

This equates to the modified Blanchard model[1] in Figure 11.5, where directive behaviour moves from high to low as people develop and are more easily empowered. When this is coupled with the appropriate level of supportive behaviour, a directing style of leadership can move through coaching and supporting to a delegating style. It must be stressed, however, that effective delegation is only possible with developed 'followers', who can be fully empowered.

One of the great mistakes in recent years has been the expectation by management that teams can be put together with virtually no training or development (S 1 in Figure 11.5) and that they will perform as a mature team (S4). The Blanchard model emphasizes that there is no quick and easy 'tunnel' from S1 to S4. The only route is the laborious climb through S2 and S3.

11.3 Stages of team development

Original work by Tuckman[1] suggested that when teams are put togther, there are four main stages of team development, the so called forming (awareness), storming (conflict), norming (co-operation), and performing (productivity). The characteristics of each stage and some key aspects to look out for in the early stages are given below:

Forming – awareness

Characteristics:

- Feelings, weaknesses and mistakes are covered up.
- People conform to established lines.
- Little care is shown for others' values and views.
- There is no shared understanding of what needs to be done.

Watch out for:

- Increasing bureaucracy and paperwork.
- People confining themselves to defined jobs.
- The 'boss' is ruling with a firm hand.

Storming – conflict

Characteristics:

- More risky, personal issues are opened up.
- The team becomes more inward-looking.
- There is more concern for the values, views and problems of others in the team.

Watch out for:

- The team becomes more open, but lacks the capacity to act in a unified, economic, and effective way.

Norming – co-operation

Characteristics:

- Confidence and trust to look at how the team is operating.
- A more systematic and open approach, leading to a clearer and more methodical way of working.
- Greater valuing of people for their differences.

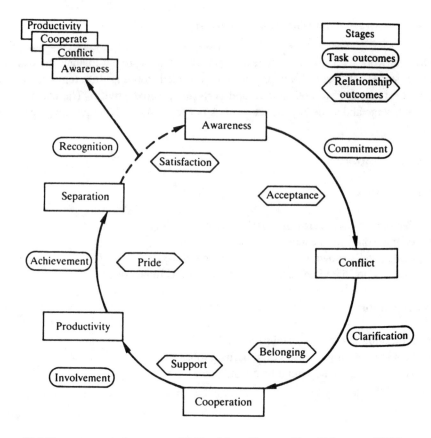

Figure 11.6 *Team stages and outcomes. (Derived from Kormanski and Mozenter, 1987)*

- Clarification of purpose and establishing of objectives.
- Systematic collection of information.
- Considering all options.
- Preparing detailed plans.
- Reviewing progress to make improvements.

Performing – productivity

Characteristics:

- Flexibility.
- Leadership decided by situations, not protocol.
- Everyone's energies utilized.
- Basic principles and social aspects of the organization's decisions considered.

The team stages, the task outcomes, and the relationship outcomes are shown together in Figure 11.6. This model, which has been modified from Kormonski and Mozenter,[2] may be used as a framework for the assessment of team peformance. The issues to look for are:

1 How is leadership exercised in the team?
2 How is decision making accomplished?
3 How are team resources utilized?
4 How are new members integrated into the team?

Teams which go through these stages successfully should become effective teams and display the following attributes.

Attributes of successful teams

Clear objectives and agreed goals

No group of people can be effective unless they know what they want to achieve, but it is more than knowing what the objectives are. People are only likely to be committed to them if they can identify with and have ownership of them – in other words, objectives and goals are agreed by team members.

Often this agreement is difficult to achieve but experience shows that it is an essential prerequisite for the effective group.

Openness and confrontation

If a team is to be effective, then the members of it need to be able to state their views, their differences of opinion, interests and problems, without fear of ridicule or retaliation. No teams work effectively if there is a cutthroat atmosphere, where members become less willing or able to express themselves openly; then much energy, effort and creativity are lost.

Support and trust

Support naturally implies trust among team members. Where individual group members do not feel they have to protect their territory or job, and feel able to talk straight to other members, about both 'nice' and 'nasty' things, then there is an opportunity for trust to be shown. Based on this trust, people can talk freely about their fears and problems and receive from others help they need to be more effective.

Co-operation and conflict

When there is an atmosphere of trust, members are more ready to participate and are committed. Information is shared rather than hidden. Individuals listen to the ideas of others and build on them. People find ways of being more helpful to each other and the group generally. Cooperation causes high morale – individuals accept each other's strengths and weaknesses and contribute from their pool of knowledge of skill. All abilities, knowledge and experience are fully utilized by the group; individuals have no inhibitions about using other people's abilities to help solve their problems, which are shared.

Allied to this, conflicts are seen as a necessary and useful part of organizational life. The effective team works through issues of conflict and uses the results to help objectives. Conflict prevents teams from becoming complacent and lazy, and often generates new ideas.

Good decision-making

As mentioned earlier, objectives need to be clearly and completely understood by all members before good decision making can begin. In making decisions effective, teams develop the ability to collect information quickly then discuss the alternatives openly. They become committed to their decisions and ensure quick action.

Appropriate leadership

Effective teams have a leader whose responsibility it is to achieve results through the efforts of a number of people. Power and authority can be applied in many ways, and team members often differ on the style of leadership they prefer. Collectively, teams may come to different views of leadership but, whatever their view, the effective team usually sorts through the alternatives in an open and honest way.

Review of the team processes

Effective teams understand not only the group's character and its role in the organization, but how it makes decisions, deals with conflicts, etc. The team process allows the team to learn from experience and consciously to improve teamwork. There are numerous ways of looking at team processes – use of an observer, by a team member giving feedback, or by the whole group discussing members' performance.

Sound inter-group relationships

No human being or group is an island; they need the help of others. An organization will not achieve maximum benefit from a collection of quality improvement teams that are effective within themselves but fight among each other.

Individual development opportunities

Effective teams seek to pool the skills of individuals, and it necessarily follows that they pay attention to development of individual skills and try to provide opportunities for individuals to grow and learn, and of course have FUN.

Once again, these ideas are not new but are very applicable and useful in the management of teams for quality improvements, just as Newton's theories on gravity still apply!

11.4   Team roles and personality types

No one person has a monopoly of 'good' characteristics. Attempts to list the qualities of the ideal manager, for example, demonstrate why that paragon cannot exist. This is because many of the qualities are mutually exclusive, for example:

Highly intelligent	*v*	Not *too* clever
Forceful and dominant	*v*	Sensitive to people's feelings
Dynamic	*v*	Patient
Fluent communicator	*v*	Good listener
Decisive	*v*	Reflective

Although no individual can possess all these and more desirable qualities, a team often does.

The overwhelming majority of behavioural research has been concerned with the individual. Since the early 1980s, however, some very valuable work has at least been done on teams, including that of Dr Meredith Belbin. Through observation over many years, both in industry and in the world of management training, Belbin identified a set of eight 'roles' which, if all present in a team, give that team the best possible chance of success. Indeed the eight roles are the only ones available in a team, they are:

Coordinator (or chairman)
Shaper
Plant (ideas generator)
Monitor – evaluator
Implementer (or worker)
Resource investigator
Teamworker
Finisher

A preponderance of a few of these roles and the absence of some within the team are a pretty good guarantee of failure, whatever the intelligence, motivation, etc., of the individuals concerned.

A few general points are worth making about team roles:

- The term 'plant' is used because this type, if 'planted' in a bogged-down group, will get it going again.
- All roles have value, and are missed when not in a team. There are no 'stars' or 'extras'.
- In small teams people can and do assume more than one role.
- The roles divide generally into outward- and inward-looking groups:

Outward-looking	*Inward-looking*
Coordinator	Implementor
Plant	Monitor-evaluator
Resource investigator	Team worker
Shaper	Finisher

- The team role for an individual is determined by the completion and analysis of Belbin's self-administered questionnaire.

Using team roles

Eight people are not required for a team, but people who are aware and capable of carrying out the roles should be present. A team will not perform so effectively if there is not a good match between the attributes of team members and their responsibilities, e.g., if the co-ordinator is actually a shaper.

Most people play different roles to suit different situations. The natural or *main* role for an individual may be a shaper, but if there is already a strong shaper in the group, it may be advisable for him/her to develop a *secondary* role.

Some roles represent *active characteristics*, e.g. the shaper 'makes things happen' and the implementor 'converts plans into tasks'. Other roles are *passive descriptions* of personality, e.g., the teamworker 'dislikes friction and confrontation' and the plant is 'forthright' and 'independent'. Groups need active members. They are not necessarily people who talk too much and dominate a meeting, but people who make a positive contribution to the proceedings.

Analysing existing groups and their performance or behaviour, using the team roles concept, can lead to improvement, e.g.

- Underachievement demands a good co-ordinator or finisher.
- Conflict within the group requires a teamworker or strong co-ordinator.
- Mediocre performance can be improved by a resource investigator, innovator or shaper.
- Error prone groups need a clever evaluator and an able organizer.

Stable organizations need a different mix of people to those operating in areas of rapid change. Different roles are more important in particular circumstances. For example, new groups need a strong shaper to get started, competitive situations demand an innovator with good ideas, and in areas of high risk a good evaluator may be needed. Teams should be analysed therefore, both in terms of what team roles members can play, and also in relation to what team skills are most needed.

The Belbin team roles concept has the merit of simplicity. The author and his colleagues believe, however, that a more complete, understandable, and helpful approach is provided by the use of the personality type indicator described in the following section.

Understanding and valuing team members – the MBTI

A powerful aid to team development is the use of the Myers-Briggs Type Indicator (MBTI).[2] This is based on an individual's preferences on four scales for:

- Giving and receiving 'energy.'
- Gathering information.

- Making decisions.
- Handling the outer world.

Its aim is to help individuals understand and value themselves and others, in terms of their differences as well as their similarities. It is well researched and non-threatening when used appropriately.

The four MBTI preferences scales, which are based on Jung's theories of psychological types, represent two opposite preferences:

- *Extroversion – Introversion* – how we prefer to give/receive energy or focus our attention.
- *Sensing – iNtuition* – how we prefer to gather information.
- *Thinking – Feeling* – how we prefer to make decisions.
- *Judgement – Perception* – how we prefer to handle the outer world.

To understand what is meant by preferences, the analogy of left and right-handedness is useful. Most people have a preference to write with either their left or their right hand. When using the preferred hand, they tend not to think about it, it is done naturally. When writing with the other hand, however, it takes longer, needs careful concentration, seems more difficult, but with practice would no doubt become easier. Most people *can* write with and use both hands, but tend to prefer one over the other. This is similar to the MBTI psychological preferences: most people are able to use both preferences at different times, but will indicate a preference on each of the scales.

In all, there are eight possible preferences – E or I, S or N, T or F, J or P, i.e. two opposites for each of the four scales. An individual's *type* is the combination and interaction of the four preferences. It can be assessed initially by completion of a simple questionnaire. Hence, if each preference is represented by its letter, a person's type may be shown by a four letter code – there are sixteen in all. For example, ESTJ represents an *extrovert* (E) who prefers to gather information with *sensing* (S), prefers to make decisions by *thinking* (T) and has a *judging* (J) attitude towards the world, i.e. prefers to make decisions rather than continue to collect information. The person with opposite preferences on all four scales would be an INFP, an introvert who prefers intuition for perceiving, feelings or values for making decisions, and likes to maintain a perceiving attitude towards the outer world.

The questionnaire, its analysis and feedback must be administered by a qualified MBTI practitioner, who may also act as external facilitator to the team in its forming and storming stages.

Type and teamwork

With regard to teamwork, the preference types and their interpretation are extremely powerful. The *extrovert* prefers action and the outer world, whilst the *introvert* prefers ideas and the inner world.

Sensing-thinking types are interested in facts, analyse facts impersonally, and use a step-by-step process from cause to effect, premise to conclusion. The *sensing-feeling* combinations, however, are interested in facts, analyse facts personally, and are concerned about how things matter to themselves and others.

Intuition-thinking types are interested in possibilities, analyse possibilities impersonally, and have theoretical, technical, or executive abilities. On the other hand, the *intuition-feeling* combinations are interested in possibilities, analyse possibilities personally, and prefer new projects, new truths, things not yet apparent.

Judging types are decisive and planful, they live in orderly fashion, and like to regulate and control. *Perceivers*, on the other hand are flexible, live spontaneously, and understand and adapt readily.

As we have seen, an individual's type is the combination of four preferences on each of the scales. There are sixteen combinations of the preference scales and these may be displayed on a *type table* (Figure 11.7). If the individuals within a team are prepared to share with each other their MBTI preferences, this can dramatically increase understanding and frequently is of great assistance in team development and good team working. The similarities and differences in behaviour and personality can be identified. The assistance of a qualified MBTI practitioner is absolutely essential in the initial stages of this work.

The five 'A' stages for teamwork

For any of these models or theories to benefit a team, the individuals within it need to become *aware* of the theory, e.g. the MBTI. They then need to *accept* the principles as valid, *adopt* them for themselves in order to *adapt* their behaviour accordingly. This will lead to individual and team *action* (Figure 11.8).

In the early stages of team development particularly, the assistance of a skilled facilitator to aid progress through these stages is necessary. This is often neglected, causing failure in so many team initatives. In such cases the net output turns out to be lots of nice warm feelings about 'how good that team workshop was a year ago', but the nagging reality that no action came out and nothing has really changed.

11.5   Implementing teamwork for quality improvement – the 'DRIVE' model

The author and his colleagues have developed a model for a structured approach to problem solving in teams, the *DRIVE* model. The mnemonic provides landmarks to keep the team on track and in the right direction:

Define   – the problem. *Output*: written definition of the task and its success criteria.

Review   – the information. *Output*: presentation of known data and action plan for further data.

Investigate – the problem. *Output*: documented proposals for improvement and action plans.

Verify   – the solution. *Output*: proposed improvements that meet success criteria.

Execute   – the change. *Output*: task achieved and improved process documented.

ISTJ	ISFJ	INFJ	INTJ
ISTP	ISFP	INFP	INTP
ESTP	ESFP	ENFP	ENTP
ESTJ	ESFJ	ENFJ	ENTJ

Figure 11.7 *MBTI type table form. Source: Isabel Briggs Myers, Introduction to Type*[2]

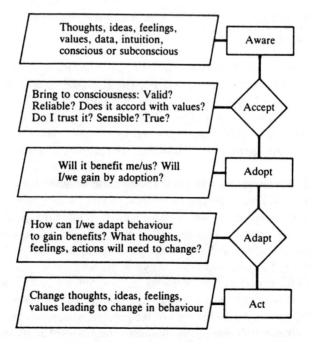

Figure 11.8 *The five 'A' stages for teamwork*

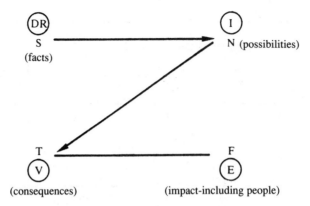

Figure 11.9 *The DRIVE model and MBTI-based problem-solving*

The DRIVE model fits well with the MBTI Z-shaped problem-solving approach. Figure 11.9 shows how the stages relate to the S-N-T-F path.

The various stages are discussed in detail in Oakland (1993).[3]

Steps in the introductions of teams

The idea of introducing problem solving groups, quality circles or quality improvement teams often makes its way into an organization through the awareness of successful results in other organizations or companies. There is no fixed methodology for starting a teamwork programme, but there are certain key points that must be considered:

1   The concept should be presented to (or come from) management and supervision, and their commitment and support enlisted. It should be possible at this stage to engage the interest and support of potential team leaders.
2   Projects should be started slowly and on a small scale. Ideally a pilot scheme, run by the most enthusiastic candidates and in the most promising areas, should be launched. Early teething troubles, doubts and worries may then be identified and resolved.
3   Selected or volunteer team or circle leaders must be trained in all aspects of group leadership, and the appropriate techniques, and they should subsequently help train the team members in the techniques required in effective problem solving. The techniques of statistical process control (SPC) should be introduced, particularly brainstorming, cause and effect analysis, Pareto analysis and charting. These concepts lay the groundwork for analysing problems in a systematic fashion, and show that the majority of the problems are concentrated into a few areas.
4   Once the causes have been determined, a solution can be proposed. This solution may affect any of the components of the process: equipment, procedures, training, input requirements or output requirements. The proposed solution should be tested by the team or circle, particularly if procedures are affected.

5 If the test of a solution proves successful, full-scale implementation can then be carried out. In the case of procedures, full documentation of the solution and management approval should be obtained. The procedure can then be communicated to all personnel concerned. Full-scale changes in equipment and other processes should occur in the same manner. The team should monitor implementation of the solution, plotting the appropriate data until the criteria for solution are met.

With the initial problems declared solved, the circle or team may then tackle another problem, and another, or be disbanded and new teams formed. The record of successful solutions will motivate other teams within the organization, and ideas should spread. As the number of teams in a company grows, new opportunities arise for stimulating interest. Some large companies organize in-house conferences of their quality improvement teams and quality circles, providing the opportunity for the publication of results and for recognition. Experience has shown that very significant improvements in areas such as energy reduction, productivity, and cost-effectiveness, in addition to quality, may be achieved by the project team approach.

One of the problems of the team approach to problem identification and solving is that sometimes the teams are organized because it is the fashionable thing to do. They either exist on paper only, or the meetings are social gatherings where nothing is learned, no projects are initiated, and people do not grow. Another common problem is that the teams attempt to solve problems without first learning the necessary techniques: enthusiasm outruns ability. Teams have enormous potential for helping to solve an organization's problems, but for them to be successful, they must follow a disciplined approach to problem solving, using proven techniques.

The team approach to problem solving works. It taps the skills and initiative of all personnel engaged in a process. This may mean a change in culture, which must be supported by management through its own activities and behaviour.

11.6   Adding the teams to the TQM model

In part 1 of this book the foundations for TQM were set down. The core of customer/supplier chains and, at every interface, a process were surrounded by the 'soft' outcomes of culture, communications, and commitment. In Parts 2 and 3 were added the hard management necessities of systems and tools. We are now ready to complete the model with the necessity of teams – the councils, the PQTs, QITs, quality circles, DPA groups, etc., which work on the processes – using the tools – to bring about continuous improvements in the systems that manage them. (Figure 11.10).

The author is grateful for the significant contribution to this chapter made by his colleagues in O&F Quality Management Consultants Ltd, Stephen Mathews, Development Director and John Glover, Senior Consultant.

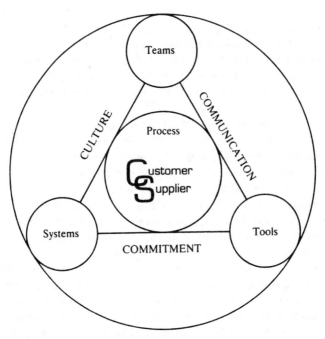

Figure 11.10 *Total quality management – teamwork added to complete the model*

Chapter highlights

The need for teamwork

- The only efficient way to tackle process improvement or complex problems is through teamwork. The team approach allows individuals and organizations to grow.
- Employees will not engage continual improvement without commitment from the top, a quality 'climate', and an effective mechanism for capturing individual contributions.
- Teamwork for quality improvement is driven by a strategy, needs a structure, and must be implemented thoughtfully and effectively.

Teamwork and action-centred leadership

- Early work in the field of human relations by McGregor, Maslow, and Hertzberg was useful to John Adair in the development of his model for teamwork and action-centred leadership.
- Adair's model addresses the needs of the task, the team, and the individuals in the team, in the form of three overlapping circles. There are specific task, team and individual functions for the leader, but (s)he must concentrate on the small central overlap area of the three circles.

- The team process has inputs and outputs. Good teams have three main attributes: high task fulfilment, high team maintenance, and low self-orientation.
- In dealing with the task, the team and its individuals, a situational style of leadership must be adopted. This may follow the Tannenbaum and Schmidt, and Blanchard models through directing, coaching, and supporting to delegating.

Stages of team development

- When teams are put together, they pass through Tuckman's forming (awareness), storming (conflict), norming (co-operation), and performing (productivity) stages of development.
- Teams that go through these stages successfully become effective and display clear objectives and agreed goals, openness and confrontation, support and trust, co-operation and conflict, good decision-making, appropriate leadership, review of the team processes, sound relationships, and individual development opportunities.

Team roles and personality types

- Valuable work on team behaviour by Belbin has identified eight team roles: co-ordinator, shaper, plant, monitor/evaluator, implementor, resource investigator, teamworker, finisher.
- Eight people are not required for a team, but the roles, either as the main or secondary individual functions, should be present. Analysing existing groups and their performance or behaviour, using the team roles concept, can lead to improvement.
- The Belbin team roles have the merit of simplicity, but a more complete, understandable, helpful approach is provided by the Myers-Briggs Type Indicator (MBTI).
- The MBTI is based on individuals' preferences on four scales for giving and receiving 'energy' (extroversion-E or introversion-I), gathering information (sensing-S or intuition-N), making decisions (thinking-T or feeling-F) and handling the outer world (judging-J or perceiving-P).
- An individual's type is the combination and interaction of the four scales and can be assessed initially by completion of a simple questionnaire. There are sixteen types in all, which may be displayed for a team on a type table.
- The five As: for any of the teamwork models and theories, the individuals must become aware, need to accept, adopt and adapt, in order to act. A skilled facilitator is always necessary.

Implementing teamwork for quality improvement – the DRIVE model

- A structured approach to problem-solving is provided by the DRIVE model: define the problem, review the information, investigate the problem, verify the solution, and execute the change which is similar to the Z-shaped MBTI stepwise problem-solving process: S-N-T-F.

- After initial problems are solved, others should be tackled – successful solutions motivating new teams. In all cases teams should follow a disciplined approach to problem-solving, using proven techniques.
- Teamwork may mean a change in culture, which must be supported by management through its activities and behaviour.

Adding the teams to the TQM model

The third and final hard management necessity – the teams – are added to the tools and systems to complete the TQM model.

References

1   See references under *TQM through people and teamwork* heading in Bibliography, pages 361–2.
2   *Ibid.*
3   John Oakland, *Total Quality Management*, 2nd Edition, Butterworth-Heinemann, 1993.

Case studies

C7

Organizing for success at Pirelli Communication Cables

Introduction

TQM is now recognized by enlightened companies as being of strategic importance in the drive for market share. Such companies may engage in a programme of publicity, employee briefings, training courses, new working practices and have a commitment to achieving excellent, and yet the much-sought-after benefits do not materialize. Instead of order there is confusion, instead of progress there is stagnation, instead of success there is failure, resulting in frustration and a belief that TQM is not the way forward to the cultural change necessary for continuous improvement.

To be successful, some companies believe that an organizational structure must be established at the outset of introducing TQM in order to create a framework which will enable quality improvement to develop and flourish. The structure itself is considered a key factor in achieving success and must be given priority attention by senior management. Such a company is Pirelli Communication Cables, a division within the Pirelli General PLC group responsible for the design, manufacturing and installation of both optical and copper communication/control cables in the UK and world markets. Pirelli Communication Cables implemented a TQM-based organizational structure several years ago. This case describes the details which have involved all employees in the company.

Organizational structure

The structure for implementing quality improvement throughout the company is shown in Figure C7.1. The structure has been designed to harness the total potential to improve at every level of the organization and, being simple, is well-understood by all employees. This means that each individual in each department can readily become involved in the quality improvement process.

The following sections describe the five key elements of the structure and explain how the element activities were integrated together to achieve continuous quality

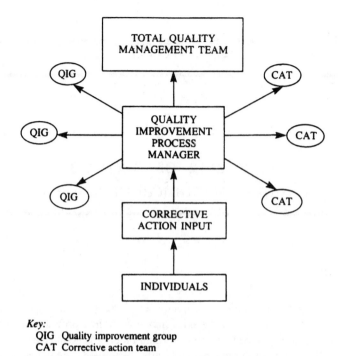

Key:
QIG Quality improvement group
CAT Corrective action team

Figure C7.1 *Organizational structure for quality improvements*

improvement. It will be shown that by implementing this structure, and by using the methodology and tools/techniques referred to, total quality concepts have been established throughout Pirelli Communication Cables.

Total Quality Management Team

The Total Quality Management Team (TQMT) consists of the General Manager, the first-line reporting managers and a specialist for facilitating the operation of the Quality Improvement Groups (QIGs) and the Corrective Action Teams (CATs). This facilitator is known as the Quality Improvement Process (QIP) Manager within Pirelli Communication Cables, to place emphasis on the nature of the activities involved.

The TQMT determines policy, establishes direction, provides support and, by example, demonstrates commitment to quality improvement. It is important that the TQMT does not act as a corrective action team or deal with specific quality issues; these are dealt with at other forums convened for that specific purpose. The TQMT operates as a steering group for the implementation of TQM, and the responsibilities for the various tasks involved are divided among the TQMT members. This is considered an essential requirement as all senior management must be actively involved and the various tasks have been divided as follows:

General Manager	Chair, Managment commitment
Marketing Manager	Communications
Technical Manager	Special events
Financial Controller	Cost of quality
Operations Manager	Tools and techniques
Purchasing Manager	Performance measures
Personnel Manager	Education, recognition
QIP Manager	QIGs, CATs
Quality Manager	Secretary, planning

The General Manager has led the way and has ensured that the TQMT members demonstrate *commitment* by acting as role models at all times. *Communications* have been specifically addressed to determine the most effective methods and media to be used to ensure all employees are kept informed of progress. Monitoring the *cost of defects* has proved to be a powerful management driver for quality improvement and *performance* has been measured whenever possible to provide a basis for QIG, CAT and individual improvement initiatives. The *education* and *recognition* of personnel has been a major task to organize and a master plan has been established to ensure timely progress was maintained. *Tools and techniques*, such as Statistical Process Control (SPC), have been introduced where appropriate and *special events* arranged, such as the initial launch of TQM and the issue of news bulletins. The task-holders have become local experts in their particular areas of responsibility and they facilitate the implementation of the action plan agreed at the TQMT meetings.

Terms of reference have been established for the TQMT in Pirelli Communication Cables, as detailed below. These have been published throughout the company to ensure the function and role of the TQMT is fully understood.

Terms of reference for the TQMT

1 To determine policy for quality improvement within the company.
2 To establish an environment where QIGs and CATs and CATs can flourish.
3 To establish procedures for measuring ongoing performance and cost of quality and ensure corrective actions are taken where appropriate.
4 Actively to support the implementation of the established policy consistently and on a continuous basis, ensuring that all disciplines/work areas are fully involved in quality improvement.
5 To hold meetings at 3-week intervals during normal working hours for approximately 1 hour to determine the implementation programme and monitor progress. Minutes will be issued of each meeting held to record decisions and actions agreed.

Quality Improvement Process Manager

The QIP Manager facilitates the day-to-day operations of the QIGs and CATs and, as such, has a major role in the ongoing success of the quality improvement process. The individual chosen was carefully selected: he was an efficient organizer, an able motivator, enthusiastic and had well-proven management experience. He was also suf-

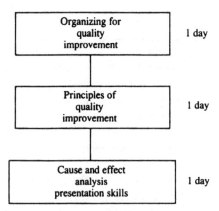

Figure C7.2 *QIG training programme*

ficiently senior in the organization to have the authority to ensure actions would be taken where required.

The QIP Manager is responsible for establishing the QIGs in the first instance and was actively involved in the training programme at the initial launch. Three days of training have been developed, as shown in Figure C7.2.

Once the groups were established, the QIP Manager provided assistance to the group leaders, ensured operating procedures were being implemented, monitored progress through the QIG meeting minutes, arranged for TQMT members to attend QIG meetings from time to time to demonstrate management commitment and interest, and organized quarterly reviews with all QIG leaders. A report is presented at each TQMT meeting to ensure top management visibility is maintained.

The second major role for the QIP Manager has been to facilitate the operation of the corrective action system and the CATs. A single interface is provided for the company in terms of processing, reporting and communicating corrective actions. This ensures that there is no duplication of effort and priorities can be established to deal with the major problems first. Corrective Action Requests (CARs) can arise either from QIGs or individuals and assistance is provided to identify the process owner and, where appropriate, to select the CAT leader. A database of personnel with specific skills is held for reference in selecting CAT members; this ensures that the 'experts' are known and serve on CATs where required. The QIP Manager keeps the TQMT informed of all CARs in progress and priorities will be decided by the TQMT when necessary.

Quality Improvement Groups

QIGs operate at all levels in the organization on a departmental basis. The QIG leader is generally the supervisor of the work area concerned, which in some cases may be a senior staff member. A team approach is adopted, however, and all QIG members are equal as far as the group operation is concerned. A QIG leader's guide has been published to provide ideas for discussion at the QIG meetings and guidance on specific topical issues.

QIGs create the framework where personnel involvement can be maximized in striving for improvement and excellence. The groups address quality issues within their specific departments/work areas, with the object purpose of reducing waste and error, enhancing performance and proposing corrective actions for those issues which cannot be resolved by the QIG concerned. They create an opportunity to resolve many of the frustrating, niggling quality issues which affect the smooth running and efficiency of day-to-day operations.

Benefits for those participating include improved morale, increased job satisfaction, stimulation of teamwork and development of skills.

In Pirelli Communication Cables a total of 25 groups has been established covering all departments on site. The number of personnel who have completed 3-day training courses for QIGs equates to 50% of the workforce; all these personnel, both white- and blue-collar, are active members of QIGs. It is planned to train the remaining 50% of the workforce to enable these people to become involved on a rotation basis.

Improvement is managed by the QIGs on a project-by-project basis. A simple recording and control system is operated by the QIG leader, which enables progress to be monitored.

Corrective Action Teams

CATs address specific CARs with the purpose of establishing a permanent and cost-effective solution. The QIP Manager facilitates the appointment of the CAT leader where appropriate; the leader will be selected for his/her skills or knowledge in dealing with a particular problem. The CAT leader selects his/her team, which should comprise no more than five members; reference to the database of skilled personnel is made to assist in this exercise. It is important that the team members invest adequate time and effort to team activities and must not compromise progress by nominating deputies. For this reason, the CARs must be carefully prioritized and resources allocated to ensure a successful closure of each request.

The CAT will address only the problem allocated for investigation and resolution. When the work is complete, the CAT will be disbanded and the CAR closed down. The QIP Manager is responsible for managing the total activity to ensure maximum use is made of the company resources. The QIP Manager will decide when a CAR can be addressed by an individual or when a CAT is required. The TQMT members may be consulted in particular cases to assist in making this decision.

CAT members are trained in tools and techniques in a similar manner to the QIGs (see Figure C7.2). More advanced courses are also being organized for the next phase of implementing TQM.

Individuals

It is important that all employees, from goods-in to goods-out, from marketing to design, from reception to delivery, are totally involved in the QIP process. The structure has, therefore, been designed to enable all individuals to contribute by applying the quality improvement principles to their own job. Every individual receives 1 day of training in these principles to provide a common understanding throughout the business of what is required. Individuals are encouraged to strive for excellence and improvement on a day-to-day basis and to raise issues either through their local QIG or by raising a CAR.

The reasons for success at Pirelli Communication Cables

Management commitment, publicity, training and improved working practices are all important elements of a TQM programme but in themselves they are insufficient to ensure success. The successful implementation of TQM requires a defined organizational structure which demands and harnesses the potential of the workforce. This can be achieved by establishing teams and groups to manage quality improvement across the company, thereby organizing for success. In this way the considerable benefits of the TQM route, i.e. achieving excellence in all aspects of business and employee performance, will be realized.

A defined organizational structure is essential if TQM is to be successfully implemented. This case shows that Total Quality has to be managed and that this can be achieved by means of senior management involvement through, in the case of Pirelli, the TQMT, by appointing a QIP manager to facilitate day-to-day operations, by establishing QIGs throughout all departments to manage local improvements, by organizing CATs to address specific company-wide problems, and by involving all employees through individual efforts and through QIGs and CARs.

TQM must be seen as a fundamental part of the business operation and not as an add-on extra. Continuous hard work, determination and persistence and a total commitment from the top down are all essential ingredients which, together with the defined structure, will ensure success in the greatest of all ambitions – to become the best. In this way the considerable benefit of the TQM route – achieving excellence in all aspects of business and employee performance – has been realized at Pirelli Communication Cables.

C8

Organization and teamwork for quality at Thomas Cork SML

Introduction

Thomas Cork S M Ltd is part of the Hartz Mountain Corporation of Harrison, New Jersey, the world's largest supplier of pet accessories. The company's principal business is the supply of complex ranges of non-food products to supermarkets. It is located in a modern purpose-built warehouse complex in Nottingham, UK, and provides a comprehensive distribution service with full merchandising support at store level.

Orders are picked in individual units, priced according to customer requirement and shipped direct to stores. The warehouse currently processes between 1 and 1.5 million units per week. Store deliveries are made by the company's own team of merchandisers who merchandise customers' fixtures and place a reorder for the next delivery.

The company operates throughout the UK and the Republic of Ireland. It employs 600 people, almost half of whom work on sales and merchandising. It currently markets and distributes around 2000 lines. These include Hartz pet accessories, Cover Girl cosmetics, Stylers haircare, Scholl footcare, Supermark stationery, Stitch & Sew sewing accessories, Rhymers babycare, Duracell batteries and a comprehensive range of housewares.

The common feature of these ranges is complexity. Many of them are ownbranded ranges for which the company is responsible for marketing and buying. Products are sourced from the UK and from around the world. The company's customer base includes Sainsbury, Tesco, Asda, Gateway, Safeway, regional multiples and Co-ops.

The company sends its merchandising teams to set up and manage display stands as part of each store's operation, adapting their approach according to the company they happen to be servicing. It is a complex and subtle relationship, in which the merchandisers have to justify by sales the space they occupy, while maintaining a wide range of products, some of which move only slowly, but are essential to the overall impression of comprehensiveness and variety.

Managing Thomas Cork calls for a knowledge of the needs and expectations of its suppliers and retailers, plus an insight into the needs and expectations of the retailers' customers, too. The demands include the utmost reliability of supply and the absolute minimum of defects and deficiencies.

Apart from the problems relating to managing 2000 products across a number of ranges, because the company's merchandisers operate within customers' stores, it has to accommodate individual customers' requirements and work within their systems. This inevitably adds considerably to the complexity of the business. For example, Thomas Cork supplies both Gateway and Tesco with more individual product lines than any other suppliers.

The need for quality management

The Chairman and Managing Director were concerned for some time about growing complexity and the problems being encountered in day-to-day management. It seemed that an inordinate amount of time was being spent on fire-fighting, and 'getting it right first time' simply did not appear to be part of the company vocabulary. The company had survived, even prospered, by 'crisis management'.

About four years ago the Chairman/Managing Director was invited to a seminar on Cost-Effective Quality Management, sponsored by the Department of Trade and

Industry. He had previously heard a good deal about Quality Management but had tended to associate this with manufacturing companies. This particular seminar soon convinced him, however, that the principles applied equally to companies involved in activities such as distribution and service.

Following discussions within the board room, they concluded that a Quality Management Programme could be very beneficial to the company and decided to proceed. Their objective was to change the culture of the business so that all the principles of Quality Management would become a natural part of the day-to-day activity, thereby enhancing the efficiency and profitability of the company.

At this stage, the Board made a number of decisions on how they should implement the programme.

1 They would take on a Quality Consultant to advise on technique and to provide guidance and assistance to help drive the programme along.
2 They agreed that the programme would be successful only if it had the total commitment of both Directors and Senior Management and that this group of people should be involved in the Quality Programme through all its stages.
3 They decided not to work to a fixed timetable, but considered that it was essential to have made sufficient progress at each stage in order to create confidence in the benefits of the programme, before moving on to the next stage.

The question now was, how should the Board of the company proceed to introduce their ideas?

The introduction

The programme began with a 2-day introduction for Directors, at which the principles and techniques of TQM were explained by the consultant. They then proceeded to redefine the company's policy and objectives. A similar exercise was carried out with the company's Senior Management and they too came up with views on the company's policies and objectives, not always the same as the Directors. This was immediately followed by a joint meeting with Directors and Senior Management, at which the final Policy Document was agreed.

A Programme Management Team (PMT) was set up at this stage to oversee the introduction of the Quality Programme. The Chairman/Managing Director acted as Chairman of the PMT and a coordinator was appointed to look after administration and to coordinate the work of the Team. All Directors and Senior Management were coopted on to the PMT.

The next stage was to identify the key problem areas which were preventing the company from operating effectively. Two exercises were carried out. The first was a Needs and Expectations exercise, which involved a large number of people from all levels and all departments within the business. Who – they asked themselves – receives my work and that of my department, and are we supplying them with what they really need and want?

The Financial Controller recalled the excitement of senior managers when they realized their opportunity to speak directly and freely to the Board. That sense of involvement and participation was extended downwards; for example, the Director responsible for transport went out with one of the lorry drivers – and came back with a checklist of questions and ideas.

The second exercise was devoted to identifying the amount of management time spent on fire-fighting. These two exercises highlighted a comparatively small number of problems which appeared to account for a large proportion of the difficulties.

In all, six key problems were identified, but it was realized that they could not all be dealt with simultaneously and it was decided that three Action Teams should be established to tackle the most pressing problem areas. Each of the Action Teams had its own Chairperson (who reported to the PMT) and Coordinator. Each team was made up by representatives from a number of departments and these were selected from different levels of management to ensure good cross-representation within the processes involved and to bring together the people best equipped to find a solution, without regard for rank or departmental boundaries. This was particularly important as it ensured that departments were working in close cooperation with common objectives. During the early stages the consultant attended PMT and Action Team meetings to provide guidance and assistance, particularly on problem-solving techniques.

The role of the Coordinator was very important. He or she was responsible for arranging meetings, for administration and, generally, acting as progress-chaser. The first task for each of the Action Teams was to define its objectives and then to tackle the particular problem allocated to them. It was also decided that all of the management needed to be informed about the programme, to stimulate their interest and to enlist their support. This was done at a 2-day management conference.

We now move into the most difficult phase of the programme. Remember, the management were already stretched trying to cope with complex day-to-day problems, endless fire-fighting and simply the job of surviving. To this the Board were to add the burden of Action Team and PMT meetings. These involved a lot of people and took up a great deal of time. Far from improving job satisfaction, the initial stage of the programme brought little but frustration and all that was offered in return was hope that things could only get better.

The Senior Management faced the problems of deciding what was important now, and how they should tell people of the important issues and stress the benefits of quality improvement.

The implementation

The importance of the PMT Coordinator and the Consultant became apparent at this stage. It was necessary to maintain strict discipline to ensure that meetings were held as planned and that reports were submitted on time.

They found that it is necessary to keep the 'day-to-day management function' and 'the improvement function' separate in the early stages of a TQM programme.

Ultimately, ongoing improvement must be the major management focus, but it is unrealistic to assume that such a cultural change can be brought in overnight. Thomas Cork's experience was that this change can be brought about by having two parallel structures working together. Soon the members of the Management Team started to question the need for two structures and resolved to create one integrated operation.

The company found that, for successful projects, training is needed in team skills. Although the management recognized that individuals are different, it was very useful to formalize the process of recognizing these differences and to concentrate on the inherent strengths and weaknesses of different personality types. Training in these concepts, together with frank discussions about the dynamics of the management team concerned, led to much stronger and more constructive management team operations.

They found it was crucial specifically to spell out the role of the PMT (or Quality Council) and to spell out the role of the Action Team. This allowed the PMT to establish a specific brief for each Action Team so that their activities became very focused. It was easy for Action Teams to drift from specific topics to attempt to resolve every issue facing the company.

One area which needed strong management was that when an Action Team had completed its task, it should be thanked publicly and disbanded. It is easy to allow an Action Team to continue after its first task has been completed, which can be quite a mistake.

People also needed constant reminders of the benefits which could be derived from the programme. The management quickly learnt that, just because they were dealing with problems in a more constructive manner using the newly acquired problem-solving techniques, there were no quick solutions and it was quite some time before workable solutions began to see the light of day. This undoubtedly was the low point of the programme. All the efforts and cost of the programme – but none of the benefits.

Slowly but surely, however, Thomas Cork began to get results. Solutions were found and, more importantly, people began to understand that, by working through problems or tackling new opportunities with well-constructed Action Teams, they could get much better results and improve efficiency and customer service. Individual managers began to set up ad hoc Action Teams to tackle problems and opportunities using the same techniques. They were also becoming more proactive in seeking opportunities to improve efficiency.

Once the full commitment of the management was secured and they began to see the benefits of the programme in terms of reduced fire-fighting and increased efficiency, it was decided that all employees should be involved. This was done by holding a Quality Week, during which all employees attended Quality Meetings. They worked with comparatively small groups so that each employee had an opportunity to participate directly in these meetings. A special edition of the company's newspaper, featuring Quality Week, was also published.

This last phase of the Quality Management Programme was launched and the company is still steadily developing programmes to involve all of the staff. There is still a long way to go but they are already seeing important contributions, particularly in the warehouse and in the sales and merchandising operations.

As far as the management is concerned, the principles of Quality Management have become a way of life. The Quality Programme is no longer run on a stand-alone basis but has been integrated into the normal management process. The PMT has been disbanded and its functions have been taken over by the Management Committee.

The managers of Thomas Cork SML are eloquent about the pain and frustration of TQM but they are unanimous that the suffering is worthwhile in the long run. 'It's not a bed of roses', warned the Chairman and Managing Director, 'or an instant revolution. We were warned that things would get worse before they got better – and that's certainly true – but I have no doubts about the benefits.'

He cites product launches as one of the areas of greatest progress. 'In the old days, there was not enough coordination of planning between departments, work fell behind schedule, and there were crises that could be solved only by throwing money at them. Sometimes, too, salesmen would make overambitious promises, and leave others to make them good. The company has now taken to heart the lesson preached by our quality consultants: that planning is the only worthwhile management activity, because it eliminates personal control (failure to delegate effectively) and fire-fighting (reacting to crises as they break).'

Interdepartmental action teams now plan every product launch in detail well in advance, according to a basic master plan. Salesmen who make rash promises are themselves made responsible for forming the action team which will fulfil them.

The Operations Director has launched a 'needs and expectations' exercise in the warehouse, where pickers have the monotonous but vital front-line job of making up the orders. It is also too easy here for a picker to be blamed for picking and packing the wrong item, when at least part of the responsibility lies with the person who put it in the wrong tray – or, more likely, with the system of working.

The Financial Controller is able to quote figures. 'We estimated the annual cost of wasted time in doing jobs twice as something between half and three-quarters of a million pounds,' he says. 'In the first 2 years of our quality programme, we have reduced these costs by half a million!'

It is this cost-effectiveness that has persuaded the Operations Director that Total Quality is more than just another gimmick. He no longer sees quality solely in terms of the product or service to the customer, but as 'part of everything everybody does'. Fundamentally, he believes, it is a matter of attitude.

What the company has achieved

1 There is a much greater spirit of cooperation between departments, with all departments working with a common purpose.
2 There has been a substantial reduction in time spent fire-fighting.
3 The company has been able to achieve a significant reduction in costs.
4 It has been possible to improve the company's profitability considerably, despite the quite difficult problems caused by the recession.

What advice may be given to companies embarking on a TQM programme?

1   Leadership must come from the top.
2   There must be complete commitment to the programme by all management.
3   The organization of the teams and the choice of personnel is crucial to success.
4   Be prepared to pass through a pain barrier before beginning to see any real benefit from the programme.
5   Avoid creating an unduly high level of expectation, otherwise there will be much disappointment and frustration during the early stages.

And finally:

- *A Quality Programme is hard work but well worth the effort.*

Discussion questions

1 The so-called process approach has certain implications for organizational structures. Discuss the main organizational issues influencing the involvement of people in process improvement.

2 Various TQM teamwork structures are advocated by many writers. Describe the role of the various 'quality teams' in the continuous improvement process. How can an organization ensure that the outcome of teamwork is consistent with its mission?

3 Describe the various types of quality teams which should be part of a total quality programme. Explain the organizational requirements associated with these and give some indication of how the teams operate.

4 A large insurance company has decided that teamwork is to be the initial focus of its TQM programme. Describe the role of the Quality Council and Process Quality Teams in managing teamwork initiatives in quality improvement.

5 Explain the difference between Quality Improvement Teams and Quality Circles. What is their role in quality improvement activities?

6 Discuss some of the factors that may inhibit teamwork activities in a TQM programme.

7 Suggest an organization for teamwork in a quality improvement programme and discuss how the important aspects must be managed, in order to achieve the best results from the use of teams. Describe briefly how the teams would proceed, including the tools they would use in their work.

8 Describe in full the various types of quality teams which are necessary in a total quality programme. Give some indication of how the teams operate at each level and using the 'DRIVE' model discuss the problem-solving approach that may be adopted.

9 Discuss the various models for teamwork within a total quality approach to business performance improvement. Explain through these models the role of the individual in TQM, and what work can be carried out in this area to help teams through the 'storming' stage of their development.

10 Team work is one of the key 'necessities' for TQM. John Adair's 'Action Centred Leadership' model is useful to explain the areas which require attention for successful teamwork. Explain the model in detail showing your understanding of each of the areas of 'needs'. Pay particular attention to the needs of the individual, showing how a technique such as the Myers Briggs Type Indicator (MBTI) or Belbin's Team Roles may be useful here.

Case study assignments

C7 Pirelli Communication Cables

Discuss the teamwork issues raised in the case study, paying particular attention to the change in culture often required for TQM implementation.

Evaluate the approach taken by the company and offer constructive criticism and suggestions for further improvement.

Critique the reasons for success listed in the case.

C8 Thomas Cork

Evaluate the key road blocks in the total quality route used by the Directors at Thomas Cork, and how they were overcome.

Part Five

TQM – The Implementation

All words, and no performance.
Philip Massinger, 1583-1640 from 'The Unnatural Combat', ca 1619

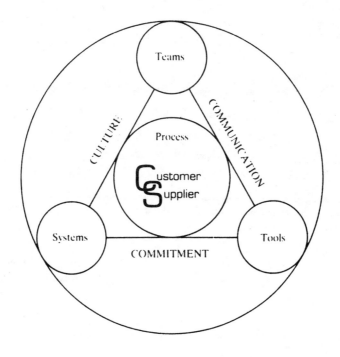

Communications
and training for quality

12.1 Communicating the total quality strategy

People's attitudes and behaviour clearly can be influenced by communication; one has to look only at the media or advertising to understand this. The essence of changing attitudes to quality is to gain acceptance for the need to change, and for this to happen it is essential to provide relevant information, convey good practices, and generate interest, ideas and awareness through excellent communication processes. This is possibly the most neglected part of many organizations' operations, yet failure to communicate effectively creates unnecessary problems, resulting in confusion, loss of interest and eventually in declining quality through apparent lack of guidance and stimulus.

Total quality management will significantly change the way many organizations operate and 'do business'. This change will require direct and clear communication from the top management to all staff and employees, to explain the need to focus on processes. Everyone will need to know their roles in understanding processes and improving their performance.

Whether a strategy is developed by top management for the direction of the business/organization as a whole, or specifically for the introduction of TQM, that is only half the battle. An early implementation step must be the clear widespread communication of the strategy.

An excellent way to accomplish this first step is to issue a total quality message that clearly states top management's commitment to TQM and outlines the role everyone must play. This can be in the form of a quality policy (see Chapter 2) or a specific statement about the organization's intention to integrate TQM into the business operations. Such a statement might read:

The Board of Directors (or appropriate title) believe that the successful implementation of Total Quality Management is critical to achieving and maintaining our business goals of leadership in quality, delivery and price competitiveness.

We wish to convey to everyone our enthusiasm and personal commitment to the Total Quality approach, and how much we need your support in our mission of process improvement. We hope that you will become as convinced as we are that process improvement is critical for our survival and continued success.

We can become a Total Quality organization only with your commitment and dedication to improving the processes in which you work. We will help you by putting in place a programme of education, training, and teamwork development, based on process improvement, to ensure that we move forward together to achieve our business goals.

The quality director or TQM co-ordinator should then assist the quality council to prepare a directive. This must be signed by all business unit, division, or process leaders, and distributed to everyone in the organization. The directive should include the following:

- Need for improvement.
- Concept for total quality.
- Importance of understanding business processes.
- Approach that will be taken.
- Individual and process group responsibilities.
- Principles of process measurement.

The systems for disseminating the message should include all the conventional communication methods of seminars, departmental meetings, posters, newsletters, etc. First line supervision will need to review the directive with all the staff, and a set of questions and answers may be suitably pre-prepared in support.

Once people understand the strategy, the management must establish the infrastructure (see Chapter 10). The required level of individual commitment is likely to be achieved, however, only if everyone understands the aims and benefits of TQM, the role they must play, and how they can implement process improvements. For this understanding a constant flow of information is necessary, including:

1   When and how individuals will be involved.
2   What the process requires.
3   The successes and benefits achieved.

The most effective means of developing the personnel commitment required is to ensure people know what is going on. Otherwise they will feel left out and begin to believe that TQM is not for them, which will lead to resentment and undermining of the whole process. The first line of supervision again has an important part to play in ensuring key messages are communicated and in building teams by demonstrating everyone's participation and commitment.

Effective TQM communications, then, have two essential components:

(a) General information about the TQM process.
(b) Regular meetings between employees and managers/supervisors.

These equate respectively to the:

(a) 'Technical' aspects of the TQM framework or model.
(b) Human and organizational aspects of launching the whole process.

TQM will clearly have a profound effect on all tasks, activities, and processes throughout the organization. It should change management style and integrate the process inputs of information, people, machines, and materials. One aspect of the communication process worthy of particular attention in this context is that between departments or functions. This is essential for establishing up-to-the-minute customer-oriented goals and building the 'house of quality' around the business processes.

The language used between departmental or functional groups will need attention in many organizations. Reducing the complexity and jargon in written and spoken communications will facilitate comprehension. When written business communications cannot be read or understood easily, they receive only cursory glances, rather than the detailed study they require. *Simplify and shorten* must be the guiding principles.

All levels of management should introduce and stress 'open' methods of communication, by maintaining open offices, being accessible to staff/employees, and taking part in day-to-day interactions and the detailed processes. This will lay the foundation for improved interactions *between* staff and employees, which is essential for information flow and process improvement. Opening these lines of communication may lead to confrontation with many barriers and much resistance. Training and the behaviour of supervisors/managements should be geared to helping people accept responsibility for their own behaviour, which often creates the barriers, and for breaking the barriers down by concentrating on the process rather than 'departmental' needs.

Resistance to change will always occur and is to be expected. Again first line management must be trained to help people deal with it. This requires an understanding of the dynamics of change and the support necessary – not an obsession with forcing people to change. Opening up lines of communication through a previously closed system, and pubicizing people's efforts to change and their results, will aid the process. Change can be – even should be – exciting if employees start to share their development, growth, suggestions, and questions. Management must encourage and participate in this by creating the most appropriate communication systems.

The key medium for motivating the employees and gaining their commitment to TQM is face-to-face communication and *visible* management commitment. Much is written and spoken about leadership, but it is mainly about communication. If people are good leaders, they are invariably good communicators. Leadership is a human interaction depending on the communications between the leaders and the followers. It calls for many skills that can be *learned* from education and training, but must be *acquired* through practice.

12.2 It's Monday – it must be training

It is the author's belief that training is the single most important factor in actually improving quality, once there has been commitment to do so. For training to be the effective, however, it must be planned in a systematic and objective manner. Quality training must be continuous to meet not only changes in technology but also changes in the environment in which an organization operates, its structure, and perhaps most important of all the people who work there.

Training cycle of improvement

Quality training activities can be considered in the form of a cycle of improvement (Figure 12.1), the elements of which are the following.

Ensure training is part of the quality policy

Every organization should define its policy in relation to quality (see Chapter 2). The policy should contain principles and goals to provide a framework within which training activities may be planned and operated. This policy should be communicated to all levels.

Allocate responsiblities for training

Quality training must be the responsibility of line management, but there are also important roles for the quality manager and his function.

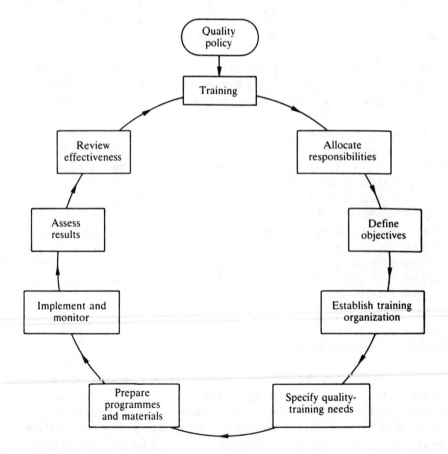

Figure 12.1 *The quality training circle*

Define training objectives

The following questions are useful first steps when identifying training objectives:

- How are the customer requirements transmitted through the organization?
- Which areas need improved performance?
- What changes are planned for the future?
- What new procedures and provisions need to be drawn up?

When attempting to set training objectives three essential requirements must be met:

1　Senior management must ensure that objectives are clarified and priorities set.
2　Defined objectives must be realistic and attainable.
3　The main problems should be identified for all functional areas in the organization. Large organizations may find it necessary to promote a phased plan to identify these problems.

Establish training organization

The overall responsibility for seeing that quality training is properly organized must be assumed by one or more designated senior executives. All managers have a responsibility for ensuring that personnel reporting to them are properly trained and competent in their jobs. This responsibility should be written into every manager's job description. The question of whether line management requires specialized help should be answered when objectives have been identified. It is often necessary to use specialists, who may be internal or external to the organization.

Specify quality training needs

The next step in the cycle is to assess and clarify specific quality training needs. The following questions need to be answered:

(a) Who needs to be trained?
(b) What competences are required?
(c) How long will training take?
(d) What are the expected benefits?
(e) Is the training need urgent?
(f) How many people are to be trained?
(g) Who will undertake the actual training?
(h) What resources are needed, e.g. money, people, equipment, accommodation, outside resources?

Prepare training programmes and materials

Quality management should participate in the creation of draft programmes, although line managers should retain the final responsibility for what is implemented, and they will often need to create the training programmes themselves.

Quality-training programmes should include:

- The training objectives expressed in terms of the desired behaviour.
- The actual training content.
- The methods to be adopted.
- Who is responsible for the various sections of the programme.

Implement and monitor training

The effective implementation of quality training programmes demands considerable commitment and adjustment by the trainers and trainees alike. Training is a progressive process, which must take into account the learning problems of the trainees.

Assess the results

In order to determine whether further training is required, line management should themselves review performance when training is completed. However good the quality training may be, if it is not valued and built upon by managers and supervisors, its effect can be severely reduced.

Review effectiveness of training

Senior management will require a system whereby decisions are taken at regular fixed intervals on:

- The quality policy.
- The quality training objectives
- The training organization.

Even if the quality policy remains constant, there is a continuing need to ensure that new quality training objectives are set either to promote work changes or to raise the standards already achieved.

The purpose of system audits and reviews is to assess the effectiveness of an organization's quality effort. Clearly, adequate and refresher training in these methods is essential if such checks are to be realistic and effective. Audits and reviews can provide useful information for the identification of changing quality training needs.

The training organization should similarly be reviewed in the light of the new objectives, and here again it is essential to aim at continuous improvement. Training must never be allowed to become static, and the effectiveness of the organization's quality training programmes and methods must be assessed systematically.

12.3   A systematic approach to quality training

Training for quality should have, as its first objective, an appreciation of the personal responsibility for meeting the 'customer' requirements by everyone from the most senior executive to the newest and most junior employee. Responsibility for the training of employees in quality rests with management at all levels and, in particular, the person nominated for the coordination of the organization's quality effort. Quality training will not be fully effective, however, unless responsibility for the quality policy rests clearly with the Chief Executive. One objective of this policy should be to develop a *climate* in which everyone is quality conscious and acts with the needs of the immediate customer in mind. Quality objectives should be stated in relation to the activities and the place of training in their achievement.

The main elements of effective and systematic quality training may be considered under four broad headings.

- Error/defect/problem prevention.
- Error/defect/problem reporting and analysis.
- Error/defect/problem investigation.
- Review.

The emphasis should obviously be on error, defect, or problem prevention, and hopefully what is said under the other headings maintains this objective.

Error/defect/problem prevention

The following contribute to effective and systematic training for prevention of problems in the organization:

1　An issued quality policy.
2　A written quality system.
3　Job specifications that include quality requirements.
4　An effective quality council or committee including representatives of both management and employees.
5　Efficient housekeeping standards.
6　Preparation and display of flow diagrams and charts for all processes.

Error/defect/problem reporting and analysis

It will be necessary for management to arrange the necessary reporting procedures, and ensure that those concerned are adequately trained in these procedures. All errors, rejects, defects, defectives, problems, waste, etc., should be recorded and analysed in a way that is meaningful for each organization, bearing in mind the corrective action programmes that should be initiated at appropriate times.

Error/defect/problem investigation

The investigation of errors, defects, and problems can provide valuable information that can be used in their prevention. Participating in investigations offers an opportunity for training. The following information is useful for the investigation:

(a) Nature of problem.
(b) Date, time and place.
(c) Product/service with problem.
(d) Description of problem.
(e) Causes and reasons behind causes.
(f) Action advised.
(g) Action taken to prevent recurrence.

Effective problem investigation requires appropriate follow-up and monitoring of recommendations.

Review of quality training

Review of the effectiveness of quality training programmes should be a continuous process. However, the measurement of effectiveness is a complex problem. One way of reviewing the content and assimilation of a training course or programme is to monitor behaviour during quality audits. This review can be taken a stage further by comparing employees' behaviour with the objectives of the quality training programme. Other measures of the training processes should be found to establish the benefits derived.

Training records

All organizations should establish and maintain procedures for the identification of training needs and the provision of the actual training itself. These procedures should be designed (and documented) to include all personnel. In many situations it is necessary to employ professionally qualified people to carry out specific tasks, e.g. accountants, lawyers, engineers, chemists, etc., but it must be recognized that all other employees, including managers, must have or receive from the company the appropriate education, training and/or experience to perform their jobs. This leads to the establishment of training records.

Once an organization has identified the special skills required for each task, and developed suitable training programmes to provide competence for the tasks to be undertaken, it should prescribe how the competence is to be demonstrated. This can be by some form of examination, test or certification, which may be carried out in-house or by a recognized external body. In every case, records of personnel qualifications, training, and experience should be developed and maintained. National vocational qualifications (NVQs) have an important role to play here.

At the simplest level this may be a record of tasks and a date placed against each employee's name as he/she acquires the appropriate skill through training. Details of attendance on external short courses, in-house induction or training schemes complete such records. What must be clear and easily retrievable is the status of training and development of any single individual, related to the tasks that he/she is likely to encounter. For example, in a factory producing contact lenses that has developed a series of well defined tasks for each stage of the manufacturing process, it would be possible, by turning up the appropriate records, to decide whether a certain operator is competent to carry out a lathe-turning process. Clearly, as the complexity of jobs increases and managerial activity replaces direct manual skill, it becomes more difficult to make decisions on the basis of such records alone. Nevertheless, they should document the basic competency requirements and assist the selection procedure.

12.4   Starting where and for whom?

Training needs occur at four levels of an organization:

- *Very senior management* (strategic decision-makers).
- *Middle management* (tactical decision-makers or implementors of policy).
- *First level supervision and quality team leaders* (on-the-spot decision-makers).
- *All other employees* (the doers).

Neglect of training in any of these areas will, at best, delay the implementation of TQM. The provision of training for each group will be considered in turn, but it is important to realize that an integrated training programme is required, one that includes follow-up activities and encourages exchange of ideas and experience, to allow each transformation process to achieve quality at the supplier/customer interface.

Very senior management

The Chief Executive and his team of strategic policy makers are of primary importance, and the role of training here is to provide awareness and instil commitment to quality. The importance of developing real commitment must be established; and often this can only be done by a free and frank exchange of views between trainers and trainees. This has implications for the choice of the trainers themselves, and the fresh-faced graduate, sent by the 'package consultancy' operator into the lion's den of a boardroom, will not make much impression with the theoretical approach that he or she is obliged to bring to bear. The author recalls thumping many a boardroom table, and using all his experience and whatever presentation skills he could muster, to convince senior managers that without the TQM approach they would fail. It is a sobering fact that the pressure from competition and customers has a much greater record of success than enlightenment, although dragging a team of senior managers down to the shop floor to show them the results of poor management was successful on one occasion.

Executives responsible for marketing, sales, finance, design, operations, purchasing, personnel, distribution, etc. must all be helped to understand quality. They must be shown how to define the quality policy and objectives, how to establish the appropriate organization for quality, how to clarify authority, and generally how to create the atmosphere in which total quality will thrive. This is the only group of people in the organization that can ensure that adequate resources are provided and they must be directed at:

1   Meeting customer requirements – internally and externally.
2   Setting standards to be achieved – zero failure.
3   Monitoring of quality performance – quality costs.
4   Introducing a good quality management system – prevention.
5   Implementing process control methods – SPC.
6   Spreading the idea of quality throughout the whole workforce – TQM.

Middle management

The basic objectives of management quality training should be to make managers conscious and anxious to secure the benefits of the total quality effort. One particular 'staff' manager will require special training – the quality manager, who will carry the responsibility for management of the quality system, including its design, operation, and review.

The middle managers should be provided with the technical skills required to design, implement, review, and change the parts of the quality system that will be under their direct operational control. It will be useful throughout the training programmes to ensure that the responsibilities for the various activities in each of the functional areas are clarifed. The presence of a highly qualified and experienced quality manager must not allow abdication of these responsibilites, for the internal 'consultant' can easily create not-invented-here feelings by writing out procedures without adequate consultation of those charged with implementation.

Middle management must receive comprehensive training on the philosophy and concepts of teamwork, and the techniques and applications of statistical process control (SPC). Without the teams and tools, the quality system will lie dormant and lifeless. It will relapse into a paper generating system, fulfilling the needs of only those who thrive on bureaucracy.

First-level supervision

There is a layer of personnel in many organizations which plays a vital role in their inadequate performance – foremen and supervisors – the forgotten men and women of industry and commerce. Frequently promoted from the 'shop floor' (or recruited as graduates in a flush of conscience and wealth!), these people occupy one of the most crucial managerial roles, often with no idea of what they are supposed to be doing, without an identity, and without training. If this behaviour pattern is familiar and is continued, then TQM is doomed.

The first level of supervision is where the implementation of total quality is actually 'managed' Supervisors' training should include an explanation of the principles of TQM, a convincing exposition on the commitment to quality of the senior management, and an explanation of what the quality policy means for them. The remainder of their training should then be devoted to explaining their role in the operation of the quality system, teamwork, SPC etc., and to gaining *their* commitment to the concepts and techniques of total quality.

It is often desirable to involve the middle managers in the training of first line supervision in order to:

- Ensure that the message they wish to convey through their tactical manoeuvres is not distorted.
- Indicate to the foreman level that the organization's whole management structure is serious about quality, and intends that everyone is suitably trained and concerned about it too. One display of arrogance towards the training of supervisors and the workforce can destroy such careful planning, and will certainly undermine the educational effort.

All other employees

Awareness and commitment at the point of production or operation is just as vital as at the very senior level. If it is absent from the latter, the TQM programme will not begin; if it is absent from the shop floor, total quality will not be implemented. The training here must include the basics of quality, and particular care should be given to using easy reference points for the explanation of the terms and concepts. Most people can relate to quality and how it should be managed, if they can think about the applications in their own lives and at home. Quality is really such common sense that, with sensitivity and regard to various levels of intellect and experience, little resistance should be experienced.

All employees should receive detailed training in the quality procedures relevant to their own work. Obviously they must have appropriate technical or 'job' training, but they must also understand the requirements of their customers. This is frequently a difficult concept to introduce, particularly in the non-manufacturing areas, and time and follow-up assistance must be given if TQM is to take hold. It is always bad management to ask people to follow instructions without understanding why and where they fit into their own scheme of things.

12.5 Follow-up

For the successful implementation of TQM, training must be followed up during the early stages. Follow-up can take many forms, but the managers must provide the lead through the design of improvement projects and 'surgery' workshops.

In introducing statistical methods of process control, for example, the most satisfactory strategy is to start small and build up a bank of knowledge and experience. Sometimes it is necessary to introduce SPC techniques alongside existing methods of control (if they exist), thus allowing comparisons to be made between the new and old methods. When confidence has been established from these comparisons, the SPC methods will almost take over the control of the processes themselves. Improvements in one or two areas of the organization's operations, by means of this approach will quickly establish the techniques as reliable methods of controlling quality.

The author and his colleagues have found that a successful formula is the in-company training course plus follow-up workshops. Usually a 20-hour seminar on TQM is followed within a few weeks by an 8-10 hour workshop at which participants on the initial training course present the results of their efforts to improve processes, and use the various methods. The presentations and specific implementation problems may be discussed. A series of such workshops will add continually to the follow-up, and can be used to initiate quality improvement teams. Wider company presence and activities should be encouraged by the follow-up activities.

Chapter highlights

Communicating the total quality strategy

- People's attitudes and behaviour can be influenced by communication, and the essence of changing attitudes is to gain acceptance through excellent communication processes.
- The strategy and changes to be brought about through TQM must be clearly and directly communicated from top management to all staff/employees. The first step is to issue a 'total quality message'. This should be followed by a signed TQM directive.
- People must know when and how they will be brought into the TQM process, what the process is, and the successes and benefits achieved. First-line supervision has an important role in communicating the key messages and overcoming resistance to change.
- The complexity and jargon in the language used between functional groups must be reduced in many organizations. Simplify and shorten are the guiding principles.
- 'Open' methods of communication and participation must be used at all levels. Barriers may need to be broken down by concentrating on process rather than 'departmental' issues.
- Good leadership is mostly about good communications, the skills of which can be learned through training but must be acquired through practice.

It's Monday – it must be training

- Training is the single most important factor in improving quality, once commitment is present. Quality training must be objectively, systematically, and continuously performed.
- All training should occur in an improvement cycle of ensuring training is part of quality policy, allocating responsibilities, defining objectives, establishing training organizations, specifying needs, preparing programmes and materials, implementing and monitoring, assessing results, and reviewing effectiveness.

A systematic approach to quality training

- Responsibility for quality training of employees rests with management at all levels. The main elements should include error/defect/problem prevention, reporting and analysis, investigation, and review.
- Training procedures and records should be established. These should show how job competence is demonstrated.

Starting where and for whom?

- Needs for integrating quality training occur at four levels of the organization: very senior management, middle management, first level supervision and quality team leaders, and all other employees.

Follow-up

- All quality training should be followed up with improvement projects and 'surgery' workshops.

Implementation of TQM and the management of change

13.1 TQM and the management of change

The author recalls the managing director of a large transportation company who decided that a major change was required in the way the company operated if serious competitive challenges were to be met. The Board of Directors went away for a weekend and developed a new vision for the company and its 'culture'. A personnel director was recruited and given the task of managing the change in the people and their 'attitudes'. After several 'programmes' aimed at achieving the required change, including a new structure for the organization, a staff appraisal system linked to pay, training programmes to change attitudes, and questionnaire surveys, very little change in actual organizational behaviour had occurred.

Clearly something had gone wrong somewhere. But what, who, where? Everything was wrong, including who needed changing, who should lead the changes and, in particular, how the changes should be brought about. This type of problem is very common in organizations desiring to change the way they operate to deal with increased competition, a changing market place, and different business rules. In this situation many companies recognize the need to move away from an autocratic management style, with formal rules and hierarchical procedures, and narrow work demarcations. Some have tried to create teams, to delegate (perhaps for the first time), and to improve communications.

Some of the senior managers in such organizations recognize the need for change to deal with the new realities of competitiveness, but they lack an understanding of how the change should be implemented. They often believe that changing the formal organizational structure, having vision or mission statements, 'culture change' programmes, training courses, and new payment systems will, by themselves, make the transformations.

In much research work carried out at the European Centre for TQM, at Bradford University Management Centre, it has been shown that there is almost an inverse relationship between successful change and having formal organization-wide change. This is particularly true if one functional group, such as personnel, 'owns' the programme.

In several large organizations in which total quality has been used successfully to effect change, the senior management did not focus on formal structures and systems, but set up *process-management* teams to solve real business or organization problems. The key to success in this area is to align the employees of the business, their roles and responsibilities with the organization and its *processes*. This is the core of process mapping or alignment. When an organization focuses on its key processes, that is the activities and tasks themselves, rather than on abstract issues such as 'culture' and 'participation', then the change process can begin in earnest.

An approach to change, based on process alignment, and starting with the mission statement, analysing the critical success factors, *and* moving on to the key or critical processes, is the most effective way to engage the staff in an enduring change process. Many change programmes do not work because they begin trying to change the knowledge, attitudes and beliefs of individuals. The theory is that changes in these areas will lead to changes in behaviour throughout the organization. It relies on a form of religion spreading through the people in the business.

What is required, however, is virtually the opposite process, based on the recognition that people's behaviour is determined largely by the roles they have to take up. If we create for them new responsibilities, team roles, and a process driven environment, a new situation will develop, one that will force their attention and work on the processes. This will change the culture. *Teamwork* is an especially important part of the TQM model in terms of bringing about change. If changes are to be made in quality, costs, market, product or service development, close co-ordination among the marketing, design, production/operations and distribution groups is essential. This can be brought about effectively only by multifunctional teams working on the processes and understanding their interrelationships. *Commitment* is a key element of support for the high levels of co-operation, initiative, and effort that will be required to understand and work on the labyrinth of processes existing in most organizations. In addition to the knowledge of the business as a whole, which will be brought about by an understanding of the mission → CSF → process breakdown links, certain *tools, techniques,* and *interpersonal skills* will be required for good *communication* around the processes. These are essential if people are to identify and solve problems as teams.

If any of these elements are missing the total quality underpinned change process will collapse. The difficulties experienced by many organizations' formal change processes is that they tackle only one or two of these necessities. Many organizations trying to create a new philosophy based on teamwork fail to recognize that the employees do not know which teams to form or how they should function as teams. Recognition that effective teams need to be formed round their process, which they begin to understand together – perhaps for the first time – and further recognition that they then need to be helped as individuals through the forming–storming–norming–performing sequence, will generate the interpersonal skills and attitude changes necessary to make the new 'structure' work.

13.2   Integrating TQM into the strategy of the business

Organizations will avoid the problems of 'change programmes' by concentrating on 'process alignment' – recognizing that people's roles and responsibilities must be related to the processes in which they work. Senior managers may begin the task of process alignment by a series of seven distinct but clearly overlapping steps. This recommended path develops a self-reinforcing cycle of *commitment, communication,* and *culture* change. The order of the steps is important because some of the activities will be inappropriate if started too early. In the introduction of total quality for managing change, timing can be critical.

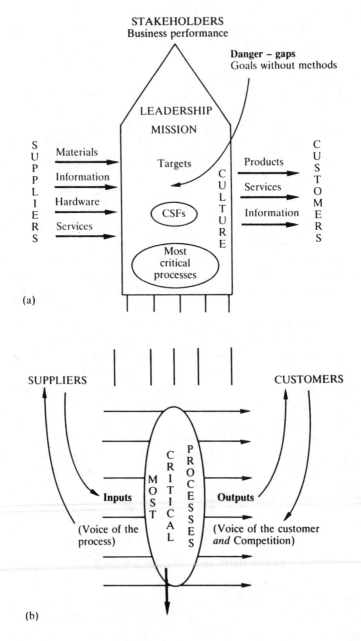

Figure 13.1 *(and opposite) From mission to process breakdown*

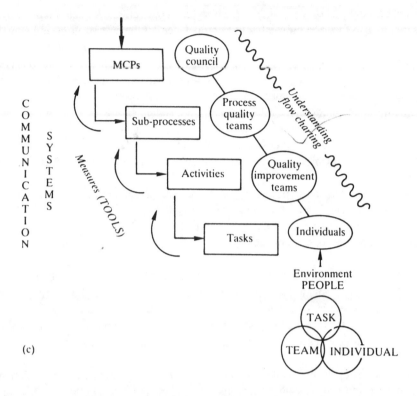

(c)

Step 1   Gain commitment to change through the organization of the top team

Process alignment requires the starting point to be a broad review of the organization and the changes required by the top management team. By gaining this shared diagnosis of what changes are required, what the 'business' problems are, and/or what must be improved, the most senior executive mobilizes the initial commitment that is vital to begin the change process. An important element here is to get the top team working as a team, and techniques such as MBTI and/or Belbin team roles will play an important part (see Chapter 11).

Step 2   Develop a shared 'mission' or vision of the business or of what change is required.

Once the top team is committed to the analysis of the changes required, it can develop a mission statement that will help to define the new process alignment, roles and responsibilities. This will lead to a co-ordinated flow of analysis of process that crosses the traditional functional areas at all levels of the organization, without changing formal structures, titles, and systems which can create resistance (Figure 13.1).

The mission statement gives a purpose to the organization or unit. It should answer the questions 'What are we here for?' or 'What is our basic purpose? and therefore must define the boundaries of the business in which the organization operates (Figure 13.1a). This will help to focus on the 'distinctive competence' of the organization, and to orient everyone in the direction of what has to be done. The mission must be documented, agreed by the top management team, sufficiently explicit to enable its eventual accomplishment to be verified, and ideally be no more than four sentences. The statement must be understandable, communicable, believable, and usable.

Some questions that may be asked of a mission statement are:

- Does it contain the need that is to be fulfilled?
- Is the need worthwhile in terms of admiration and identification, both internally and externally?
- Does it take a long term view, leading to, for example, commitment to new product or service development, or training of personnel?
- Does it take into account all the 'stakeholders'?
- Will the purpose remain constant despite changes in top management?

It is important to establish in some organizations whether or not the mission is survival. This does not preclude a longer term mission, but the short term survival mission must be expressed, if it is relevant. The management team can then decide whether it wishes to continue long term strategic thinking. If survival is a real issue, the author and his colleagues would advise against concentrating on the long term planning initially.

There must be open and spontaneous discussion during generation of the mission, but there must in the end be convergence on one statement. If the mission statement is wrong, everything that follows will be wrong too, so a clear understanding is vital.

Step 3   Define the measurable objectives, which must be agreed by the team, as being the quantifiable indicators of success in terms of the mission.

The mission provides the vision and guiding light and sets down the core values, but it must be supported by measurable objectives that are tightly and inarguably linked to it. These will help to translate the directional and sometimes 'loose' statements of the mission into clear targets, and in turn to simplify management's thinking. They can later be used as evidence of success for the team, in every direction, internally and externally.

Step 4   Develop the mission into its critical success factors (CSFs) to coerce and move it forward

The development of the mission is clearly not enough to ensure its implementation. This is the 'danger gap' into which many companies fall, because they do not foster the skills needed to translate the mission through its CSFs into the critical processes. Hence they have 'goals without methods', and TQM is not integrated properly into the business. At this stage of the process strong leadership from the top is crucial. Commitment to the change, whatever it may be, is always imbalanced; some senior managers may be antagonistic, some neutral, others enthusiastic or worried about the proposed changes.

Once the top managers begin to list the CSFs, they will gain some understanding of what the mission or the change requires. The first step in going from mission to CSFs is to brainstorm all the possible impacts on the mission. In this way thirty to fifty items, ranging from politics to costs, from national cultures to regional market peculiarities, may be derived.

The CSFs may now be defined – what the organization must accomplish to achieve the mission, by examination and categorization of the impacts. There should be no more than eight CSFs, and no more than four if the mission is survival. They are the minimum key factors or subgoals that the organization *must have* or *need*, and which together will achieve the mission. They are not the how, and are not directly manageable – they may be in some cases statements of hope or fear – but they provide direction and the success criteria. In CSF determination a management team should follow the rule that each CSF is *necessary*, and that together they are *sufficient* for the mission to be achieved.

Some examples of CSFs may clarify understanding.

- We must have right-first-time suppliers.
- We must have motivated, skilled people.
- We need new products that satisfy market needs.
- We need new business opportunities.
- We must have best-in-the-field product quality.

The list of CSFs should be an agreed balance of strategic and tactical issues, each of which deals with a 'pure' factor, the use of *and* being forbidden. It will be important to know when the CSFs have been achieved through Key Performance Indicators (KPIs), but the more important next step is to use the CSFs to enable the identification of the *processes*.

Step 5 Break down the critical success factors into the key or critical process and gain process ownership

This is the point at which the top management team have to consider how to institutionalize the mission or the change in the form of processes that will continue to be in place, after any changes have been effected (Figure 13.1b).

The key, critical, or business processes describe what actually is or needs to be done so that the organization meets its CSFs. As with the CSFs and the mission, each process *necessary* for a given CSF must be identified, and together the processes listed must be *sufficient* for the CSFs to be accomplished. To ensure that *processes* are listed, they should be in the form of verb plus object, such as 'research the market', 'recruit competent staff', or 'measure supplier performance'.

Each business process should have an owner who is a member of the management team that agree the CSFs. The business processes identified frequently run across 'departments' or functions, yet they must be measurable.

The questions will now come thick and fast. Is the process currently carried out? By whom? When? How frequently? With what performance and how well compared with competitors? The answers to these will force process ownership into the business. The process owner should form a process quality team to take the next steps in quality improvement. Some form of prioritization, by means of process 'quality' measures, is necessary at this stage to enable effort to be focused on the key areas for improvement. This may be carried out by a form of matrix analysis[1] or some other means. The outcome should be a set of 'most critical processes' (MCPs), which receive priority attention for improvement.

The first stage in understanding the critical processes is to produce a set of processes of a common order of magnitude. Some processes identified by the quality council may break into two or three critical processes; others may be already at the appropriate level. This method will ensure that the change becomes entrenched, the critical processes are identified and that the right people are in place to own or take responsibility for them; and it will be the start of getting the process-team organization up and running.

Step 6 Break down the critical processes into sub-processes, activities and tasks and form improvement teams around these.

Once an organization has defined and mapped out the critical processes, people need to develop the skills to understand how the new process structure will be analysed and made to work. The very existence of new process quality teams (PQTs) with new goals and responsibilities will force the organization into a learning phase. The changes should foster new attitudes and behaviours.

An illustration of the breakdown from mission through CSFs and critical processes to individual tasks may assist in understanding the process required:

Mission

Two of the statements in a well known quality management consultancy's mission statement are: 'Gain and maintain a position as Europe's foremost management consultancy in the development of organizations through the management of change' and 'provide the consultancy, training and facilitation necessary to assist with making the continuous improvement of quality an integral part of our customers' business strategy.'

↓

Critical success factor

One of the CSFs that clearly relates to this is 'We need a high level of awareness of our company in the market place'.

↓

| Critical process |

One of the critical processes that clearly must be done particularly well to achieve this CSF is to 'Promote, advertise, and communicate the company's business capability'.

↓

| Sub-process |

One of the sub-processes resulting from a breakdown of this critical process is 'Prepare the company's information pack'.

↓

| Activity |

One of the activities contributing to this sub-process is 'Prepare *one* of the subject booklets, i.e. TQM, SPC or quality systems'.

↓

| Task |

One of the tasks that contributes to this is 'Write the detailed leaflet for any particular seminar', e.g.: 'One-day or three-day seminars on TQM or SPC, or quality system advisory project'.

Individuals, tasks, and teams

Having broken down the processes into sub-processes, activities, and tasks in this way, we can now link them with the Adair model of action-centred leadership and teamwork.

The *tasks* are performed, at least initially, by individuals. For example, some*body* has to sit down and draft out the first version of a seminar leaflet. There has to be an understanding by the individual of the task and its position in the hierarchy of processes. Once the initial task has been performed, the results must be checked against the activity of co-ordinating the promotional booklet – say for TQM. This clearly brings in the team, and there must be interfaces between the needs of the *tasks*, the *individuals* who performed them and the *team* concerned with the *activities*.

Using the hierarchy of processes, it is possible to link this with the hierarchy of quality teams. Hence:

Quality council – mission – CSFs – critical processes.
Process quality teams – critical processes.

Quality improvement (or functional) teams (QITs) – sub-processes.
QITs – activities.
QITs and quality circles/Kaizen teams/individuals – tasks.

Performance measurement and metrics

Once the processes have been analysed in this way, it should be possible to develop metrics for measuring the performance of the processes, sub-processes, activities, and tasks. These must be meaningful in terms of the inputs and outputs of the processes, and in terms of the customers and of suppliers to the processes (Figure 13.1c).

At first thought, this form of measurement can seem difficult for processes such as preparing a sales brochure or writing leaflets advertising seminars, but, if we think carefully about the *customers* for the leaflet-writing tasks, these will include the *internal* ones, i.e. the consultants, and we can ask whether the output meets their requirements. Does it really say what the seminar is about, what its objectives are and what the programme will be? Clearly, one of the 'measures' of the seminar leaflet-writing task could be the number of typing effors in it, but is this a *key* measure of the performance of the process? Only in the context of office management is this an important measure. Elsewhere it is not.

The same goes for the *activity* of preparing the subject booklet. Does it tell the 'customer' what TQM or SPC is and how the consultancy can help? For the *sub-process* of preparing the company brochure, does it inform people about the company and does it bring in enquiries from which customers can be developed? Clearly, some of these measures require *external market research*, and some of them *internal research*. The main point is that metrics must be developed and used to reflect the *true performance* of the processes, sub-processes, activities, and tasks. These must involve good contact with external and internal customers of the processes. The metrics may be quoted as *ratios*, e.g. number of customers derived per number of brochures mailed out. Good data-collection, record-keeping, and analysis are clearly required.

It is hoped that this illustration will help the reader to:

- Understand the breakdown of processes into sub-processes, activities, and tasks.
- Understand the links between the process breakdowns and the task, individual and team concepts.
- Link the hierarchy of processes with the hierarchy of quality teams.
- Begin to assemble a cascade of flowcharts representing the process breakdowns, which can form the basis of the quality system and communicate what is going on throughout the business.
- Understand the way in which metrics must be developed to measure the true performance of the process, and their links with the customers, suppliers, inputs and outputs of the processes.

This whole concept/structure is represented in Figure 13.1c. The changed patterns of co-ordination, driven by the process maps, should increase collaboration and information sharing.

Clearly the senior and middle managers must provide the right support. Once employees, at all levels, identify what kinds of new skill are needed, they will ask for the formal training programmes in order to develop those skills further. This is a key area, because the teamwork around the processes will ask more of employees, so they will need increasing support from their managers.

This has been called 'just-in-time' training, which describes very well the nature of the process required. Such training is quite different from the blanket or carpet-bombing training associated with many unsuccessful change programmes, which targets competencies or skills but does not change the organization's patterns of collaboration and co-ordination.

Step 7   Monitor and adjust the process alignment in response to difficulties in the change process

Change must create something that did not exist before, namely a 'learning organization' capable of adapting to a changing competitive environment. One must also learn how to monitor and modify the new behaviour to maintain the change-sensitive environment.

Some people will, of course, find great difficulty in accepting the changes, and perhaps will be incapable of doing so, in spite of all the direction, support, and peer pressure brought about by the process alignment. There will come a time to replace those managers and staff who cannot function in the new organization, after they have had a good opportunity to make the changes. These decisions are of course never easy, especially where valuable technical skills are owned by the people who have difficulty working in the new participatory, process-driven organization.

When people begin to understand what kind of manager and employee/staff the new organization needs, and this often develops slowly and from experience of seeing individuals succeed and fail, they should begin to accept the need to replace or move people to other parts of the organization.

13.3   Summarizing the steps

If a top-management team has attended at least a 1-day workshop on TQM, the initial key steps may be summarized in Figure 13.2 together with their links to commitment, communications and culture change, through project work and correct follow-up. This must all be done within the continuous improvement cycle to avoid the 'danger gaps' shown in Figure 13.3.

13.4   Continuous improvement

Never ending or continuous improvement is probably the most powerful concept to guide management. It is a term not well understood in many organizations, although that must begin to change if those organizations are to survive. To maintain a wave of interest in quality, it is necessary to develop generations of managers who not only understand but are dedicated to the pursuit of never-ending improvement in meeting external and internal customer needs.

C			Initial key steps following one day seminar for top management
O			• Formation of quality council (Top-management team)
M			• TQM 'Attitude' survey – Profile of organization
M	**C**		– Quality costs – Strengths/weaknesses
I	**O**		• Two-day strategic planning workshop (quality council)
T	**M**		– Charter – Mission statement
M	**M**		– Quality policy – Critical success factors
E	**U**		– Critical processes – Implementation action plan
N	**N**		• Formation of process quality teams and/or site steering committees
T	**I**		• Teamwork seminar for quality council (may precede strategic planning workshop)
	C		• Identify team facilitators
	A	**C**	• Run specific training and team-forming workshops
	T	**U**	• Company-wide awareness training on customer/supplier interfaces
	I	**L**	• Implementation/improvement projects for quality policy deployment
	O	**T**	– Quality costing
	N	**U**	– Customer/supplier framework – DPA
		R	– Systems – Techniques
		E	• Feedback/follow-up workshops throughout implementation

Figure 13.2 *TQM implementation*

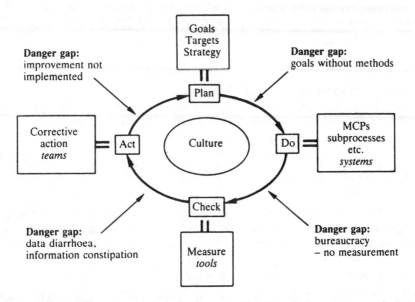

Figure 13.3 *TQM implementation – all done with the Deming continuous improvement cycle*

The concept requires a systematic approach to quality management that has the following components:

- *Planning* the processes and their inputs.
- *Providing* the inputs.
- *Operating* the processes.
- *Evaluating* the outputs.
- *Examining* the performance of the processes.
- *Modifying* the processes and their inputs.

This system must be firmly tied to a continuous assessment of customer needs, and depends on a flow of ideas on how to make improvements, reduce variation, and generate greater customer satisfaction. It also requires a high level of commitment, and a sense of personal responsibility in those operating the processes.

The never-ending improvement cycle ensures that the organization learns from results, standardizes what it does well in a documented quality management system, and improves operations and outputs from what it learns. But the emphasis must be that this is done in a planned, systematic, and conscientious way to create a climate – a way of life – that permeates the whole organization.

There are three basic principles of never-ending improvement:

- Focusing on the *customer*.
- Understanding the *process*.
- All *employees* committed to quality.

1   Focusing on the customer

An organization must recognize, throughout its ranks, that the purpose of all work and all efforts to make improvements is to serve the customers better. This means that it must always know how well its outputs are performing, in the eyes of the customer, through measurement and feedback. The most important customers are the external ones, but the quality chains can break down at any point in the flows of work. Internal customers therefore must also be well served if the external ones are to be satisfied.

2   Understanding the process

In the successful operation of any process it is essential to understand what determines its performance and outputs. This means intense focus on the design and control of the inputs, working closely with suppliers, and understanding process flows to eliminate bottlenecks and reduce waste. If there is one difference between management/ supervision in the Far East and the West, it is that in the former management is closer to, and more involved in, the processes. It is not possible to stand aside and manage in never-ending improvement. TQM in an organization means that everyone has the determination to use their detailed knowledge of the processes and make improvements, and use appropriate statistical methods to analyse and create action plans.

3   All employees committed to quality

Everyone in the organization, from top to bottom, from offices to technical service, from headquarters to local sites, must play their part. People are the source of ideas and innovation, and their expertise, experience, knowledge, and co-operation have to be harnessed to get those ideas implemented.

When people are treated like machines, work becomes uninteresting and unsatisfying. Under such conditions it is not possible to expect quality services and reliable products. The rates of absenteeism and of staff turnover are measures that can be used in determining the strengths and weaknesses, or management style and people's morale, in any company.

The first step is to convince everyone of their own role in total quality. Employers and managers must of course take the lead, and the most senior executive has a personal responsibility for quality. The degree of management's enthusiasm and drive will determine the ease with which the whole workforce is motivated.

Most of the work in any organization is done away from the immediate view of management and supervision, and often with individual discretion. If the co-operation of some or all of the people is absent, there is no way that managers will be able to cope with the chaos that will result. This principle is extremely important at the points where the processes 'touch' the outside customer. Every phase of these operations must be subject to continuous improvement, and for that everyone's co-operation is required.

Never-ending improvement is the process by which greater customer satisfaction is achieved. Its adoption recognizes that quality is a moving target, but its operation actually results in quality.

13.5   A model for total quality management

The concept of total quality management is basically very simple. Each part of an orga-nization has customers, whether within or without, and the need to identify what the customer requirements are, and then set about meeting them, forms the core of a total quality approach. This requires the three hard management necessities: a good quality management system, tools such as statistical process control (SPC), and teamwork. These are complementary in many ways, and they share the same requirement for an uncompromising commitment to quality. This must start with the most senior management and flow down through the organization. Having said that, teamwork, SPC, or the quality system, or all three, may be used as a spearhead to drive TQM through an organization. The attention to many aspects of a company's operations – from purchasing through to distribution, from data recording to control chart plotting – which are required for the successful introduction of a good quality system, or the implementation of SPC, will have a 'Hawthorne effect', concentrating everyone's attention on the customer–supplier interface, both inside and outside the organization.

Total quality management calls for consideration of processes in all the major areas:

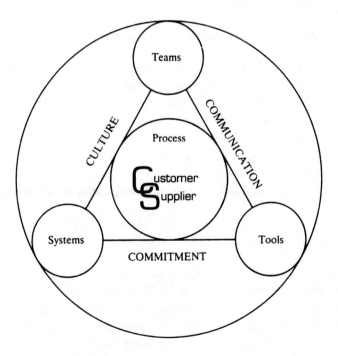

Figure 13.4 *Total quality management model*

marketing, design, procurement, operations, distribution, etc. Clearly, these each require considerable expansion and thought, but if attention is given to all areas, using the concepts of TQM, then very little will be left to chance. Much of industry and commerce would benefit from the improvements in quality brought about by the approach represented in Figures 13.1 and 13.4. This approach will ensure the implementation of the management commitment represented in the quality policy, and provide the environment and information base on which teamwork thrives.

Chapter highlights

TQM and the management of change

- Senior managers in some organizations recognize the need for change to deal with increasing competitivness, but lack an understanding of how to implement the changes.
- Successful change is effected not by focusing on formal structures and systems, but by aligning process management teams. This starts with writing the mission statement, analysis of the critical success factors (CSFs) and understanding the critical or key processes.

Integrating TQM into the strategy of the business/the steps

- Senior management may begin the task of process alignment through seven steps to a self-reinforcing cycle of commitment, communication, and culture change.
- The first three steps are gain commitment to change, develop a shared mission or vision of the business or desired change, and define the measurable objectives.
- The remaining four steps comprise developing the mission into its CSFs; understanding the key or critical processes and gaining ownership; breaking down the critical processes into sub-processes, activities and tasks; and monitoring and adjusting the process alignment in response to difficulties in the change process.

Continuous improvement

- Managers must understand and pursue never-ending improvement. This should cover planning and operating processes, providing inputs, evaluating outputs, examining performance, and modifying processes and their inputs.
- There are three basic principles of continuous improvement: focusing on the customer, understanding the process, and seeing that all employees are committed to quality.

A model for TQM

- In the model for TQM the customer–supplier chains form the core, which is surrounded by the hard management necessities of a good quality system, tools, and teamwork.

Reference

1 See, for example, Hardaker, M. and Ward, B. K., 'Getting Things Done – how to make a team work', *Harvard Business Review*, Nov/Dec. 1987, pp. 112-119.

Case study

C9

Implementing TQM at the University of Bradford Management Centre

Introduction

The University of Bradford's Management Centre is one of Europe's oldest and largest business schools. The Management Centre pursues an extensive programme of research that has earned an international reputation in many fields of study. It is a fully integrated business school, providing comprehensive and innovative programmes of management education for undergraduates, postgraduates and postexperience students. The interaction of students, experienced managers and staff, with diverse educational and industrial backgrounds, provides a stimulating and creative environment.

The Management Centre has a matrix structure with eight Professors, responsible for the subject groups of Economics, Financial Management, Credit Management, International Business, Marketing, Organizational Behaviour, Production and Operations Management, and TQM, whilst non-professorial Programme Chairs manage the undergraduate, postgraduate (MBA), full- and part-time, doctoral, and executive development (EDP) programmes. There is also a Director and Assistant Director of the Centre who are both Professors. The Director, Assistant Director, Programme Chairmen, and some Professors also sit on an Executive Committee, which is the decision-making body of the Management Centre.

There are approximately 80 full-time equivalent academic and related staff, 50 non-academic staff, 500 undergraduates, 300 full-time and part-time MBA students, and 30 doctoral students on site. Almost 2000 executives and managers from industry, commerce and the public sector pass through the EDP each year on various types of short-course programmes, including the executive MBA.

The Management Centre is part of the University of Bradford, although it is physically separated from the main campus. It is set in a pleasant site of approximately 13 acres with a mixture of historically old and new buildings.

The establishment of the industry-funded European Centre for Total Quality Management (ECTQM) in 1987 was a major innovation. The ECTQM is actively involved in research, teaching and advisory work in all areas of quality management. A wide range of students, including those on EDPs, experience TQM training and education at Bradford. The Centre is a member of the European Foundation for Quality Management (EFQM) and the TQM group are involved in many EFQM activities.

The 1990s is a very challenging phase in the life of the Management Centre. Business schools generally operate in an increasingly competitive environment and the Management Centre's future success will depend on the commitment of all its staff to the organization of its key processes. It was decided to introduce TQM into the Management Centre itself, using the expertise of the European Centre for TQM, in order to prepare for this challenge.

Awareness and organization of TQM

The then nine Professors held two TQM Strategic Planning Workshops to examine the feasibility of introducing TQM into the Management Centre.

A model of TQM (Figure 13.4), developed at the ECTQM, was adopted for implementation at the Management Centre. This conceptual model views the customer–supplier relationship and the processes that link them as being a core value of TQM. Continuous improvement of processes to deliver increasing customer satisfaction is central to the TQM philosophy. To achieve this there are certain requirements that must be in place. A commitment to a culture of continuous improvement is an essential element and this is facilitated by effective two-way communications. Actual process improvement is achieved by teams that are supported by good systems and use the tools of TQM.

The consensus view was that TQM at the Centre should involve:

- Everyone striving to meet customer requirements – internally and externally.
- Managing business processes.
- Continuous improvement in everything we do.
- Open, good communications.
- Participative management style and involvement of everyone.
- Documented, auditable systems for the way we do things.
- Teamwork, built around our processes.
- Training and education in the identification of processes and the tools and techniques of improvement.
- Empowering people to act wherever improvements can be made.

It was recognized that the necessary culture change would happen slowly and that the Management Centre's Total Quality Culture would not be built overnight. There was a strong belief among the Professors that the TQM approach could be used at the Centre in a disciplined approach to never-ending improvement.

It was also recognized that to devise and implement a TQM process takes considerable time and dedication and it must be given the status of an executive project. It was also essential that any TQM initiatives be fully integrated into the Management Centre's operating philosophy and management systems. The Professors suggested to the Executive Committee that the Centre should embark seriously on a TQM implementation programme, but pointed out that the commitment would be continually questioned and be weakened – perhaps destroyed – by the failure of the senior management to support the initiatives.

Implementing the TQM programme

The Quality Council

It was decided that a Quality Council (QC) should be formed to guide the TQM process. The QC's role is described below.

Purpose

To evolve the Centre's culture into one of Total Quality, thereby ensuring that we identify, understand, and achieve our mission.

Charter and responsibilities

The members of the QC were drawn from various levels in the organization. It works within the strategic framework laid down by the Professors and the Executive Committee. The membership is the Director, two Professors (including the Professor of TQM as facilitator, and chairperson) two Programme Chairmen, a lecturer, a secretary and a computer officer (technician).

Their responsibilities include:

- Updating the mission statement.
- Identifying the critical success factors.
- Providing overall strategic direction on TQM for the Management Centre.
- Establishing plans for TQM implementation.
- Setting up Process Quality Teams and Quality Action Teams to make improvements.
- Reviewing progress and plans for quality improvement.
- Revising plans for the development of TQM and process improvement.

The QC does not act as a senior problem-solving group. It holds meetings monthly, following the meeting of the Executive Committee to review quality strategy, implementation, progress and improvement.

The first tasks of the QC was to review the previous mission statement. It was found to contain suitable components for the development of a new mission statement, and the Critical Success factors (CSFs). The CSFs are the key factors that an organization must have to achieve its mission. They are the building blocks of the mission. These were set down as follows, including a list of stakeholders.

Mission statement

- To be a growing centre of excellence in teaching and research in the disciplines of management.
- To improve the practice of management, worldwide.

Critical success factors

1 We must have a Higher Education Funding Council (HEFC) research rating of 5.
2 We need a demonstrably excellent reputation for an innovative practical approach.
3 We must have products and services which meet current and future market needs.
4 We need financial independence.
5 We need an excellent infrastructure.
6 We must have a stimulating and rewarding work environment.
7 We must achieve a critical mass of quality staff.
8 We need quality inputs.

These were deemed to be all *necessary* and together *sufficient* for the mission to be achieved. Some are directly measurable (e.g. HEFC research rating); some are aspirations, hopes or fears.

Stakeholders

These are:

1 Students.
2 Staff:
   (a) academic.
   (b) others.
3 State.
4 Industry/business/public organizations.
5 Professions.
6 The University.

Current Aims were derived from the mission and CSFs as follows:

1 *Stakeholders*: To achieve a HEFC research rating of 5. To improve the management processes in the external world by research, teaching and advisory work.
2 *Customers*: To be the number one UK business school, in terms of the services and products offered to targeted markets.
3 *Employees*: To be a total quality business school which fully involves and develops all employees. This would revolve around never-ending improvement of processes to meet customers' requirements completely. To empower employees and teams to act in making continuous improvements.

The QC also identified 28 critical processes. These are the activities which must be carried out especially well in order for the CSFs to be achieved. The Council then produced a process quality matrix in order to prioritize critical processes for improvement. This identifies which processes have a high impact on each CSF. Again the necessary and sufficiency rule applies. The matrix also showed the subjective quality ranking given by the Council to each process on the scale:

A Excellent performance
B Good performance
C Fair performance
D Bad performance
E Embryonic processes

A second matrix showed the results of this work – a plot of the quality of each process against the number of CSF imports. Shaded zones of the matrix gave the critical processes in most urgent need of attention, i.e. those processes offering the greatest opportunity.

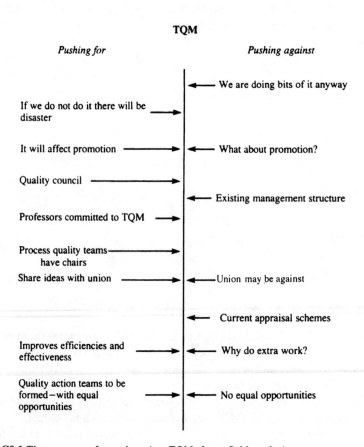

TQM

Pushing for   *Pushing against*

◄──── We are doing bits of it anyway

If we do not do it there will be disaster ────►

It will affect promotion ────►   ◄──── What about promotion?

Quality council ────►

◄──── Existing management structure

Professors committed to TQM ──►

Process quality teams have chairs ────►

Share ideas with union ────►   ◄──── Union may be against

◄──── Current appraisal schemes

Improves efficiencies and effectiveness ────►   ◄──── Why do extra work?

Quality action teams to be formed – with equal opportunities ────►   ◄──── No equal opportunities

Figure C9.1 *The pressures for and against TQM: force-field analysis*

All 28 processes were grouped under seven headings and these main groupings given generic titles. Seven Process Quality Teams were set up to manage these processes. The critical processes and quality/impact matrix are shown in Appendix A and B. The QC prepared a force field diagram for the pressures for and against TQM at the Management Centre (Figure C9.1)

Teamwork for quality improvement

Involvement in quality improvements was cascaded down through the organization using a structured team approach involving Process Quality Teams (PQTs) and Quality Action Teams (QATs).

The teamwork structure, which is shown in Figure C9.2, ensures the widest possible involvement in the TQM process and its effective implementation. The role of these teams is described below.

Process Quality Teams

The PQTs own and manage the process improvements.

Purpose

To define certain business processes and to set them up to run perfectly. Each PQT Chair will form a team of approximately eight staff. Their responsibilities will include:

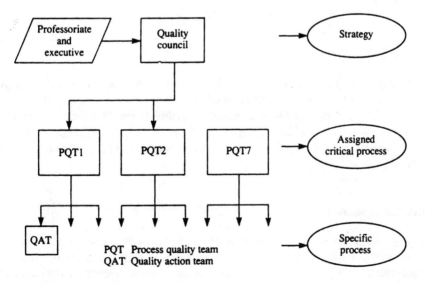

Figure C9.2 *Organization for TQM*

- Breaking down and describing the assigned critical processes.
- Prioritizing and selecting processes for improvement.
- Setting up QATs.
- Reviewing and supporting QAT activity.

Quality Action Teams

The detailed improvements will be carried out by QATs.

Purpose

To define and improve a particular process assigned by a PQT.

Composition

Six to 10 members of staff, selected by a Team Leader, representing all those involved in the assigned process. The team leader will be selected and asked by the PQT to form the team, preferably using a flowchart of the process. It is hoped that every employee at the Management Centre will be involved in quality improvement through a QAT (or PQT) at some point.

Responsibilities include:

- Drawing a flowchart of the process to identify its customers and suppliers.
- Identifying measurement points.
- Measuring and comparing results with requirements.
- Improving the process and documenting it.

The TQM survey

It was agreed at the senior level that only by measurement would people know when the Centre had succeeded in its mission and in meeting its aims. To measure that start point, a survey of the staff's perceptions of quality at the Management Centre was carried out. The survey addressed all the key areas of the Bradford TQM model.

A summary of the survey findings as reported back to the Management Centre staff is shown below.

External customers

Although we believe we know who are our customers (75% agree or strongly agree), we do not generally believe that we are completely clear what are our customer's requirements (72%). There is some level of disagreement amongst ourselves about whether we:

1   are *good at keeping up* with the changing needs of our customers;
2   *respond better to customers'* problems now than a *year ago*;
3   are *better than our competitors* at giving customers what they want;
4   work to improve our ability to *measure* how well we meet customer requirements;
5   are *committed* to serving customer needs.

This may reflect our different individual areas of activity – executive development, postgraduate, undergraduate, doctoral, marketing, finance, quality, etc. The overall medians of this group of questions, however, suggest some dissatisfaction with our performance here. One quite negative point is that we are not strong on detection and correction – 73% of respondents disagree with the statement that we do whatever it takes to satisfy a dissatisfied customer. In quality management this is not even 'right second time', and it may be costing us a fortune in lost business.

Internal customer–supplier relationships

There is a split in the Centre with regard to:

1   knowing the *standards* required;
2   *other people/groups creating unnecessary work;*
3   *work* received from others being *correctly done;*
4   *internal customers* receiving equal treatment to external customers.

Feedback, however, seems to be a problem for the majority, with 74% feeling that they do not get information about problems with their work in sufficient time to deal with them, and 66% suggesting that their group does not receive feedback from other groups or course managers about how well their requirements are met. Perhaps we need something in addition to the simple questionnaires completed by students (or delegates) who attend our courses and programmes.

Staff investment, development and reward

There are some very positive pointers here; 84% believe that efforts to improve quality are recognized by their boss, 59% of respondents are asked about their ideas for improvement, and 72% feel their boss encourages full use of their skills and abilities. On the negative side, however, 68% feel they do not get the training they need to improve the quality of their work, and 75% are not always provided with what they need to do their job correctly. This is probably linked to the fact that 75% do not feel that doing good work is rewarded and 67% say that the Management Centre is not committed to the development of its people.

A change is clearly needed here if quality improvement is to stand a chance at the Centre. It is nice to know, however, that 63% of the respondents take pride in the place!

Systems, tools/techniques and teams

One or two highlights here are that 88% of the respondents do not feel that senior staff have established a clear policy and strategy to improve quality (yet!). Clearly people cannot wait for TQM to do this!

On the prevention versus detection issue, we are well over to the detection side of things, with 86% saying that we do not prevent problems before they happen and 78% agreeing that we often make the same mistakes twice in the Centre.

There is a big cry for better and well-documented systems: 97% of respondents say that our system and procedures are not well-documented and up to date. We also do not have records which clearly demonstrate the extent to which we meet customer requirements, according to 79% of respondents.

This is clearly an area which requires massive improvement, particularly if we aspire to BS5750/ISO9000 (Quality Systems) certification, which is rapidly gaining ground in the education sector.

With regard to *data collection* and *measuring the capability* of our processes and *performance*, we do not feel that we are doing very well here. In all, 76% believe we do not represent data in a clear and meaningful way, and that we do not always analyse the collected data and information so that appropriate action can be taken. Even without this type of analysis taking place:

- 75% of respondents believe that our system, procedures and processes are not capable of meeting our customers' requirements.
- 71% disagree with the statement that we have means of knowing the causes of our performance variation.
- 87% do not believe we understand and measure our process capabilities.
- 69% think we act on hunches.
- 85% do not agree that we keep accurate records of how quality has improved.
- 88% do not believe we have consistent standards for measuring quality.

This lack of a systematic approach to quality performance measurement and information is directly against what we preach to our customers, but then 72% do not agree that we accept work only when we know we can deliver the customer's requirements.

Teamwork at the Management Centre also gets a bad rating: not a lot of teamwork in handling problems (65%), missed opportunities, room for improvement. Lack of coordination (89%) and lack of trust and dependence on each other (68%) are the negative aspects of this data, but responses to the other teamwork questions showed something of a split in opinion.

Generally speaking, many positive things were revealed in this survey, e.g. people taking a pride in the Management Centre, but the survey also highlighted many areas for improvement. Deficiencies in teamwork, communication, systems and measurement were identified. The most alarming statistic was that 88% of the respondents did not feel that the senior staff had established a clear policy and strategy to improve quality. Clearly this illustrated that the ground was fertile for a TQM initiative.

The TQM training programme

The TQM training programme commenced with a teamwork workshop for the Executive Committee and the Professoriate (Figure C9.3). The senior team profile had previously been exposed to the Myers-Briggs Type Indicator (MBTI), which is a psychological measure that attempts to explain the central aspects of people's personality, both to the individuals themselves and to their colleagues. An understanding of the MBTI measures helps to promote effective teamwork. This profile was reviewed at the workshop together with the TQM concepts and models. The action plan for implementation of TQM at the Management Centre was also reviewed.

All staff have also taken part in a series of 1-day workshops which were led by the Professor of TQM and facilitated by members of his department.

The objectives of the workshops were:

- to enable staff to share information on their work and associated quality problems;
- to develop the staff's understanding of the concept of TQM;
- to have fun;
- to start building more effective teamwork for quality improvement.

The outcome of these workshops was that staff were encouraged to participate in the TQM process at the individual and team level. The team approach to continuous improvement, described above, was launched by the QC, once a core of staff had been trained. All staff were asked to do some work on improvement immediately on an individual basis, using the tools and techniques of TQM learnt on their workshops.

Further training on process improvement methods was provided to the individual teams on an 'as-needed' basis. It was expected, however, that academic staff at a management centre should be familiar with techniques such as flow-charting, force-field analysis, Pareto analysis, brainstorming, cause-and-effect analysis, and the use of simple data presentation methods.

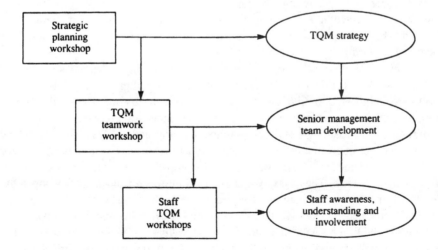

Figure C9.3 *The training programme*

The way ahead

The first phase of the TQM programme was concerned with obtaining the commitment of the Professoriate and Executive Committee to the principles of TQM. This commitment to TQM has been reinforced by the following statement from the Director of Bradford Management Centre, Professor David Weir:

> We are entering a very challenging competitive phase in the life of the Centre, and we are committed to creating a quality environment. Our success over the next few years depends on our ability to liberate the enormous positive energy within the Centre to meet our customers' requirements. Universities, old and new, all over the UK, Europe and the world, will have to adopt never-ending quality improvement processes to succeed. We want to be one of the first departments to use TQM to gain a clear competitive advantage over our competitors.

A strategy for implementing TQM was developed at a strategic planning workshop. A team-building workshop was used to weld the Professoriate and Executive Committee into an effective senior management team. A QC has been formed to guide the programme. The commitment to TQM was communicated to all the Management Centre's staff through a series of TQM workshops. The development of a TQM culture has started to evolve.

How will the necessary improvements be effected in these areas? Some of the 'harder' tools and techniques of TQM will undoubtedly be called into play. The role of quality management systems such as ISO9000 can make a significant contribution to improvement. The review of existing formal and informal procedures and the adoption of best practices is a fundamental step in the TQM process. It is important to produce a documented system of what is actually done. The danger in all improvement activities is that people prefer to improve processes first before writing down what is done. This results in an indisciplined approach and progress is usually not sustained. Measurement and recording systems required by a good-quality system will also result in more effective operations. Many organizations in the educational sector are considering the contribution of ISO9000 to quality improvement. At a recent QC meeting it was decided to begin the process of registering the Management Centre's quality system for independent third-part certification to ISO9000.

The combined effect of good systems and people working in teams using the tools and techniques of TQM sustain the process of continuous improvement. The PQTs and QATs are empowered to drive the improvement process forward. The results of many team projects have been implemented, e.g. the new induction process.

Initiating and sustaining a TQM programme in a large and well-established academic institution raises many interesting questions. Hopefully, the TQM initiative at Bradford is fully integrated into the Management Centre's operating philosophy and management systems. The TQM awareness level of all staff has been developed by a systematic training programme. As the programme evolves, further development of the Quality Model may be required. The contribution to quality improvement of the various elements of the European Quality Model will be evaluated. The ultimate success of the programme will depend upon people working effectively together, with the shared values of TQM, to achieve the shared aims critical to the future of the Bradford

Management Centre. However, some significant milestones have already been passed, e.g. the Management Centre has achieved one of its major critical success factors, namely a research rating of 5.

Appendix C9.A

Critical processes owned by Process Quality Teams (PQTs)

The 28 critical processes at the Management Centre have been grouped under the various PQTs as follows:

Critical process number	Critical Success Factor/ quality rank	
		Teaching and Staff Development PQT
1*	3E	Reward groups and individuals for performance
4	5C	Develop teaching performance
5	5C	Develop staff
7	6B	Recruit and retain top-quality researchers and teachers
14*	5D	Communicate and involve people within the Centre
26*	8E	Manage ownership of the mission
		Strategic Planning PQT
2	5C	Introduce a strategic planning process
8*	5D	Measure and control performance
21*	6E	Research market place for requirements
27	5C	Manage new business development
		Research and Dissemination PQT
3	5B	Obtain research funding
6	5B	Convert research into publications
19*	5E	Provide direct advice to improve management (do consulting)
28	5B	Conduct research

Critical process number	Critical Success Factor/ quality rank	
		Corporate Development PQT
9	5C	Recruit quality students
13	7B	Form international alliances
18*	4E	Create business relationships and alumni
27	5C	Manage new business development
		External Networks, Information and Promotion PQT
10*	5D	Advertise and promote the Centre's activities
11*	7E	Undertake regular competitor analysis
12*	7C	Manage external winning relationships
17*	6C	Communicate externally
		Facilities Development PQT
20*	6D	Have fun
22	5C	Research technological innovations
24	2D	Make the Management Centre beautiful
25	4C	Have appropriate course materials
		Finance PQT
15	5B	Manage University relationship (negotiate terms with)
16	7B	Invest in infrastructure
23*	7C	Generate general income

*Processes in most urgent need of attention (shaded zone in Appendix B).

Appendix C9.B

Critical processes – impact/quality matrix

Appendix B: Critical processes – impact/quality matrix

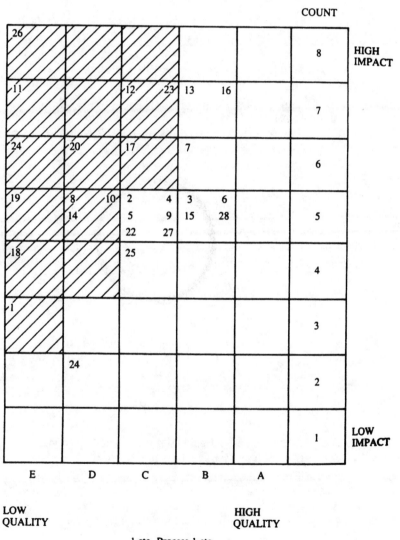

COUNT

	E	D	C	B	A		
26						8	HIGH IMPACT
11		12	23	13 16		7	
24	20	17	7			6	
19	8 10	2 4	3 6			5	
	14	5 9	15 28				
		22 27					
18		25				4	
1						3	
	24					2	
						1	LOW IMPACT

E   D   C   B   A

LOW
QUALITY

HIGH
QUALITY

1 etc. Process 1 etc.

Discussion questions

1 You have just been appointed the Production Manager of a small chemical company. You are shocked at the apparent disregard for procedures which have been laid down. This is particularly noticeable amongst the younger/newer members of the work force.

Briefly outline your responsibility in the area of quality and describe how you could proceed to improve the situation.

2 You have just joined a company as the Quality Executive.

The method of quality control is based on the use of inspectors who return about 15% of all goods inspected for modification, rework or repair. The monthly cost accounts suggest that the scrap rate of raw materials is equivalent to about 10% of the company's turnover and that the total cost of employing the inspectors is equal to about 15% of the direct labour costs.

Outline your plan of action over the first 12 months.

3 You have recently been appointed as Transport Manager of the haulage division of an expanding company and have been alarmed to find that maintenance costs seem to be higher than you would have expected in an efficient organization.

Outline some of the measures that you would take to bring the situation under control.

4 TQM has been referred to as 'a rain dance to make people feel good without impacting on bottom line results'. It was also described as 'flawed logic that confuses ends with means, processes with outcomes'. The arguments on whether to focus on budget control through financial management or quality improvement through process management clearly will continue in the future.

Discuss the problems associated with taking a financial management approach which has been the traditional method used in the West.

5 (a) Discuss what is meant by taking a process management approach? What are the key advantages of focusing on process improvement?
(b) Discuss how TQM can impact on bottom line results.

6 You are a management consultant who has been invited to make a presentation on Total Quality Management to the board of directors of a company employing around 200 people. They are manufacturers of injection moulded polypropylene components for the automotive and electronics industries, and they also produce some lower technology products, such as beverage bottle crates.

As they supply Ford Motor Company and have achieved their Q1 approval, the board have asked you to stress the role of quality systems and statistical process control (SPC) in TQM.

Prepare your presentation, including references to appropriate models as visual aids.

7 Describe the key stages in integrating total quality management into the strategy of an organization. Illustrate your answer by reference to one of the following organizations:

The Rover Group, Exxon Chemical, The British Army – Equipment Support Organization (ESO), National and Provincial Building Society.

8 What are the critical elements of integrating total quality management or business improvement into the strategy of an organization? Illustrate your approach with reference to an organization with which you are familiar, or which you have heard about and studied.

9 You are the new Quality Director of part of ICI. Some members of the top management team have had some brief exposure to TQM, and you have been appointed to lay down plans for its implementation.

Set down plans for the process which you would initiate to achieve this. Your plans should include reference to any training needs, outside help and additional internal appointments required, with timescales.

10 You are the new Quality Director of ONE of the following:

    National Westminster Bank
    Bradford Royal Infirmary
or University of Leeds

The members of your top management team have had some brief exposure to TQM and you have been appointed to lay down plans for its implementation.

Choose any of the above organizations and set down plans for the process which you would initiate to achieve this. Your plans should be as fully developed as possible in the time allowed and include reference to any training needs, outside help and additional internal appointments required, with a realistic timescale.

Case study assignments

C9 University of Bradford, Management Centre

Evaluate the approach used by the Management Centre for general application in the public sector – health, education, armed services, social services, Inland Revenue services, etc.

Discuss the issues of measurement in an organization such as this one, and evaluate the approach taken at Bradford.

How should the senior team at the Centre develop their thinking to sustain the momentum of total quality?

Three American gurus

A small group of American quality experts or 'gurus' have, in the past, advised industry throughout the world on how it should manage quality. The approaches of Philip B. Crosby, W. Edwards Deming, and Joseph M. Juran, their similarities and differences, are presented briefly here.

Philip B. Crosby

Crosby's four absolutes of quality:

- Definition – conformance to requirements.
- System – prevention.
- Performance standard – zero defects.
- Measurement – price of non-conformance.

He offers management fourteen steps to improvement:

1 Make it clear that management is committed to quality.
2 Form quality improvement teams with representatives from each department.
3 Determine where current and potential quality problems lie.
4 Evaluate the cost of quality and explain its use as a management tool.
5 Raise the quality awareness and personal concern of all employees.
6 Take actions to correct problems identified through previous steps.
7 Establish a committee for the zero defects programme.
8 Train supervisors to actively carry out their part of the quality improvement programme.
9 Hold a 'zero defects day' to let all employees realize that there has been a change.
10 Encourage individuals to establish improvement goals for themselves and their groups.
11 Encourage employees to communicate to management the obstacles they face in attaining their improvement goals.
12 Recognize and appreciate those who participate.
13 Establish quality councils to communicate on a regular basis.
14 Do it all over again to emphasize that the quality improvement programme never ends.

W. Edwards Deming

Deming's fourteen points for management are the following:

1 Create constancy of purpose towards improvement of product and service.
2 Adopt the new philosophy. We can no longer live with commonly accepted levels of delays, mistakes, defective workmanship.
3 Cease dependence on mass inspection. Require, instead, statistical evidence that quality is built in.
4 End the practice of awarding business on the basis of price tag.
5 Find problems. It is management's job to work continually on the system.
6 Institute modern methods of training on the job.
7 Institute modern methods of supervision of production workers. The responsibility of foremen must be changed from numbers to quality.
8 Drive out fear, so that everyone may work effectively for the company.
9 Break down barriers between departments.
10 Eliminate numerical goals, posters, and slogans for the workforce asking for new levels of productivity without providing methods.
11 Eliminate work standards that prescribe numerical quotas.
12 Remove barriers that stand between the hourly worker and his right to pride of workmanship.
13 Institute a vigorous programme of education and retraining.
14 Create a structure in top management that will push every day on the above thirteen points.

Joseph M. Juran

Juran's ten steps to quality improvement are the following:

1 Build awareness of the need and opportunity for improvement.
2 Set goals for improvement.
3 Organize to reach the goals (establish a quality council, identify problems, select projects, appoint teams, designate facilitators).
4 Provide training.
5 Carry out projects to solve problems.
6 Report progress.
7 Give recognition.
8 Communicate results.
9 Keep score.
10 Maintain momentum by making annual improvement part of the regular systems and processes of the company.

A comparison

One way to compare directly the various approaches of the three American gurus is in tabular form. Table A.1 shows the differences and similarities, classified under 12 different factors.

Table A.1 *The American quality gurus compared*

	Crosby	Deming	Juran
Definition of quality	Conformance to requirements	A predictable degree of uniformity and dependability at low cost and suited to the market	Fitness for use
Degree of senior-management responsibility	Responsible for quality	Responsible for 94% of quality problems	Less than 20% of quality problems are due to workers
Performance standard/motivation	Zero defects	Quality has many scales. Use statistics to measure performance in all areas. Critical of zero defects	Avoid campaigns to do perfect work
General approach	Prevention, not inspection	Reduce variability by continuous improvement. Cease mass inspection	General management approach to quality – especially 'human' elements
Structure	Fourteen steps to quality improvement	Fourteen points for management	Ten steps to quality improvement
Statistical process control (SPC)	Rejects statistically acceptable levels of quality	Statistical methods of quality control must be used	Recommends SPC but warns that it can lead to tool-driven approach
Improvement basis	A 'process', not a programme. Improvement goals	Continuous to reduce variation. Eliminate goals without methods	Project-by-project team approach. Set goals
Teamwork	Quality improvement teams. Quality councils	Employee participation in decision-making. Break down barriers between departments	Team and quality circle approach
Costs of quality	Cost of non-conformance. Quality is free	No optimum – continuous improvement	Quality is not free – there is an optimum

Table A.1 *(continued)*

	Crosby	Deming	Juran
Purchasing and goods received	State requirements. Supplier is extension of business. Most faults due to purchasers themselves	Inspection too late – allows defects to enter system through AQLs. Statistical evidence and control charts required	Problems are complex. Carry out formal surveys
Vendor rating	Yes *and* buyers. Quality audits useless	No – critical of most systems	Yes, but help supplier improve
Single sources of supply		Yes	No – can neglect to sharpen competitive edge.

Appendix B

TQM Bibliography

General quality management and TQM

Bank, J., *The Essence of Total Quality Management*, Prentice Hall, Hemel Hempstead (UK), 1992.

Caplen, R. H., *A Practical Approach to Total Quality Control* (5th edn), Business Books, London, 1988.

Crosby, P. B., *Quality is Free*, McGraw-Hill, New York, 1979.

Crosby, P. B., *Quality Without Tears*, McGraw-Hill, New York, 1984.

Dale, B. G. and Plunkett, J. J. (eds), *Managing Quality*, Philip Alan, Hemel Hempstead (UK), 1990.

Deming, W. E., *Out of the Crisis*, MIT, Cambridge, Mass. (USA), 1982.

Deming, W. E., *The New Economies*, MIT, Cambridge, Mass. (USA), 1993.

Edosomwam, J. A., *Productivity and Quality Improvement*, IFS, Bedford (UK), 1988

Feigenbaum A. V., *Total Quality Control* (3rd edn, revised), McGraw-Hill, New York, 1991.

Garvin, D. A., *Managing Quality: the strategic competitive edge*, The Free Press (Macmillan), New York, 1988.

Hakes, C. (ed), *Total Quality Improvement: the key to business improvement*, Chapman & Hall, London, 1991.

Hutchins, D., *In Pursuit of Quality*, Pitman, London, 1990.

Hutchins, D., *Achieve Total Quality*, Director Books, Cambridge (UK), 1992.

Ishikawa, K. (translated by D. J. Lu), *What is Total Quality Control? the Japanese Way*, Prentice-Hall, Englewood Cliffs, NJ (USA), 1985.

Macdonald, J. and Piggot, J., *Global Quality: the new management culture*, Mercury Books, London, 1990.

Mann, N. R., *The Keys to Excellence: the story of the Deming philosophy*, Prestwick Books, Los Angeles, CA (USA), 1985.

Murphy, J. A., *Quality in Practice*, Gill and MacMillan, Dublin, 1986.

Popplewell, B. and Wildsmith, A., *Becoming the Best*, Gower, Aldershot (UK), 1988.

Price, F., *Right Every Time*, Gower, Aldershot (UK), 1990.

Sarv Singh Soin, *Total Quality Control Essentials – key elements, methodologies and managing for success*, McGraw-Hill, New York, 1992.

Wille, E., *Quality: achieving excellence*, Century Business, London, 1992.

Zairi, M., *Total Quality Management for Engineers*, Woodhead, Cambridge (UK), 1991.

Leadership and commitment

Adair, J., *Not Bosses but Leaders: how to lead the successful way*, Talbot Adair Press, Guildford (UK), 1987.

Adair, J., *The Action-Centred Leader*, Industrial Society, London, 1988.

Adair, J., *Effective Leadership* (2nd edn), Pan Books, London, 1988.

Crosby, P. B., *Running Things*, McGraw-Hill, New York, 1986.

Juran, J. M., *Juran on Leadership for Quality: an executive handbook*, The Free Press (Macmillan), New York, 1989.

Townsend, P. L. and Gebhardt, J. E., *Commit to Quality*, J. Wiley Press, New York, 1986.

Townsend, P. L. and Gebhardt, J. E., *Quality in Action – 93 lessons in leadership, participation and measurement*, J. Wiley Press, New York, 1992.

Customers, suppliers and service

Albin, J. M., *Quality Improvement in Employment and other Human Services – managing for quality through change*, Paul Brookes Pub. (USA), 1992.

Cook, S., *Customer Care – implementing total quality in today's service driven organization*, Kogan Page, London, 1992.

Groocock, J. M., *The Chains of Quality*, John Wiley, Chichester (UK), 1986.

King Taylor, L., *Quality: total customer service* (a case study book), Century Business, London, 1992.

Lash, L. M., *The Complete Guide to Customer Service*, J. Wiley Press, New York, 1989.

Mastenbrock, W. (ed)., *Managing for Quality in the Service Sector*, Basil Blackwell, Oxford (UK), 1991.

Zeithaml, V. A., Parasuraman, A. and Berry, L. L., *Delivering Quality Service: balancing customer perceptions and expectations*, The Free Press (Macmillan), New York, 1990.

Design, innovation, and QFD

Adair, J., *The Challenge of Innovation*, Talbot Adair Press, Guildford (UK), 1990.

Fox, J., *Quality Through Design*, MGLR, 1993.

Juran, J. J., *Juran on Quality by Design*, Free Press, New York, 1992.

Marsh, S., Moran, J., Nakui, S. and Hoffherr, G. D., *Facilitating and Training in QFD*, ASQC, Milwaukee, WI (USA), 1991.

Zairi, M., *Management of Advanced Manufacturing Technology*, Sigma Press, Wilmslow (UK), 1992.

Quality planning, JIT, and POM

Ansari, A. and Modarress, B., *Just-in-time Purchasing*, The Free Press (Macmillan), New York, 1990.

Bineno, J., *Implementing JIT*, IFS, Bedford (UK), 1991.

Harrison, A., *Just-in-Time Manufacturing in Perspective*, Prentice-Hall, Englewood Cliffs, NJ (USA), 1992.

Hutchins, D., *Just-in-Time*, Gower, Aldershot (UK), 1988.

Juran, J. M. (ed), *Quality Control Handbook*, McGraw-Hill, New York, 1988.

Juran, J. M. and Gryna, F. M., *Quality Planning and Analysis* (2nd edn), McGraw-Hill, New York, 1980.

Muhlemann, A. P., Oakland, J. S. and Lockyer, K. G., *Production and Operations Management* (6th edn), Pitman, London, 1992.

Voss, C. A. (ed), *Just-in-Time Manufacture*, IFS Publications, Bedford (UK), 1989.

Quality systems

Dale, B. G. and Oakland, J. S., *Quality Improvement Through Standards*, Stanley Thornes, Cheltenham (UK), 2nd Edn, 1994.

Hall, T. J., *The Quality Manual – the application of BS5750 ISO 9001 EN 29001*, John Wiley, Chichester (UK), 1992.

Rothery, B., *ISO 9000*, Gower, Aldershot (UK), 1991.

Stebbing, L., *Quality Assurance: the route to efficiency and competitiveness* (2nd edn), John Wiley, Chichester (UK), 1989.

The Baldrige and European Quality Award criteria

Brown M. G., *Baldrige Award Winning Quality: how to interpret the Malcolm Baldrige Award criteria* (2nd edn), ASQC, Milwaukee, WI (USA), 1992.

EPQM (European Foundation for Quality Management), *The European Model for TQM – guide to self assessment*, 1995.

Hart, W. L. and Bogan, C. E., *The Baldrige: what it is, how it's won, how to use it to improve quality in your company*, McGraw-Hill, New York, 1992.

Mills Steeples, M., *The Corporate Guide to the Malcolm Baldrige National Quality Award*, ASQC, Milwaukee, WI (USA), 1992.

NIST (US Dept. of Commerce, National Institute of Standards and Technology), *Malcolm Baldrige National Quality Award Criteria*, 1995.

Quality costing, measurement and benchmarking

Bendell, Tony, *Benchmarking for Competitive Advantage*, Longman, 1993.

Camp, R. C., *Benchmarking: the search for industry best practices that lead to superior performance*, ASQC Quality Press, Milwaukee, WI (USA), 1989.

Dale, B. G. and Plunkett, J. J., *Quality Costing*, Chapman and Hall, London, 1991.

Dixon, J. R., Nanni, A. and Vollmann, T. E., *The New Performance Challenge – measuring operations for world class competition*, Business One Irwin, Homewood (USA), 1990.

Hall, R. W., Johnson, H. Y. and Turney, P. B. B., *Measuring Up – charting pathways to manufacturing excellence*, Business One Irwin, Homewood (USA), 1991.

Kaplan, R. W. (ed), *Measures for Manufacturing Excellence*, Harvard Business School Press, Boston, Mass. (USA), 1990.

Kinlaw, D. C., *Continuous Improvement and Measurement For Total Quality – a team-based approach*, Pfieffer & Business One (USA), 1992.

Porter, L. J. and Rayner, P., 'Quality costing for TQM', *International Journal of Production Economics*, **27**, pp. 69-81, 1992.

Spendolini, M. J., *The Benchmarking Book*, ASQC, Milwaukee, WI (USA), 1992.

Talley, D. J., *Total Quality Management: performance and cost measures*, ASQC, Milwaukee, WI (USA), 1991.

Zairi, M., *Competitive Benchmarking*, TQM Practitioner Series, Technical Communications (Publishing), Letchworth (UK), 1992.

Zairi, M., *TQM-Based Performance Measurement*, TQM Practitioner Series, Technical Communication (Publishing), Letchworth (UK), 1992

Zairi, M., *Measuring Performance for Business Results*, Chapman and Hall, 1994.

Zairi, M. and Leonard, P., *Practical Benchmarking – the complete guide*, Chapman and Hall, 1994.

Tools and techniques of TQM (including SPC)

Bhote, K. R., *World Class Quality – using design of experiments to make it happen*, AMACOM, New York (USA), 1991.

Carlzon, J., *Moments of Truth*, Ballinger, Cambridge, Mass. (USA), 1987.

Caulcutt, R., *Data Analysis in the Chemical Industry, Vol. 1: Basic Techniques*, Ellis Horwood, Chichester (UK), 1989.

Caulcutt, R., *Statistics in Research and Development* (2nd edn)., Chapman and Hall, London, 1991.

Joiner B., *Fourth Generation Management*, McGraw-Hill, 1994.

Neave, H., *The Deming Dimension*, SPC Press, Knoxville (USA), 1990.

Oakland, J. S. and Followell, R. F., *Statistical Process Control: a practical guide* (2nd edn), Butterworth-Heinemann, Oxford (UK), 1990.

Price, F., *Right First Time*, Gower, London, 1985.

Ryuka Fukuda, *CEDAC – a tool for continuous systematic improvement*, Productivity Press, Cambridge, Mass (USA), 1990.

Wheeler, D., *Understanding Variation*, SPC Press, 1993.

Shingo and Taguchi methods

Bendell, T., Wilson, G. and Millar, R. M. G., *Taguchi Methodology with Total Quality*, IFS, Bedford (UK), 1990.

Lagothetis, N., *Managing for Total Quality – from Deming to Taguchi and SPC*, Prentice-Hall, Englewood Cliffs, NJ (USA), 1990.

Ranjit, Roy, *A Primer on the Taguchi Method,* Van Nostrand Reinhold, New York, 1990.

Shingo, S., *Zero Quality Control: source inspection and the Poka-yoke system*, Productivity Press, Stamford, Conn. (USA), 1986.

TQM through people and teamwork

Adair, J., *Effective Teambuilding* (2nd edn), Pan Books, London, 1987.

Aubrey, C. A. and Felkins, P. K., *Teamwork: involving people in quality and productivity improvement*, ASQC, Milwaukee, WI (USA), 1988.

Belbin, R. M., *Management Teams: why they succeed or fail*, Butterworth-Heinemann, Oxford (UK), 1981.

Blanchard, K. and Hersey, P., *Management of Organizational Behaviour: Utilizing Human Resources* (4th edn), Prentice-Hall, Englewood Cliffs, NJ (USA), 1982.

Briggs Myers, I., *Introduction to Type: a description of the theory and applications of the Myers Briggs Type Indicator*, Consulting Psychologists Press, Palo Alto (USA), 1987.

Choppin, J., *Quality Through People: a blueprint for proactive total quality management*, IFS, Kempston (UK), 1991.

Collard, R., *Total Quality: success through people*, Institute of Personnel Management, Wimbledon (UK), 1989.

Dale, B. G. and Cooper, C., *Total Quality and Human Resources – an executive guide*, Blackwell, Oxford (UK), 1992.

Hutchins, D., *The Quality Circle Handbook*, Gower, Aldershot (UK), 1985.

Kormanski, C., 'A situational leadership approach to groups using the Tuckman Model of Group Development', *The 1985 Annual: Developing Human Resources*, University Associates, San Diego (USA), 1985.

Kormanski, C. and Mozenter, A., 'A new model of team building: a technology for today and tomorrow', *The 1987 Annual: Developing Human Resources*, University Associates, San Diego (USA), 1987.

Krebs Hirsh, S., *MBTI Team Building Program, Team Member's Guide*, Consulting Psychologists Press, Palo Alto, CA (USA), 1992.

Krebs Hirsh, S. and Kummerow, J. M., *Introduction to Type in Organizational Settings*, Consulting Psychologists Press, Palo Alto, CA (USA), 1987.

McCaulley, M. H., 'How individual differences affect health care teams', *Health Team News*, **1** (8), pp. 1-4, 1975.

Masaaki, I., *Kaizen: the key to Japanese competitive success*, McGraw-Hill, New York, 1986.

Robson, M., *Quality Circles, a practical guide* (2nd edn), Gower, Aldershot (UK), 1989.

Scholtes, P. R., *The Team Handbook*, Joiner Associates, Madison, NY (USA), 1990.

Shetty, Y. K. and Buehler, V. M. (eds), *Productivity and Quality Through People* (case studies), Quorum Books, London, 1985.

Tannenbaum, R. and Schmidt, W. H., 'How to choose a leadership pattern', *Harvard Business Review*, May-June, 1973.

Tuckman, B. W. and Jensen, M. A., 'Stages of small group development revisited', *Group and Organizational Studies*, **2** (4), pp. 419-427, 1977.

Wellins, R. S., Byham, W. C. and Wilson, J. M., *Empowered Teams*, Jossey Bass, Oxford (UK), 1991.

Whitley, R., *The Customer Driven Company*, Business Books, London, 1991.

Cross-functional process improvement

Dimaxcescu, D., *The Seamless Enterprise – making cross-functional management work*, Harper Business, New York, 1992.

Francis, D., *Unblocking the Organisational Communication*, Gower, Aldershot (UK), 1990.

Hammer, M. and Champy, J., *Re-engineering the corporation*, Nicholas Brearley, 1993.

Harrington, H. J., *Business Process Improvement*, McGraw-Hill, New York, 1991.

Rummler, G. A. and Brache, A. P., *Improving Performance: how to manage the white space on the organisation chart*, Jossey-Bass Publishing, San Francisco, CA (USA), 1990.

Senge, P. M., *The Fifth Discipline*, Century Business, 1990.

Implementing TQM

Atkinson, P. E., *Creating Culture Change: the key to successful total quality management*, IFS, Bedford (UK), 1990.

Ciampa, D., *Total Quality – a user's guide for implementation*, Addison-Wesley, Reading, Mass. (USA), 1992.

Crosby, P. B., *The Eternally Successful Organization*, McGraw-Hill, New York, 1988.

Cullen, J. and Hollingham, J., *Implementing Total Quality*, IFS (Publications), London, 1987.

Fox, R., *Six Steps to Total Quality Management*, McGraw-Hill, NSW (Australia), 1991.

Gitlow, H. S., and Gitlow, S. J., *The Deming Guide to Quality and Competitive Position*, Prentice-Hall, New Jersey (USA), 1987.

Hardaker, M. and Ward, B. K., 'Getting things done – how to make a team work', *Harvard Business Review*, pp. 112-119, Nov/Dec. 1987.

Hiam, A., *Closing the Quality Gap – lessons from America's leading companies*, Prentice-Hall, Englewood Cliffs, NJ (USA), 1992.

Morgan C. and Murgatroyd, S., *Total Quality Management in the Public Sector*, Open University Press, 1994.

Munro-Faure, L. and Munro-Faure, M., *Implementing Total Quality Management*, Pitman, London, 1992.

Saylor, J. H., *Total Quality Management Field Manual*, McGraw-Hill, New York, 1992.

Scherkenbach, W. W., *The Deming Route to Quality and Productivity: road maps and road blocks*, Mercury Press/Fairchild Publications, Rockville, Md (USA), 1986.

Scherkenbach, W. W., *Deming's Road to Continual Improvement*, SPC Press, Knoxville (USA), 1991.

Schuler, R. S. and Harris, D. L., *Managing Quality – the primer for middle managers*, Addison-Wesley, Reading, Mass. (USA), 1992.

Spenley, P., *World Class Performance Through Total Quality*, Chapman and Hall, London, 1992.

Tennor, A. R. and De Toro, I. J., *Total Quality Management – three steps to continuous improvement*, Addison-Wesley, Reading, Mass. (USA), 1992.

Tunks, R., *Fast Track to Quality*, McGraw-Hill, New York, 1992.

British Standards related to TQM

BS 600:1935 'The application of statistical methods to industrial standardisation and quality control'

BS 2564:1955 'Control chart technique when manufacturing to a specification, with special reference to articles machined to dimensional tolerances'

BS 2846:Parts 1 to 7:1976-1991 (ISO 2602, Part 2; ISO 3207, Part 3; ISO 2854, Part 4; ISO 3494, Part 5; ISO 3301, Part 6; ISO 5479, Part 7) 'Guide to statistical interpretation of data'

BS 4891:1972 'A guide to quality assurance'

BS 5700:1984 'Guide to process control using quality control chart methods and cusum techniques'

BS 5701:1980 'Guide to number-defective charts for quality control'

BS 5703:Parts 1 to 4:1980-1982 'Guide to data analysis and quality control using cusum techniques'

BS 5750:Parts 0 to 13 (with gaps):1987 to 1994 (ISO 9001, Part 1; ISO 9002, Part 2; ISO 9003, Part 3; ISO 9004-2, Part 8; ISO 900-3, Part 13) 'Quality systems' (BS EN ISO 9000 series)

BS 5760:Parts 0 to 7:1981-1991 'Reliability of systems, equipment and components'

BS 5781:Parts 1 to 2:1988 'Measurement and calibration systems'

BS 6000:1972 (ISO 2859) 'Guide to the use of BS 6001, sampling procedures and tables for inspection by attributes'

BS 6001:Parts 1 to 3:1984 to 1991 (ISO 2859-1) 'Sampling procedures for inspection by attributes'

BS 6002:1979 (ISO 2859-2) 'Specification for sampling procedures and charts for inspection by variables for per cent defective'

BS 6143:Parts 1 to 2:1990-1992 (ISO 2859-3) 'Guide to the economies of quality'

BS 7000:1989 'Guide to managing product design'

BS 7165:1991 'Recommendations for achievement of quality in software'

BS 7229:Parts 1 to 3:1991 (ISO 10011) 'Guide to quality systems auditing'

BS 7850:Parts 1 to 2:1992 'Total quality management'

BS 9000:Parts 1 to 8:1989-1991 'General requirements for a system for electronic components of assessed quality'

BS Published Document PD 3542:1991 'The role of standards in company quality management'

Index